Praise for *Fit for Developing Software*

"The unique thing about *Fit for Developing Software* is the way it addresses the interface between customers/testers/analysts and programmers. All will find something in the book about how others wish to be effectively communicated with. A Fit book for programmers wouldn't make sense because the goal is to create a language for business-oriented team members. A Fit book just for businesspeople wouldn't make sense because the programmers have to be involved in creating that language. The result is a book that should appeal to a wide range of people whose shared goal is improving team communications."

—Kent Beck, Three Rivers Institute

"Even with the best approaches, there always seemed to be a gap between the software that was written and the software the user wanted. With Fit we can finally close the loop. This is an important piece in the agile development puzzle."

—Dave Thomas, coauthor of *The Pragmatic Programmer*

"Ward and Rick do a great job in eschewing the typical, overly complicated technology trap by presenting a simple, user-oriented, and very usable technology that holds fast to the agile principles needed for success in this new millennium."

—Andy Hunt, coauthor of *The Pragmatic Programmer*

"Florida Tech requires software engineering students to take a course in programmer testing, which I teach. Mugridge and Cunningham have written a useful and instructive book, which will become one of our course texts."

—Cem Kaner, Professor of Software Engineering, Florida Institute of Technology

"Rick and Ward continue to amaze me. Testing business rules is a fundamentally hard thing that has confounded many, and yet these two have devised a mechanism that cuts to the essence of the problem. In this work they offer a simple, thorough, approachable, and automatable means of specifying and testing such rules."

—Grady Booch, IBM Fellow

"By providing a simple, effective method for creating and automating tabular examples of requirements, Fit has dramatically improved how domain experts, analysts, testers, and programmers collaborate to produce quality software."

—Joshua Kerievsky, founder, Industrial Logic, Inc., and author of *Refactoring to Patterns*

"Agile software development relies on collaborating teams, teams of customers, analysts, designers, developers, testers, and technical writers. But, how do they work together? Fit is one answer, an answer that has been thoroughly thought through, implemented, and tested in a number of situations. Primavera has significantly stabilized its product line using Fit, and I'm so impressed by the results that I'm suggesting it to everyone I know. Rick and Ward, in their everlasting low-key approach, have again put the keystone in the arch of software development. Congratulations and thanks from the software development community."

—Ken Schwaber, Scrum Alliance, Agile Alliance, and codeveloper of Scrum

"Fit is the most important new technique for understanding and communicating requirements. It's a revolutionary approach to bringing experts and programmers together. This book describes Fit comprehensively and authoritatively. If you want to produce great software, you need to read this book."

—James Shore, Principal, Titanium I.T. LLC

"There are both noisy and quiet aspects of the agile movement and it is often the quieter ones that have great strategic importance. This book by Ward and Rick describes one of these absolutely vital, but often quieter, practices—testing business requirements. A renewed focus on testing, from test-driven development for developers to story testing for customers, is one of the agile community's great contributions to our industry, and this book will become one of the cornerstones of that contribution. Stories are done-done (ready for release) when they have been tested by both developers (done) and customers (done-done). The concepts and practices involved in customer story testing are critical to project success and wonderfully portrayed in this book. Buy it. Read it. Keep it handy in your day-to-day work."

—Jim Highsmith, Director of Agile Software Development & Project Management Practice, Cutter Consortium

"I have been influenced by many books, but very few have fundamentally changed how I think and work. This is one of those books. The ideas in this book describe not just how to use a specific framework in order to test our software, but also how we should communicate about and document that software. This book is an excellent guide to a tool and approach that will fundamentally improve how you think about and build software—as it has done for me."

—Mike Cohn, Mountain Goat Software, author of *User Stories Applied*

"Fit is a tool to help whole teams grow a common language for describing and testing the behavior of software. This books fills a critical gap—helping both product owners and programmers learn what Fit is and how to use it well."

—Bill Wake, independent consultant

"Over the past several years, I've been using Fit and FitNesse with development teams. They are not only free and powerful testing tools, they transform development by making the behavior of applications concrete, verifiable, and easily observable. The only thing that has been missing is a good tutorial and reference. Rick Mugridge and Ward Cunningham's *Fit For Developing Software* fits the bill. Essentially, two books in one, it is a very readable guide that approaches Fit from technical and nontechnical perspectives. This book is a significant milestone and it will make higher software quality achievable for many teams."

—Michael C. Feathers, author of *Working Effectively with Legacy Code,* and consultant, Object Mentor, Inc.

"Wow! This is the book I wish I had on my desk when I did my first story test-driven development project. It explains the philosophy behind the Fit framework and a process for using it to interact with the customers to help define the requirements of the project. It makes Fit so easy and approachable that I wrote my first FitNesse tests before I even I finished the book.

"For the price of one book, you get two, written by the acknowledged thought leaders of Fit testing. The first is written for the nonprogramming customer. It lays out how you can define the functionality of the system you are building (or modifying) using tabular data. It introduces a range of different kinds of 'test fixtures' that interpret the data and exercise the system under test. While it is aimed at a nontechnical audience, even programmers will find it useful because it also describes the process for interacting with the customers, using the Fit tests as the focal point of the interaction.

"The second 'book' is targeted to programmers. It describes how to build each kind of fixture described in the first book. It also describes many other things that need to be considered to have robust automated tests—things like testing without a database to make tests run faster. A lot of the principles will be familiar to programmers who have used any member of the xUnit family of unit testing frameworks. Rick and Ward show you how to put it into practice in a very easy-to-read narrative style that uses a fictitious case study to lead you through all the practices and decisions you are likely to encounter."

—Gerard Meszaros, ClearStream Consulting

Fit for Developing Software

Robert C. Martin Series

The mission of this series is to improve the state of the art of software craftsmanship. The books in this series are technical, pragmatic, and substantial. The authors are highly experienced craftsmen and professionals dedicated to writing about what actually works in practice, as opposed to what might work in theory. You will read about what the author has done, not what he thinks you should do. If the book is about programming, there will be lots of code. If the book is about managing, there will be lots of case studies from real projects.

These are the books that all serious practitioners will have on their bookshelves. These are the books that will be remembered for making a difference and for guiding professionals to become true craftsman.

Managing Agile Projects
Sanjiv Augustine

Working Effectively with Legacy Code
Michael C. Feathers

Agile Java™: Crafting Code with Test-Driven Development
Jeff Langr

Agile Software Development: Principles, Patterns, and Practices
Robert C. Martin

UML For Java™ Programmers
Robert C. Martin

Fit for Developing Software: Framework for Integrated Tests
Rick Mugridge and Ward Cunningham

Agile Software Development with SCRUM
Ken Schwaber and Mike Beedle

Extreme Software Engineering: A Hands on Approach
Daniel H. Steinberg and Daniel W. Palmer

For more information, visit http://www.phptr.com/martinseries

Fit for Developing Software

Framework for Integrated Tests

Rick Mugridge

Ward Cunningham

PRENTICE
HALL
PTR

Prentice Hall Professional Technical Reference

Upper Saddle River, NJ • Boston • Indianapolis • San Francisco
New York • Toronto • Montreal • London • Munich • Paris • Madrid
Capetown • Sydney • Tokyo • Singapore • Mexico City

The publisher offers excellent discounts on this book when ordered in quantity for bulk purchases or special sales, which may include electronic versions and/or custom covers and content particular to your business, training goals, marketing focus, and branding interests. For more information, please contact:

  U.S. Corporate and Government Sales
  (800) 382-3419
  corpsales@pearsontechgroup.com

For sales outside the U.S., please contact:

  International Sales
  international@pearsoned.com

Visit us on the Web: www.phptr.com

Library of Congress Cataloging-in-Publication Data:

Mugridge, Rick.
    Fit for developing software : framework for integrated tests / Rick Mugridge, Ward Cunningham.
        p.   cm.
    Includes bibliographical references and index.
    ISBN 0-321-26934-9 (pbk. : alk. paper)
    1. Computer software—Evaluation. 2. Software engineering. I. Cunningham, Ward.
II. Title.
    QA76.76.E93M84 2005
    005.3′028′7—dc22   2005005894

ISBN 0-321-26934-9
Text printed in the United States on recycled paper at Courier in Westford, Massachusetts.
First printing, June 2005

To **Jackie** and **Anna**, lights of my life.

—Rick

To **Gary Goldberg**, the first business analyst to sit with me
and make better software together.

—Ward

Contents

Foreword   xxi

Preface   xxiii

Acknowledgments   xxv

About the Authors   xxvii

1. Introduction   1

1.1   The Need for Fit   1

1.2   The Value of Fit Tables   2

1.3   Fit and Business Roles   3

1.4   Organization of the Book   5

1.5   The Book's Use of Color   6

PART I   Introducing Fit Tables   7

2. Communicating with Tables   9

2.1   Fit Tables   9

2.2   Tables for Communicating   10

2.3   Tables for Testing   11

2.4   Tables, Fixtures, and a System Under Test   11

2.5   Reading Fit Tables   11

3. Testing Calculations with `ColumnFixture` Tables   13

3.1   Calculating Discount   13

3.2   Reports: Traffic Lights   14

3.3   Calculating Credit   16

3.4   Selecting a Phone Number   19

3.5   Summary   20

3.6   Exercises   21

4. Testing Business Processes with `ActionFixture` Tables   23
4.1   Buying Items   23
4.2   Actions on a Chat Server   26
4.3   Summary   28
4.4   Exercises   29

5. Testing Lists with `RowFixture` Tables   31
5.1   Testing Lists Whose Order Is Unimportant   31
5.2   Testing Lists Whose Order Is Important   34
5.3   Summary   36
5.4   Exercises   36

6. Testing with Sequences of Tables   39
6.1   Chat Room Changes   39
6.2   Discount Group Changes   43
6.3   Summary   46
6.4   Exercises   47

7. Creating Tables and Running Fit   49
7.1   Using Spreadsheets for Tests   49
7.2   Organizing Tests in Test Suites   50
7.3   Using HTML for Tests   52
7.4   Summary   54
7.5   Exercises   55

8. Using FitNesse   57
8.1   Introduction   57
8.2   Getting Started   58
8.3   Organizing Tests with Subwikis   61
8.4   Test Suites   62
8.5   Ranges of Values   63
8.6   Other Features   64
8.7   Summary   64
8.8   Exercises   64

9. Expecting Errors   67
9.1   Expected Errors with Calculations   67
9.2   Expected Errors with Actions   69
9.3   Summary   69

10. FitLibrary Tables   71

10.1   Flow-Style Actions with `DoFixture`   71

10.2   Expected Errors with `DoFixture`   74

10.3   Actions on Domain Objects with `DoFixture`   75

10.4   Setup   76

10.5   `CalculateFixture` Tables   78

10.6   Ordered List Tables   78

10.7   Testing Parts of a List   79

10.8   Summary   79

10.9   Exercises   80

11. A Variety of Tables   81

11.1   Business Forms   81

11.2   Testing Associations   82

11.3   Two-Dimensional Images   83

11.4   Summary   85

11.5   Exercises   85

PART II   Developing Tables for RentAPartySoftware   **87**

12. Introducing Fit at RentAPartySoftware   89

12.1   RentAPartySoftware   89

12.2   Development Issues   90

12.3   An Initial Plan   90

12.4   The Cast   91

12.5   The Rest of This Part   92

12.6   Summary   92

12.7   Exercises   93

13. Getting Started: Emily and Don's First Table   95

13.1   Introduction   95

13.2   Choosing Where to Start   95

13.3   The Business Rule   96

13.4   Starting Simple   97

13.5   Adding the Grace Period   98

13.6   Adding High-Demand Items   99

13.7   Reports   100

13.8   Seth's Return   101

13.9   Summary   101

13.10   Exercises   102

14. Testing a Business Process: Cash Rentals   103
14.1   Introduction   103
14.2   Cash Rentals   104
14.3   Split and Restructure   107
14.4   Which Client   109
14.5   Summary   111
14.6   Exercises   112

15. Tests Involving the Date and Time   115
15.1   Introduction   115
15.2   Charging a Deposit   115
15.3   Dates   118
15.4   Business Transactions   119
15.5   Sad Paths   121
15.6   Reports   122
15.7   Summary   124
15.8   Exercises   124

16. Transforming Workflow Tests into Calculation Tests   127
16.1   Introduction   127
16.2   Testing Calculations Instead   128
16.3   Using Durations   131
16.4   Reports   132
16.5   Summary   133
16.6   Exercises   134

17. Story Test-Driven Development with Fit   137
17.1   Introduction   137
17.2   The Stories   139
17.3   The First Storytests   140
17.4   The Planning Game   143
17.5   Adding to the Storytests   147
17.6   Progress During the Iteration   148
17.7   Exploratory Testing at Iteration End   151
17.8   Summary   151
17.9   Exercises   153

18. Designing and Refactoring Tests to Communicate Ideas   155

18.1   Principles of Test Design   155
18.2   Fit Tests for Business Rules   156
18.3   Workflow Tests   161
18.4   Calculation Tests   165
18.5   List Tests   167
18.6   Tests and Change   168
18.7   Automation of Tests   170
18.8   Summary   170

19. Closing for Nonprogrammers   171

19.1   The Value of Fit Tables   171
19.2   Getting Fit at RentAPartySoftware   171

PART III   Introducing Fit Fixtures   175

20. Connecting Tables and Applications   177

20.1   Writing Fixtures   177
20.2   Fixtures and Traffic Lights   178

21. Column Fixtures   179

21.1   Fixture CalculateDiscount   179
21.2   Extending Credit   182
21.3   Selecting a Phone Number   184
21.4   ColumnFixture in General   185
21.5   Summary   186
21.6   Exercises   186

22. Action Fixtures   187

22.1   Buying Items   187
22.2   Changing State of Chat Room   190
22.3   ActionFixture in General   192
22.4   Summary   193
22.5   Exercises   194

23. List Fixtures   195

23.1   Testing Unordered Lists   195
23.2   Testing Ordered Lists   197
23.3   Testing a List with Parameters   201

23.4   Summary   202
23.5   Exercises   202

24. Fixtures for Sequences of Tables   203
24.1   Chat Room Fixtures   203
24.2   Discount Group Fixtures   208
24.3   Summary   211
24.4   Exercises   212

25. Using Other Values in Tables   213
25.1   Standard Values   213
25.2   Values of Money   214
25.3   Values in FitNesse and the Flow Fixtures   217
25.4   Summary   217
25.5   Exercises   217

26. Installing and Running Fit   219
26.1   Installing Fit and FitLibrary   219
26.2   Running Fit on Folders   219
26.3   Running Fit on HTML Files   220
26.4   Running Tests During the Build   220
26.5   Other Ways to Run Tests   220
26.6   Summary   221

27. Installing FitNesse   223
27.1   Installation   223
27.2   Locating the Code   223
27.3   Larger-Scale Use with Virtual Wiki   224
27.4   Debugging FitNesse Tests   224
27.5   Summary   225
27.6   Exercises   225

28. FitLibrary Fixtures   227
28.1   Flow-Style Actions with `DoFixture`   227
28.2   `DoFixtures` as Adapters   231
28.3   Using `SetFixture`   232
28.4   Expected Errors with `DoFixture`   232
28.5   Actions on Domain Objects with `DoFixture`   234
28.6   `DoFixture` in General   237
28.7   Setup   239

28.8   CalculateFixture Tables   242
28.9   Ordered-List Tables   243
28.10   Testing Parts of a List   244
28.11   Using Other Values in Flow Tables   245
28.12   Summary   245
28.13   Exercises   245

29. Custom Table Fixtures   247
29.1   Business Forms   247
29.2   Testing Associations   248
29.3   Two-Dimensional Images   251
29.4   Summary   252

PART IV   Developing Fixtures for RentAPartySoftware   253

30. Fixtures and Adapting the Application   255
30.1   Introduction   255
30.2   The Programmers' Perspective   255
30.3   System Architecture   256
30.4   Test Infecting for Improvements   258
30.5   The Rest of This Part   260

31. Emily's First Fixture   261
31.1   The Table   261
31.2   Developing the Fixture   262
31.3   Summary   265
31.4   Exercises   266

32. Fixtures Testing Through the User Interface   267
32.1   Introduction   267
32.2   Spike   269
32.3   The Fixtures   270
32.4   The Adapter   271
32.5   Showing Others   274
32.6   Summary   275

33. Restructuring the System for Testing   277
33.1   Test Infecting   277
33.2   Slow Tests   278

33.3   Setup   278
33.4   Barriers to Testing   280
33.5   Transactions   282
33.6   Transaction Fixture   283
33.7   Split Domain and Data Source Layers   285
33.8   Reduce Interdependencies   286
33.9   Summary   287

34. Mocks and Clocks   289
34.1   Introduction   289
34.2   Changing the Date   291
34.3   Time-Related Object Interactions   292
34.4   Date Formatting   292
34.5   Changing the Application in Small Steps   293
34.6   Summary   294

35. Running Calculation Tests Indirectly   295
35.1   Testing Directly   295
35.2   Testing Indirectly   297
35.3   Summary   300

36. Closing for Programmers at RPS   301
36.1   The Value of Fit Tables   301
36.2   Getting Fit at RPS   301

PART V   Custom Development   **305**

37. The Architecture of Fit   307
37.1   Running Fit   307
37.2   Parse Tree   308
37.3   `doTable()`   309
37.4   Counts in Class `Fixture`   310
37.5   The `Fixture` Subclasses   310
37.6   `TypeAdapter`   311
37.7   Summary   312
37.8   Exercises   312

38. Developing Custom Fixtures   313
38.1   Using `SetUpFixture`   313

38.2   SetUpFixture   314
38.3   ImageFixture   314
38.4   Summary   316

39. Custom Runners   319
39.1   Runners   319
39.2   Calculator Runner   319
39.3   Reading Tests from a Text File   320
39.4   Reading Tests from a Spreadsheet   322
39.5   Summary   324

40. Model-Based Test Generation   325
40.1   Symmetries: Operations That Cancel Each Other   325
40.2   Generate a Simple Sequence   326
40.3   Generate an Interleaved Sequence   329
40.4   Summary   332
40.5   Exercises   332

PART VI   Appendices   **333**

A. Background Material   335
A.1   Testing   335
A.2   Agile Software Development   335
A.3   Ubiquitous Language   336

B. Book Resources Web Site   337

C. Fit and Other Programming Languages   339
C.1   Table Portability   339
C.2   Other Programming Languages   339

Bibliography   341
Index   345

Foreword

If you know of Fit as a testing tool, you don't need me to convince you that this book is important. You know that Fit is a tool used to write what I call "business-facing" tests, tests that help everyone believe that the software really will deliver business value. You may also know that Fit has been used mostly by early-adopter projects, the ones that are always pushing the envelope of their abilities, but that it's poised for mainstream acceptance.

And what is one of the things a tool needs to move into the mainstream? Authoritative texts, so that new users can quickly benefit from everything the scattered early adopters have learned through trial and error. That's what you're holding: a book by Fit's creator and one of the world's foremost Fitsters.

But Fit is more than a testing tool. Used to its fullest extent, it's a tool for *surprise*. Let me circle around to what I mean by that.

> To create a supple, knowledge-rich design calls for a versatile, shared team language, and a lively experimentation with language that seldom happens on software projects.
> —Eric Evans, *Domain-Driven Design* [Eva04, p. 24]

A software project is a place where different cultures come together. Some people face toward the business and its concerns; other people face toward the computer and its demands. To an expert in financial trading, a "bond" is something that's tangled up in all sorts of explicit and implicit legal, social, historical, and emotional meanings. To programmers, a Bond is an object in their program that they're trying to *keep* from getting too tangled up with other objects, lest their brains explode. Somehow, these people have to work together, and they do it by creating a shared language.

Most of that creation happens through the conversation that threads through the whole project. But some of it happens through writing.

> Ever since I can remember I have belonged to the zoological species of those for whom thought takes shape as I write.
> —Louis Aragon

Fit is a tool for people to sit down and collaboratively create tests. Tests are special things. Spoken conversation is free to be abstract, and it often is, but tests are relentlessly concrete. It's a struggle to express so precisely what you want. And it's in such struggle that creative surprise happens. You push against the world. The world pushes back. You shift your position—maybe you're not using the right words, maybe you could break the problem down differently—and push again. Repeat, maybe until it seems you'll never get it right. And then, suddenly, you push and the resistance is gone. Eureka! You've figured out how to say something that the businesspeople, the programmers, and the computer can all work with.

> By relieving the brain of all unnecessary work, a good notation sets it free to concentrate on more advanced problems.... Civilization advances by extending the number of important operations which we can perform without thinking about them.
> —A. N. Whitehead, *An Introduction to Mathematics*

It's not just through concreteness that Fit helps. When we think of what we want the computer to do, we tend to think linearly: "First I do A, so the computer will do B. Then I'll do C, so the computer will do D." It's natural to write tests the same way. But Fit uses a tabular format that encourages you to play around with both horizontal and vertical space as you look for a better way to lay out what the program is to do. When you find it, the details will drop away, handled behind the scenes, and you'll be surprised by what they obscured: overlooked special cases, conflicting needs, regularities that you can exploit, and the like.

A really top-notch software project is a strange beast. It's both relentlessly focused on delivering business value *and* ever prepared for that moment when what you know falls into a new configuration, and great new paths forward open up. For the latter to happen, you need tools, practices, habits, and patterns of communication that keep the funding flowing while gently jiggling what you know. Fit is such a tool, and this is the book that will open it up to you.

Read on.

Brian Marick
February 2005

Preface

Fitness, agility, and balance apply as much to software development as they do to athletic activities. We can admire the movements of a highly skilled dancer, skier, or athlete. Gracefulness comes from wasting no energy on unnecessary tension or balance recovery, so that effort can be focused exactly where it is needed, exactly when it is needed. The expert is continuously making small adjustments to stay aligned and in balance. Agile responses to unexpected changes distinguish the expert from the nonexpert, as their rebalancing adjustments are fluid and subtle and go unnoticed by nonexperts.

Injury, pain, distractions, and poor concentration can wreck balance, reducing the expert's ability to respond well in a focused way. Much more effort is required to perform even at a substandard level.

A high degree of fitness and practice is needed in order to build the required concentration, balance, agility, and focused power. This, inevitably, is a process of refinement over time, with attention given to more subtle aspects of risk assessment and response as expertise increases.

The achievements of athletes have continued to improve over time, sometimes through changes that break assumptions about the activity or how best to train. Big changes are often met with skepticism but will slowly become accepted as the norm as they prove their worth.

When we look at the efforts of most software developers, we see a lot of energy being wasted. In the rush to get software completed, there is often little time to reflect on how to improve the way we do things, how to get that special fitness, balance, and agility that allow us to be graceful in our intellectual efforts in order to achieve inspired results with less effort.

We get unbalanced when we have to fix old bugs, losing flow. We often have to speculate about what's needed, and feedback is too slow. Our software becomes less than elegant and is difficult to change, with tensions and stresses building up in us and in our software.

This book is intended to help improve your fitness and agility in two areas of software development where we can make huge improvements to current practice. First, improving communication between the people who need the software and the people who develop it, as well as show you how to express the business rules that are at the heart of a software solution. Second, how to use automated testing to provide immediate and effective feedback so we can maintain balance and agility and avoid "injury."

The book also questions some common assumptions about the way in which software is developed. But we don't expect that you'll make a big leap of faith: We start with current practice and show how you make small yet effective improvements.

Just like the dancer and the athlete, you will have to do more than simply read about how to do this. It is also necessary to practice.

Rick Mugridge
Ward Cunningham

Acknowledgments

Many thanks for many excellent suggestions to reviewers Dave Astels, Lisa Crispin, Brian Marick, Robert C. Martin, Kay Pentecost, and Bill Wake. Thanks to Carl Rivas, Keith Nicholas and Tom Poppendieck for helpful review comments.

Many thanks to the staff at Pearson Education, especially Paul Petralia and Tyrrell Albaugh.

Rick Mugridge

Very special thanks to Jackie Tyrrell and Anna Tyrrell for encouragement, feedback, and support through the writing process.

Many thanks to Dave Mugridge for feedback and encouragement. Thanks to Ewan Tempero for writing the original Chat server tests that ended up in Fit, for help with the Sokoban example, and for discussions about approaches to Web testing. Thanks to John Hamer for introducing me to Dot and PSTricks and for help with obscure LaTex issues. Thanks to Ian Mitchell for stressing the importance of testing the essence of business rules. Thanks to Sharron of McEntee Party Hire, Papakura, for background information on the business of renting party items.

Thanks to Robert Ensor and the students of SOFTENG 306 at the University of Auckland, who built the PartyHire system in a third-year group project in 2004, based on Fit tests that I supplied. Their questions helped me to tune my thinking about expressing and refining business rules as tests.

Thanks for discussions and help from Frank Westphal, Joshua Kerievsky, Micah Martin, David Hussman, Angela Martin, and Diana Larsen. Thanks to good feedback from the participants at the XP2004, ADC2004, and XPAU 2004 Fit tutorials. Thanks to Geoff Bache and Jennitta Andrea for discussions about testing frameworks. Thanks to Hubert Baumeister for sharing his experience in using Fit tests in his project class. Thanks to the members of the AgileAuckland group, and its predecessor, for lots of good discussions about agility.

Thanks to the University of Auckland for the half-year sabbatical in 2003, which allowed me time for attending conferences and for the initial writing.

Many thanks to Ward Cunningham, my coauthor, for creating Fit, such a powerful and elegant tool. Thanks also to Fit enthusiasts Jim Shore, John Roth, Micah Martin, Robert C. Martin, Chris Wheeler, Friedrich Brunzema, and others on the fit-dev email group for many interesting discussions about Fit and its evolution.

Special thanks to Brian Marick, whose clear thinking on the role of business-facing tests is inspiring.

Ward Cunningham

Thanks to Gary Goldberg, whose tests made the first version of this test framework sing.

Thanks to Martin Fowler, who coaxed me to write another version, and to Emmet Murphy and Dave Rice, who helped write it.

Thanks to Brian Dorsey, who got me thinking about HTML as a file format and helped with another version.

Thanks to Eric Evans, who suggested a public project, and Kent Beck, who made me do it.

Thanks to Bret Pettichord, James Bach, Brian Marick, and Cem Kaner, who helped me understand my work's relation to the larger field of testing. Thanks to Jim Shore and Ken Dicky, who sat in my office and wrote translations, and to Dave Smith, Simon Michael, Dave Thomas, Paul Chisholm, Michael Feathers, Dave Astels, Brian Ingerson, Martin Chernenkoff, and Steven Newton, who did them on their own.

Thanks to Frank Westphal, Joshua Kerievsky, Bob Martin, Bjorn Freeman-Benson, Wilkes Joiner, Jim Weaver, and my coauthor Rick Mugridge, who shared their first fixtures.

Thanks to Charlie Poole, Francesco Cirillo, and Erik Lundh, who helped me make the first Fit tutorial and take it on tour.

Thanks to all the people on the fit-dev, agile-testing, and software-testing lists, all the people at the PNWSQC, XP2003, XPAU, ADC, JAOO, and OOPSLA workshops and tutorials, and all the members of xpdx.org.

About the Authors

Rick Mugridge has been involved in software development for many years. He is an Associate Professor in Computer Science at the University of Auckland, where he has taught agile software development to engineering students since 2001. He also researches and consults to the software industry on various topics, including agile software development, (story) test-driven development, automated testing, software tools, software architecture, and user interfaces.

Rick has applied Fit to defining business rules and testing in a wide range of areas. He developed the FitLibrary, which was released in February 2005. He runs his own consulting company, Rimu Research.

Ward Cunningham is an architect in Microsoft's patterns and practices group, where he focuses on social aspects of technical knowledge. He is a founder of Cunningham & Cunningham, Inc., and has served as Director of R&D at Wyatt Software and as Principle Engineer in the Tektronix Computer Research Laboratory. Ward is well known for his contributions to the developing practice of object-oriented programming, the variation called Extreme Programming, and the communities supported by his WikiWikiWeb. Ward hosts AgileManifesto.org. He is a founder of the Hillside Group and has served as the first program chair of the Pattern Languages of Programs conference, which it sponsors.

CHAPTER 1

Introduction

1.1 The Need for Fit

Two major, interconnected tasks essential to the value and quality of a software application are

- Helping to think about and *communicate* through concrete examples what is needed in a software application

- Automatically *testing*, from a *business perspective*, that the application is doing what is expected and that it continues to do so as it grows in functionality

Often, however, these two tasks are carried out poorly, leading to breakdowns in each step along the way from an identified business need to a running application.

- The business needs are not well understood by those who want the system, owing to a lack of a clear way of thinking about these needs and, more generally, of communicating them.

- The business needs are not well understood by the developers, and so the application doesn't solve the right problem.

- The application is of low quality. It is difficult for users to understand and contains frequent faults that users have to work around. Updates are treated with suspicion because they're likely to cause more trouble than they're worth.

- The more it evolves, the more the application becomes difficult to change. It becomes fragile and easy to break. The developers start to fear making changes. They add redundant code rather than revising the existing code.

Fit (Framework for Integrated Tests) is a powerful framework for automated testing to help solve such problems. Fit is especially well suited to testing from a business perspective, using tables for representing tests and for reporting the results of automatically checking those tests. This tabular form enables people with no programming background to write tests and thereby help guide overall development of a needed system. Fit is a general-purpose, open-ended framework that's easy to extend for expressing various sorts of tests.

This book shows how to begin to solve several pervasive problems in developing software:

- Communicating with clarity between the various stakeholders and the developers. What does the system do, and what should it do?
- Focusing with precision on what needs to be done next.
- Knowing when something has been completed.
- Supporting the inevitable restructuring of the code as the system evolves.
- Ensuring that we know quickly when completed work is broken by mistake.

Our focus is on understanding business rules and expressing them with concrete examples in test tables. We distinguish two sorts of business rules:

1. Business rules that calculate something or make decisions, such as a business rule that determines the discount on a purchase
2. Business process, or workflow, rules, which specify how some action is carried out and what the outcomes should be, such as a workflow rule for what happens when a user creates and enters a chat room when connected to a chat server

We show how Fit can be incorporated into software development practices, filling a serious gap. This can be done through small steps, avoiding the risks of "big-bang" change. We show that choosing and structuring test examples are crucial. Test examples not only enhance communication between the stakeholders and the developers but also are central to automatic testing. Expressing the tests well in Fit tables begins the design process and allows for managing the inevitable changes in what is needed from the software.

1.2　The Value of Fit Tables

Fit tables help solve three major problems in software development:

1. Communication: providing a way for people who want a system to discuss and communicate that need in a concrete way. Too often, developed software is unsuited for its purpose because our understanding of what is needed and what is possible has remained vague and has not been able to evolve, owing to a lack of feedback.

    Written requirements alone are inadequate, especially when they have to be completed without feedback from the development process. Guesses often have to be made about what is important for the future, and many opportunities for gaining business value are not realized.

    It is easy to have misunderstandings with written requirements, leading to the wrong software being built. Having concrete tests that are based on realistic examples from the business domain help build a common understanding of the business needs.

2. Agility: keeping the software in good shape by supporting design changes that are essential as the needs of the business change. Automated tests help define those changes and help ensure that any changes to the software do not break previously satisfied requirements.

    As we'll see in Chapter 17, Fit tests can also help focus the development process, with a major aim of providing the most useful feedback as early as possible to enable businesspeople to guide the development in the best direction, according to their latest understanding of the problem and the solution.

3. Balance: spending less time on gaining balance with fixing problems by reducing the number and severity of problems, catching them early, and making sure they don't return.

    As we'll see in Part II, Fit tests can be introduced in small, focused steps for an existing software product that has lost balance but that needs to support change. Gaining and retaining balance is the key to agility: the ability to respond quickly to business or organizational change.

1.3 Fit and Business Roles

Fit is relevant to people in four types of business roles.

1.3.1 Businesspeople, Business Analysts, and Systems Analysts

You want a better way to influence the software development process. Too often, people misunderstand what's required. The developers expect you to make decisions about details when you're still trying to sort out the value of various approaches to solving important business issues.

This book will help you see the value of well-expressed examples that help clarify business rules. Realistic examples will help everyone involved better understand what's needed of the system. You will learn how to develop concrete examples in tables, a design process that helps people to communicate with clarity about what's needed. With successful experience, you will find that many of your frustrations with the development process will be reduced, as important enhancements happen more quickly.

1.3.2 Managers

You see a lot of wasted effort, with much rework being done. The bugs have grown to an extent that you need special tools to track them. Staff people are stressed, have lower morale, and seem reluctant to respond quickly to changes that are important for business. As the software has grown, it seems to limp more and more. You may be concerned about losing the confidence of upper management when it comes to in-house development.

This book will teach you how tests can improve communication about business rules between the people who understand the rules and those who incorporate them into a software system. You will realize that the introduction of Fit tests will require careful change management. Once Fit tables become established successfully, you will begin to see benefits in improved morale and software quality and in faster response to change. You plan for the day when the bug-tracking software can be retired; it's now clear that a lot of unnecessary work was centered on it.

1.3.3   Testers

Although automated tests would be great, there's not been time to get started on automation. Or, much of the automation you've used has been too fragile, with GUI (graphical user interface) changes invalidating many tests. Many expensive tools are available, but it's not easy to determine how much value they will provide. It's a struggle to work out what the system should do, and there is never enough time to carry out tests before the panic at the end of a release. Users are reporting too many bugs, and it takes time to filter out the ones that make sense. Manual testing is necessary in many parts of the system because it is simply too difficult to automate, and many errors are not picked up.

This book will teach you that testing can be an essential part of the software development process, not something tacked on in a rush at the end of a release. Rather than testing after the fact, your role will shift to the front. You will play a role in helping business analysts to structure and write tests that help spell out business rules. You will also use the table structures to develop sets of tests that provide good coverage, based on your knowledge of what is likely to go wrong. You will find that your tests will change in character as the impact of the Fit tests propagates throughout the development cycle. As tests cover more of the software and as regression testing becomes a daily occurrence, you will find fewer bugs returning after they have been "fixed." You will have more time to focus on finding those difficult bugs rather than on the many trivial ones that used to slip through.

This book does not try to teach testing. Instead, the book aims to leverage the general testing skills that you have already by using Fit for automated testing of business rules.

1.3.4   Programmers, Software Architects, and Software Engineers

It can be difficult to get answers at the right time to your questions about what's needed; this means that you simply have to guess and change it later. The pressure is always on to change a large, complex piece of software. It takes longer to make changes and to fix bugs as the system grows. Often, a bug fix simply leads to more bugs (in 16 percent of the time, according to Steve McConnell [McC99]). You know from experience that it's unwise to change some parts of the system; inevitably, bugs result. So you tend to add similar code, because changing what's there is risky.

This book will teach you that Fit tests can improve your fitness to develop software. Fit tables can provide you with a clearer understanding of what's needed. Some of the design decisions about the whole system will be affected or driven by businesspeople, but that's OK, as you will have more time to focus on the hard architectural design decisions. The tests give you more confidence that you have completed a task and that you haven't broken any other code in the process. This encourages you to use a unit-testing framework, such as JUnit, for your programmer tests, as you appreciate the value of clarifying with tests what is needed beforehand. You are relieved to at last feel confident about tackling the mess that has built up in the tangle of software, as you have the tests to support your refactorings. As the quality improves, you find that you spend less and less of your time on rework and fixing bugs. Enhancements now go smoothly, with much less effort.

In order to communicate with testers and business stakeholders, you will need to read Fit tests, and understand how they evolve. And you will be needed to develop the "glue" code that connects those tests to the system under test.

1.4 Organization of the Book

This book is centered on the use of the Fit framework for developing tests that nonprogrammers can read and write and that can be automated by developers. The rest of this book is organized into five parts.

Business-oriented Part I and Part II focus on the design of Fit tables, based on business rules. These parts are relevant to everyone who has an interest in using Fit, including programmers. Part III and Part IV focus on the development of fixtures that mediate between the Fit tables and the system under test, as well as the impact on that system. Part V focuses on custom development with Fit. These three parts contain technical material for programmers.

- Part I introduces the idea of Fit tables for testing and shows simple examples of several types of tests. We leave the more complex issues that arise in the design of Fit tables until Part II. This part requires no programming background.

- Part II shows by example how Fit tests are developed. We cover the issues that arise in the step-by-step integration of Fit tables for testing a "legacy"[1] system in RentAPartySoftware, a fictitious software company. We now start looking at more complex issues that arise in the development of tests. This part requires no programming background.

- Part III introduces the use of fixtures to mediate between the Fit tables of Part I and the system under test. We leave the issues that arise in adapting a system to enable testing until Part IV. This part is for those with a programming background.

- Part IV covers the development of fixtures corresponding to the tables introduced in Part II. We explain how to manage the changes to the system under test to enable testing. This part is for those with a programming background.

---

[1] By "legacy," we mean a system that lacks test support and hence lacks rejuvenation.

- Part V covers the development of custom Fit fixtures, runners, and test generators. This part is for those with a programming background.

The appendices are as follows.

- Appendix A provides access to background information on testing and other topics related to this book.
- Appendix B provides information on accessing the various resources related to this book.
- Appendix C briefly covers Fit and programming languages other than Java.

1.5   The Book's Use of Color

Because colors are important in the reports of Fit tables (see Section 3.2 for more details), the text of this book is printed in black and green.

Other colors are also important in certain Fit screen dumps (see Figure 2.1, for example). In those cases, full-color versions of figures are provided on the inside cover.

PART I

INTRODUCING FIT TABLES

CHAPTER 2

Communicating with Tables

2.1 Fit Tables

Fit tables can enhance our communication about what is needed in a software system. Fit uses tables for writing tests and for reporting the results of automatically checking those tests. This tabular form enables people with a business or organizational background to help guide the overall development of a needed system by writing concrete examples that also serve as tests.

For example, the report for a Fit table for testing discounts is shown in Figure 2.1 (see also Plate 1). This table consists of several tests, with each row showing what discount is expected for a given amount. This example is explained in Chapter 3.

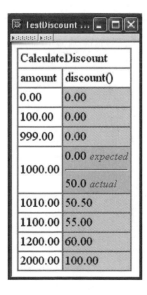

Figure 2.1 Fit Report for TestDiscount

2.2   Tables for Communicating

As we saw in Chapter 1, Fit tables help solve three major problems in software development: Communication, Agility, and Balance. Fit tables aid communication between the people who want a software system and those who develop it. Test tables also apply to the ongoing development of new features in existing software products and systems. Rather than talking in vague terms about what is required or how a system works, businesspeople can use concrete examples in tables to help be specific. For example, the requirement "Charge fairly for rental items, using the rental scheme that is best for the customer" is rather vague and requires considerable questioning or guesswork for a programmer to handle. Further, it's not clear when it has been completed.

Stories and examples are a powerful way to communicate. We often need good, clear examples before we're ready to discuss the general case. These examples help us to agree on terminology and to refine or create a "ubiquitous language" [Eva04]. It is effective to have people with different backgrounds discussing those cases, looking at them from different perspectives, and sketching out concrete examples that can turn into Fit tests.

The programmers can see more clearly what's needed, driving their development from the tests, and know when they're done. The testers can see what other cases need to be considered at the start, when everyone is thinking about it. The businesspeople have specifics to discuss and to reconsider, to gain agreement about business needs and the relative value to be gained from developing features in a software system to support those needs.

Our focus in this book is on expressing tests for business rules. We are interested in two types of business rules:

1. Those that define how *calculations* are made, such as for discounts, or how *decisions* are made, such as whether to send a payment demand

2. Those that define the *business processes* that are incorporated into a software system, such as the steps used to admit a patient to a hospital

We often need a mixture of tests for such rules, because we want to ensure that business calculations are also being made correctly within the context of a business process.

Tables are used, rather than plain text or a programming language, because the rows and columns of a table provide a clear and simple structure. Placing a value in the cell of a table is very simple, and many people are used to using tables in spreadsheets, Web pages, and other documents. As we discuss in the following chapters, once the structure of a table is clear, using that table, or another like it, to add concrete examples is straightforward. Finally, as we saw in Figure 2.1, Fit provides feedback from running tests by coloring the cells in the reported test table (Plate 1).

2.3   Tables for Testing

Fit tables are structured so that they can also act as automated tests that are run against an application system, which we call the *system under test*. Specific information is provided in Fit tables to enable them to be used in testing. The *fixture* of a table determines how it will be used in automated testing.

In the next three chapters, we see three main families of fixtures that make use of the table structure in different ways. Later chapters introduce other sorts of fixtures and show how new table structures can be invented to enable business rules to be expressed as clearly as possible. Together, a variety of table types are used to express business rules that are to be incorporated in the software under development.

2.4   Tables, Fixtures, and a System Under Test

Figure 2.2 shows the main testing ingredients that we will be exploring throughout this book. At the top are three Fit tables that contain data for one or more tests. In the middle are three fixtures, each of which is responsible for checking that the tests in their table are satisfied by the system under test, which is at the bottom.

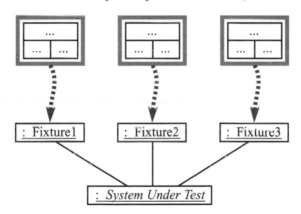

Figure 2.2 Fit Tables Test Applications

We begin with some simple examples of Fit tables for testing. Such tests are for checking various business rules, those elements of a software application that most interest businesspeople.

2.5   Reading Fit Tables

A reading knowledge of Fit tables is needed in order to undertake the social process of creating and evolving tests with Fit. Chapters 3, 4, and 5 look at examples of tests using tables based on the three core Fit fixtures:

1. ColumnFixture tables, for testing calculations (Chapter 3)
2. ActionFixture tables, for testing that things happen on actions (Chapter 4)
3. RowFixture tables, for testing lists or other collections of things (Chapter 5)

The remaining chapters of Part I further develop the basics of reading Fit test tables:

- Using sequences of tables (Chapter 6)
- Creating tables and running Fit on them (Chapter 7)
- Using FitNesse, a Web-based environment for creating, managing, and running Fit tables (Chapter 8)
- Managing several issues that arise in testing (Chapter 9)
- Using flow-style fixture tables (Chapter 10)
- Using examples of other table structures (Chapter 11) to show by example that custom table structures may be used to better express some tests

The process and people aspects of developing Fit tests are examined in Part II. Fit tables need some support from programmers to connect the tests through to the system under test. Corresponding to the tables and tools developed in Part I, programmer-specific details are given in Part III, which covers writing the fixture code and installing Fit and FitNesse.

Note

Fit was developed by Ward Cunningham and released in 2002.

Details of the history of Fit development are available at http://fit.c2.com/wiki.cgi?FrameworkHistory.

CHAPTER 3

Testing Calculations with `ColumnFixture` Tables

We often want to test that calculations are being carried out correctly, according to some business rule. Tables of concrete examples help us to understand business needs and communicate what's required. Here, we will focus on how to read such Fit tests; later, we will show how to write them.

We begin with two simple examples that test calculations by using tables of type `ColumnFixture`, which is designed to do this.

These tests are rather abstract in that they say nothing about how someone using the system under test will see the consequences of this business rule. In Chapter 4, we'll see tests that are more aligned to the step-by-step use of the system under test.

3.1   Calculating Discount

The business rule for our first example follows.

> A 5 percent discount is provided whenever the total purchase is greater than $1,000.

We use examples in a table to help define the relationship between the amount and the discount for several cases. For example, when the amount is $1,100, the discount is $55. Figure 3.1 shows a simple set of tests for the part of a system that calculates discounts.

The *fixture*, `CalculateDiscount`, is named in the first row of the table. The fixture determines how the examples in the table are to be tested automatically against the system under test.

As this is a `ColumnFixture` table, the second row is a *header* row, which labels the *given* and *calculated* value columns. Here, the *amount* column holds the *given* values, and the *discount()* column holds the *calculated* results that are expected.[1]

---

[1] The label for a *calculated* result column has () after the name.

Column labels in the header row serve two purposes.

1. They help us to understand the examples in the table.

2. They are used when the examples are automatically tested by Fit.

CalculateDiscount	
amount	*discount()*
0.00	0.00
100.00	0.00
999.00	0.00
1000.00	0.00
1010.00	50.50
1100.00	55.00
1200.00	60.00
2000.00	100.00

Figure 3.1 Fit Table for Testing Discount (with an Error)

The remaining eight *test rows* of the table are our test cases, which are checked one at a time. For the first test case, the given value under **amount** is 0, and so a *calculated* value of 0 under **discount()** is expected. The second test case is independent of the first; the *given* **amount** is 100, and so the *calculated* **discount()** is expected to be 0. And so on.

Fit runs the tests, one row at a time, against the system under test. Fit begins with the third row of the table, providing the *given* value of 0.00 to the application. Fit checks that the result calculated by the application, based on that **amount**, is 0.00, as *expected*.

3.2   Reports: Traffic Lights

When Fit is run, it produces a report. The table cells are colored to show the results of the tests, so that we can tell which tests passed and which failed. This makes it easy to see which tests went right and which went wrong. Fit uses a traffic light metaphor for the colors in the report.

- *Green:* Test passed.

- *Red:* Test failed to meet expectations. Additional information may be provided.

- *Yellow:* Part of a test is not completely implemented, or something else went wrong.

- *Gray:* Parts of tables that have not been processed for some known reason, perhaps because a test is not completely implemented.

Other cells are left unmarked unless something goes wrong. A reported table may have rows added to it to provide extra information about failing tests.

The results of the tests in Figure 3.1 are reported as shown in Figure 3.2 (see also Plate 1). The passing tests, whose calculated value of *discount()* is as expected, are green. The report contains a single failing test. This failed test is red because the system under test is incorrect when the amount is 1,000.00. The actual value that was calculated by the system under test (50.0) is added to the report.

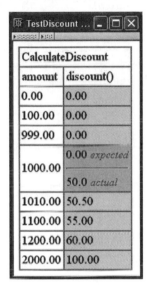

Figure 3.2 Fit Report for TestDiscount

Tip

The ordering of the test rows in this particular table is not important for automated testing, as the tests are independent. However, the order is important to the people who read and write such tests.

Are there any questions at this stage?

Questions & Answers

Are these tests, or are they requirements?
They're both. The concrete examples help us to think about and communicate the important requirements to software developers. As the examples are in a suitable form, they can also be used to automatically test that the resulting software application does what's expected.

But the tests can't *define* all situations.

That's right; we use concrete examples to give an idea of the general case. They need to be augumented with other forms of communication: general statements of the underlying business rules and discussion between the people concerned.

What if the business rules are not well understood or are changing?

Creating the examples helps to focus on the essence of the rules. Examples serve as a way to sort out how we want to talk about the important issues that a system has to deal with. It can be easier to discuss business issues in the context of specific examples rather than trying to deal with generalities. The examples help to break down the important cases so that we don't have to deal with everything all at once. (We cover the dynamics of this process in detail in Part II.)

If the business rules are changing, we need a way to express those changes and to talk about them. That may mean simply adding new examples to cover new cases. Or it may mean changing our terminology because the essence of the rules has to be altered. Either way, as we see in Chapter 18, it's important that we can change the Fit tests as the world changes.

What happens if you put something other than a number in a cell?

When the wrong sort of data is in a table cell, an *error* is marked with yellow in the report that Fit produces.

Can we use values other than numbers?

Yes; in general, a cell table can contain any sort of values, such as text strings, dates, times, and simple lists. See Section 3.4 for an example that uses simple lists.

Programmers: The fixture code for the tests here is given in Section 21.1 on p. 179.

3.3   Calculating Credit

Here's the business rule for our second example of using a `ColumnFixture` table to test calculations.

> Credit is allowed, up to an amount of $1,000, for a customer who has been trading with us for more than 12 months, has paid reliably over that period, and has a balance owing of less than $6,000.

Again, we use a table to define whether credit will be extended, based on the values of the various given characteristics of our customers. A small set of tests for this business rule is shown in Figure 3.3.

The first row of the table names `CalculateCredit`, the *fixture*, which determines how the examples in the table are to be tested automatically against the system under test. In this book, we follow a convention that fixtures that test calculations have `Calculate` in their name.

CalculateCredit				
months	*reliable*	*balance*	*allow credit()*	*credit limit()*
14	true	5000.00	true	1000.00
0	true	0.00	false	0.00
24	*false*	0.00	false	0.00
18	true	*6000.00*	false	0.00
12	true	5500.00	true	1000.00

Figure 3.3 Fit Table for Testing Credit

The second (header) row of this table, as usual, labels the *given* and *calculated* value columns for testing creditworthiness. Two columns have *calculated* values: `allow credit()` and `credit limit()`. The given value of `reliable` and the calculated value of `allow credit()` will be either true or false. As is usual with `ColumnFixture` tables, the test rows are independent of one another.

In Figure 3.3, the four cell values in *italics* indicate that credit is refused. Test writers can format Fit tables to better organize them, as we'll see later, and format cells values of special interest to highlight them.

Fit reports the results as shown in Figure 3.4 (see also Plate 2). In each *test row* of the report, the two cells for the calculated results that are expected are marked. The tests in the first four rows are *right* and are marked in green. The last row of the table fails, with two cells marked *wrong*, in red.

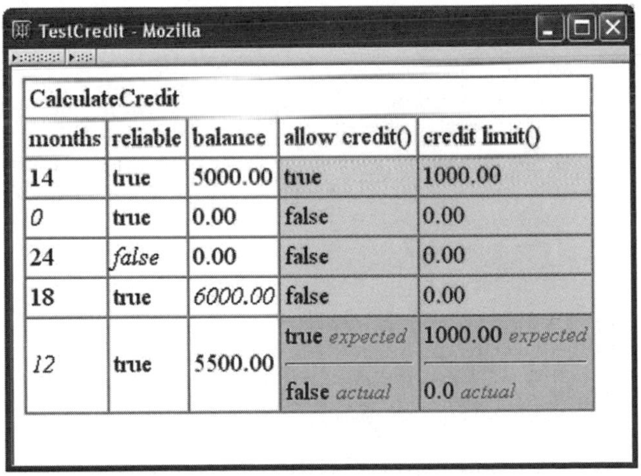

Figure 3.4 Fit Report for TestCredit

In general, a test can fail for several reasons. For example, in the report in Figure 3.4, the failing test itself could be incorrect, or the business rule may be stated incorrectly for the case of exactly 12 months.

Looking Ahead

Note that we don't test the business rule with specific customers; we have abstracted away from the table how we determine those characteristics for particular customers. We discuss such design issues for tables in Chapter 18.

This set of examples is fine for giving a sense of the business rule. However, they are incomplete from a tester's perspective. We'd need more tests to make sure that the business rule has been understood and implemented correctly in software. Testers have expertise in the art of choosing such test cases.

These tests are also badly organized. It's not easy to see what the rows are testing and what is missing. We take up this issue in Chapter 18.

You may have noticed the subtle redundancy between the two calculated fields. The value of *credit limit ()* always depends, effectively, on the value of *allow credit ()*. *Redundancy*, and why we want to avoid it in the design of tables, is discussed in Chapter 18.

Finally, in some situations, the rows of a ColumnFixture table are not independent, by choice, as we show in Section 4.1 on p. 23 and in Chapter 13.

Questions & Answers

What if we want to use *yes* and *no* instead of *true* and *false*?
They can be used instead in FitNesse (Chapter 8), where *yes*, *y*, *1*, and + can also be used for true. Anything else is false.

What if a *given* number is negative, which is not valid in the application?
We take up this issue in Chapter 9.

What's a *fixture*?
A fixture is the "glue" that connects the tests in a Fit table to your application.

From a programmer's point of view, a fixture names the software that is responsible for running the tests in the table against the system under test. Different fixtures may do different sorts of tests. Part III covers this in detail.

Will a whole test sequence be included in one table? Some of our tests go on for many pages.
No, not necessarily. We'll see in Chapter 6 that a test sequence may consist of many tables of varying types.

Programmers: The fixture code for the tests here is given in Section 21.2 on p. 182.

3.4   Selecting a Phone Number

Our third example illustrates the use of simple lists in tests. The business rule for this example is very simple.

> The first phone number in the list of supplied phone numbers will normally be used for communicating with the client.

A single test is shown in Figure 3.5. The *phones* column contains a comma-separated list of phone numbers. The *calculated* column *first()* selects the first one in the list.

CalculateFirstPhoneNumber	
phones	*first()*
(209)373 7453, (209)373 7454	(209)373 7453

Figure 3.5 Fit Table for Testing First Phone

When the elements of a list are more complex, such as containing details of each order item within an order, this approach doesn't work. A RowFixture table can be used instead, as discussed in Chapter 5.

Questions & Answers

What if an element in the list contains a comma (,)?
In that case, a RowFixture tables could be used, as covered in Chapter 5. If you wanted to use such lists in a ColumnFixture, a programmer would need to write some fixture code to handle that specially, as we discuss in Chapter 25.

What happens if the phone list is empty?
The business rule doesn't cover that situation, but it does need to be defined. We take up this issue in Chapter 9, when we talk about handling various expected errors.

Programmers: The fixture code for the tests here is given in Section 21.3 on p. 184.

3.5 Summary

- Fit tests are defined in tables.

- ColumnFixture tables are good for specifying the expected *calculated* value based on the *given* value in a row.

- The test writer gets to choose the names of the labels in the header row, such as *phones* and *first()*.

- Each row of a ColumnFixture table represents an independent test when it's used for testing the same calculations on different data. We'll see ColumnFixture tables in Section 4.1, where the rows are not independent, and so their order is important.

- When Fit runs a test, it produces a report. This report gives feedback on the test by marking parts of the input table according to what passed.

- We've seen several examples of ColumnFixture tables; the second table had two *calculated* columns.

The next chapter introduces action-style tables. However, if you'd like to start using Fit on ColumnFixture examples first, you may like to look now at Chapter 7.

Questions & Answers

We have lots of tests in text files. We wouldn't want to make tables from them.
You don't need to do so. As we'll see in Chapter 7, tests in other input formats can be fed into Fit. However, some straightforward programming will be required for custom data formats (as discussed in Chapter 39).

Our existing tests all center on the process of using the system. There are no "calculation" tests.
Often, tests are written in this way because the only way to check them has been to run the system through the user interface and carry out a sequence of steps. When we look more closely at those tests, we often get an inkling of the underlying business rules.
As discussed in Part II and especially Chapter 18, we aim to extract those essential business rules and express them independently of the work flow. That extraction has several benefits. We gain clarity about the rules. By expressing them succinctly, we can more easily discuss the rule and see what cases (examples) we may need to add or change as the business changes. It is much faster to create the (short) examples, as they can ignore the workflow. The tests are not dependent on the user interface, which is often the part of a system that changes the most. Those tests can be made to run much faster, if necessary.

But that assumes that we can test the business rules in isolation!
Yes, it seems to assume that. We discuss various ways for programmers to manage this in Chapter 33.

How do we decide on suitable tests for our application?
We'll cover that in some depth in Part II, once we've seen several examples of various sorts of tests. The process of writing tests usually starts from thinking about the important things in your business domain and what you want to say about them. That's what we're calling "business rules." In some cases, they're quite obvious; in others, they come out of clear thinking about what's needed by exploring with concrete examples.

If you now want to see how Fit tests are created, skip ahead and read Chapters 12 and 13. The chapters after those two may not make complete sense; you will probably need to come back and read more of the chapters in this part first.

How do the programmers know what to do with a Fit table I've written?
To write the fixture code, they may need to talk to you about what you intend with the test. After that, they'll know what to do with similar tables.

3.6   Exercises

Answers to selected exercises are available on the book Web site; see Appendix B for details.

1. The business rule from Section 3.1 on p. 13 is as follows: "A 5 percent discount is provided whenever the total purchase is greater than $1,000." Using this business rule, color in Figure 3.6, based on the traffic light colors in Section 3.2 on p. 14. Do so as it would be reported by Fit, according to whether the tests pass. You don't need to bother to insert *actual* values where a test value is *wrong*.

CalculateDiscount	
amount	*discount()*
1.00	0.00
10.00	0.50
1400.00	75.00
20000.00	200.00

Figure 3.6 Color in the Table

2. The business rule from Section 3.3 on p. 16 is as follows: "Credit is allowed, up to an amount of $1,000, for a customer who has been trading with us for more than 12 months, has paid reliably over that period, and has a balance owing of less than $6,000." Color in Figure 3.7, using this business rule, as in the previous exercise.

3. Create a `ColumnFixture` table for the following.

   Percentages of dollar amounts are rounded to the nearest cent.

CalculateCredit				
months	*reliable*	*balance*	*allow credit()*	*credit limit()*
13	true	5900.00	true	1000.00
12	true	0.00	false	1000.00
24	false	1000.00	false	0.00
18	false	6000.00	true	1000.00

Figure 3.7 Color in the Table

4. Create a `ColumnFixture` table for this business rule.

    We charge for time, based on the charge rate of the consultant, in units of whole hours and with a minimum charge of $5,000.

5. Create a `ColumnFixture` table for a simple business rule that is relevant to you and that involves simple calculations.

CHAPTER 4

Testing Business Processes with `ActionFixture` Tables

An `ActionFixture` table tests that a sequence of actions made to a system have the desired effects. For example, pressing keys on a simple calculator leads to changes in the numbers shown on the calculator display. `ActionFixture` uses the metaphor of a *device* to control the test; values can be entered into input fields, buttons pressed (clicked), and output fields checked against expected values. In this chapter, we look at two simple examples of using `ActionFixture` tables

4.1   Buying Items

Here's the business rule for the first example of an `ActionFixture` table.

> A user selects a number of items to buy. The total price is accumulated for those items.

Figure 4.1 shows a simple table for testing. The first row is the fixture name, as usual: in this case, `ActionFixture`. The second row of the table *starts* `BuyActions`. This starts the application under test, which will accumulate the total price.

fit.ActionFixture		
start	BuyActions	
check	total	00.00
enter	price	12.00
press	buy	
check	total	12.00
enter	price	100.00
press	buy	
check	total	112.00

Figure 4.1 Fit Table for Testing Buying Items

The third row, and those that follow, carry out the following *action* sequence:

1. *check* that the *total* is initially 00.00

2. *enter* a *price* of 12.00

3. *press* the *buy* button to buy an (unspecified) item of price 12.00

4. *check* that the *total* is now 12.00, as expected

5. *enter* a second *price* of 100.00

6. *press* the *buy* button to buy an item of price 100.00

7. *check* that the *total* is now 112.00, as expected

The *actions* in the rows of the table are carried out in the order given. The columns of the table as a whole serve only to split up each of the rows into cells.

The resulting report is shown in Figure 4.2. Only the *check* results are marked, with the green showing that the *total* value was as expected each time.

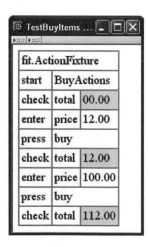

Figure 4.2 Fit Report for TestLineItems

Underlying this `ActionFixture` is a device model; it's not a real device and is not intended to be testing through the user interface. We can imagine that after the *start*, the device model is like that shown in Figure 4.3 for TestLineItems. The device model is made up of:

1. An input field for *enter*ing the *price*

2. A *buy* button to *press*

3. A display for *check*ing the *total*

The device shown in Figure 4.4 is after the first six actions in Figure 4.1, just before the *buy* button is pressed.

Figure 4.3 Initial Device

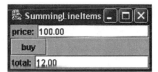

Figure 4.4 Device After Five Actions

Questions & Answers

The seventh row changes the *price* in Figure 4.1 to 100.00. What happens if that row is removed?
Because the *price* has not been changed to 100.00, another 12.00 will be added to the *total*, resulting in the *check* in the last row being wrong (24.00 instead of 112.00).

Do you mean that we should test through the user interface?
No, we don't mean to imply that; the terminology of `ActionFixture` simply uses a device interface as a metaphor.

It's best to avoid testing through the user interface, as that is difficult and leads to tests that break when the user interface changes. We'll have lots more to say about that in Part II.

Are there other actions?
`ActionFixture` has the actions *start*, *enter*, *press*, and *check*. However, as we'll see in Chapter 11, `DoFixture` tables may have any actions you wish.

What happens if the *start* action is missing?
That could mean that the system under test has not been started and so an error would be given. However, we'll see in Chapter 6 that a *start* action is not usually used in the middle of a sequence of tables.

What happens if the entered data is wrong?
If the entered data is of the wrong format, such as a date instead of a number, Fit signals the error in the table directly. If the application under test rejects it, such as the *price* should not be negative, Fit signals that in the table.

What if we want to test that an invalid date is rejected, as expected?
We cover this general topic later, in Section 9.1 on p. 67.

Couldn't the tests in Figure 4.1 be done with a `ColumnFixture`?
Yes, you're right. We could do it as in Figure 4.5, where the *total()* accumulates.

BuyActionsWithColumn	
price	*total()*
12.00	12.00
100.00	112.00

Figure 4.5 Fit `ColumnFixture` Table for Testing Buying Items

Programmers: The fixture code for the tests here is given in Section 22.1 on p. 187.

4.2   Actions on a Chat Server

The business rule for changes to a chat server, our second example of `ActionFixture`, follows.

> A chat user connects, creates a new chat room, and enters it. Another user connects and enters the same room. Check that the room has two occupants.

A simple table for testing this is shown in Figure 4.6. The second row of the table *start*s `ChatServerActions`, starting the application under test. In this book, fixtures that test actions have *Action* in their names.

The third row, and those that follow, carry out the following *action* sequence:

1. *enter* a *user* name of anna

2. *press* the *connect* button to connect user anna to the chat server

3. *enter* a *room* name of lotr

4. *press* the *new room* button for anna to create a new room named lotr on the chat server

fit.ActionFixture		
start	ChatServerActions	
enter	user	anna
press	connect	
enter	room	lotr
press	new room	
press	enter room	
enter	user	luke
press	connect	
press	enter room	
check	occupant count	2

Figure 4.6 Fit Table for Testing a Chat Server

5. *press* the *enter room* button for anna to enter lotr, the new chat room

6. *enter* a *user* name of luke

7. *press* the *connect* button to connect user luke to the chat server

8. *press* the *enter room* button for luke to enter the lotr room

9. *check* that the *occupant count* for the lotr room is 2

After all actions have been carried out, the device model for this is as shown in Figure 4.7. The resulting Fit report is shown in Figure 4.8.

Figure 4.7 Device After All Actions

Note

In deciding on concrete examples and working out how to express them in tables, we use and invent terminolgy for discussing important things in the business domain. *Domain-Driven Design* [Eva04] shows how this language is formed through a dialogue among the various stakeholders about what is required of a software system.

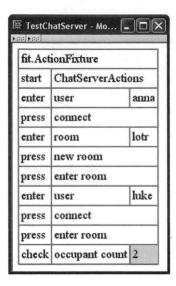

Figure 4.8 Fit Report for TestChatServer

Questions & Answers

Can comments be put in the tables?
Yes, it is valuable to include discussion with the tables. We'll first see the use of such documentation in Chapter 6, when we look at sequences of tables.

Why tables?
That's an interesting question. Tables provide just enough structure and no more, helping to organize information, including tests. As we'll see in the next chapter, Fit associates tables with tests and ignores all other information when running those tests. Written requirements are rarely structured enough to permit automated testing.

In addition, rows and cells of a table can be colored and have extra information added in a Fit report, giving feedback in the same form as the tests.

Programmers: The fixture code for the tests here is given in Section 22.2 on p. 190.

4.3   Summary

- `ActionFixture` tables are good for carrying out a series of actions and tests on a system that changes state.

- Four actions can be carried out in an **ActionFixture** table: *start*, *enter*, *press*, and *check*.

- The *enter*, *press*, and *check* actions operate on various *fields*, such as *total* and *new room*. The names of these *fields* are chosen by the test writer.

- We have seen two examples in which the tests make changes to the state of a system and check that the system responds as expected to those changes.

- In our first example, each time an item is bought, we expect the total to increase by the price of that item.

- In our second example, when a connected user enters a room, we expect to see them counted as an occupant of that room. We continue with this example in Chapter 6.

4.4 Exercises

Answers to selected exercises are available on the book Web site; see Appendix B for details.

1. The business rule from Section 4.1 on p. 23 is as follows: "A user selects a number of items to buy. The total price is accumulated for those items." Color in Figure 4.9 according to this rule, based on the traffic light colors in Section 3.2 on p. 14. Do so as it would be reported by Fit, according to whether the tests pass. You don't need to bother to insert *actual* values where a test value is *wrong*.

fit.ActionFixture		
start	BuyActions	
check	total	00.00
enter	price	45.00
press	buy	
check	total	55.00
enter	price	100.00
press	buy	
check	total	145.00
enter	price	100.00
check	total	255.00

Figure 4.9 Color in the Table

2. Let's write a new test related to the test in Section 4.2 on p. 26: "Anna creates a second room and moves to it." You make the business decision as to whether she is only in the latest room or is in both.

3. Choose a simple sequence of steps in a business process that is relevant to you, and write a test using an **ActionFixture** table.

CHAPTER 5

Testing Lists with RowFixture Tables

RowFixture tables are designed for testing that the results of a search or a query of the system under test are as expected. Such tables can also test that the expected elements of a list—group, list, sequence, set, or bag of things—are present in the system under test. For example, we may wish to test that all the outstanding orders for a customer are as expected. The rows together form a single group, unlike the independent rows of a ColumnFixture table.

Using RowFixture tables we now look at examples that test lists. In the next chapter, we'll see how to combine such tables with other types of tables in a Fit test.

5.1 Testing Lists Whose Order Is Unimportant

Here's the business rule for chat room occupants, our first example.

> A chat room user may ask for a list of all users currently in chat rooms.
> The list includes the chat room name and the user name.

This business rule is related to the one in Section 4.2 on p. 26. A Fit table to test that the current occupants of the chat room are as expected, such as after the actions of Figure 4.6 on p. 27, is shown in Figure 5.1.

The first row names the fixture *OccupantList*, which determines from the system under test the list that is to be tested against the table rows after the second row. In this book, we use the convention that all fixtures related to testing lists include *List* in their names.

The second, header row of the Fit table in Figure 5.1 labels the columns with the two *expected*[1] field names for the elements of the list. Two further rows are for

---

[1] Unlike with ColumnFixture, the labels for *expected* fields in RowFixture tables usually do not include ().

the two expected occupants of the chat room. The order of these two rows does not need to be the same as their *actual* order in the system under test.

OccupantList	
user	*room*
anna	lotr
luke	lotr

Figure 5.1 Fit Table for Testing Occupants of a Chat Room

When Fit runs the tests in Figure 5.1, the report shown in Figure 5.2 results, with both rows correct and marked with green. This tells us that two elements are in the collection and that they match the rows given in the table.

Figure 5.2 Fit Report for TestOccupants

The report in Figure 5.3 (see also Plate 3) results from a different test, in which the expected rows don't match that actual collection. As usual, unexpected values are marked with red.

Figure 5.3 Fit Report for TestOccupants

Questions & Answers

What happens if there are more occupants than expected?
Fit reports the unexpected elements from the actual list as *surplus*. These elements are added to the bottom of the reported `RowFixture` table as extra rows. We'll see an example of that shortly.

What if we expect no elements?
In that case, the table has no *expected* rows, as shown in Figure 5.4. The test would fail, with two surplus elements being reported in red, as shown in Figure 5.5 (see also Plate 4).

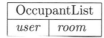

Figure 5.4 Table for Testing That There Are No Occupants

Figure 5.5 Fit Reporting Surplus Occupants

What if we want to check the occupants only in a particular room?
We can do that by providing the room name in the first row, after the fixture name, as shown in Figure 5.6. In general, we can provide one or more values as *arguments* in the fixture row for any fixture.

OccupantListInRoom	lotr
user	
anna	
luke	

Figure 5.6 Table for Testing the Occupants of a Selected Room

Can we make the tests ignore whether the names are uppercase?
Yes, a programmer can handle that easily in the fixture.

What if the order of the occupant rows *is* important?
We cover order in the next example.

Programmers: The fixture code for the tests here is given in Section 23.1 on p. 195.

5.2   Testing Lists Whose Order Is Important

Here's the business rule for discount groups, our second example.

> The discount percentage that is provided depends on a customer's projected future value (high, medium, low), how much is owed, and the total amount of any one purchase. As the specifics of discount groups will change from time to time, their defining values will be stored in a configuration file.

This description is not easy to follow, a situation that often arises with requirements documents. We'll see that the following examples in this chapter and in the next will help clarify what's really required.

At this stage, we simply check that the current discount groups are stored in order, as expected, in the file. The fixture *DiscountGroupOrderedList*, a RowFixture, is named in the first row of Figure 5.7. The header row labels the five *expected* field values of each element in the list, from *order* to *discount percent*.

DiscountGroupOrderedList				
order	*future value*	*max owing*	*min purchase*	*discount percent*
1	low	0.00	0.00	0
2	low	0.00	2000.00	3
3	medium	500.00	600.00	3
4	medium	0.00	500.00	5
5	high	2000.00	2000.00	10

Figure 5.7 **RowFixture** Table That Tests Order Explicitly

We have included a column *order* here to be explicit about the order of the elements in the file. (This value doesn't occur in the file, so it is added by the fixture.) Fit runs the table and compares the table rows with the elements of the list in the system under test. The report resulting from Figure 5.7 is shown in Figure 5.8.

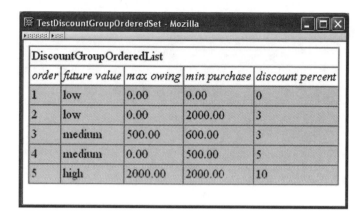

Figure 5.8 Report

Questions & Answers

What if two rows in the table are the same?
That's OK. There would need to be two matching rows in the actual list for the test to pass.

Does the order of the columns in the table have to match the order of the values in the actual collection?
No. And it is not necessary to include all columns if they are not of interest in a particular test. This is illustrated by Figure 5.9, which passes.

DiscountGroupArrayList	
discount percent	*future value*
0	low
3	low
3	medium
5	medium
10	high

Figure 5.9 Table That Tests Some Column Values

Programmers: The fixture code for the tests here is given in Section 23.2 on p. 197.

Note

For now, we have ignored how the discount groups are changed. We
have simply tested that they are all as expected at a certain point in time. In
Section 6.2 on p. 43, we show a sequence of tests that checks that additions
to the discount groups are stored correctly.

Note that we're not testing that the discount groups are being handled
correctly when discounts are calculated in the software; other tests are needed
to do that. For example, either of the "medium" discount groups may apply,
but which takes priority? We take this up in Section 6.2 on p. 43.

5.3   Summary

- We often need to test collections, especially after carrying out some actions
  on a system under test, to check that an appropriate change has occurred.

- `RowFixture` tables are good for checking the elements of a list.

- Where the order of the list is important, a table column is needed to give the
  order.

- We see in Section 10.6 on p. 78 that `ArrayFixture` tables can also be used
  to check that the elements are in the correct order.

- We see in Section 10.7 on p. 79 that `SubsetFixture` tables check that all
  the expected elements in the table occur in the actual collection but ignore
  surplus elements.

5.4   Exercises

Answers to selected exercises are available on the book Web site; see Appendix B
for details.

1. Using the business rule from Section 5.1 on p. 31 and the known occupants
    from Figure 5.1, color in Figure 5.10. Do so as it would be reported by Fit,
    according to whether the tests pass. You don't need to bother to insert *actual*
    values where a test value is *wrong*. You can add any rows inserted in the
    report if you wish.

2. Color in Figure 5.11, using the business rule from Section 5.2 on p. 34, as in
    the previous exercise.

3. Create a `RowFixture` table for a list of things that is relevant to you.

4. What is the type of the table shown in Figure 5.12, assuming that it is one
    of the three standard table types: `ColumnFixture` (C), `RowFixture` (R), or
    `ActionFixture` (A)?

OccupantList	
user	*room*
anna	lotr
luke	Lotr
warren	shrek

Figure 5.10 Color in the Table

DiscountGroupList			
future value	*max owing*	*min purchase*	*discount percent*
low	0.00	0.00	0
medium	500.00	600.00	3
medium	0.00	500.00	5
low	0.00	500.00	5

Figure 5.11 Color in the Table

5. What type of table is shown in Figure 5.13?

6. Select the type of table—ColumnFixture (*C*), RowFixture (*R*), or ActionFixture (*A*)—that you would expect to use for testing any of the following that interest you; make any appropriate assumptions.

   a. The tax paid depends on income and total (allowed) expenses.

   b. Does a nasty letter need to be sent to a slow payer to ask for immediate payment (or else)?

   c. Is this a valid URL?

   d. Test a sequence of moves in a chess playing program, along with an indication of *check* and *checkmate*.

   e. Is a number negative or not?

CardHandList	
suit	*card*
heart	ace
heart	queen
diamond	king
diamond	7
club	king
club	jack
club	10
club	9
club	4
spade	ace

Figure 5.12 Identify the Type of the Table

CalculateMoney		
money	*multiplier*	*result()*
0.00	5	0.00
12.00	5	60.00
24.00	1	24.00
100	15	1500.00

Figure 5.13 Identify the Type of the Table

f. Test that a Google search has listed your special home page.

g. Are the pieces in the right position on the chessboard at the start of a game?

h. Are all the customers in the list, along with correct addresses and phone numbers?

i. Calculate the logarithm of a number.

j. Is the history of debit and credit transactions correct?

k. Is a date value formatted correctly?

CHAPTER 6

Testing with Sequences of Tables

A single table is usually not sufficient to define a test. In this chapter, we show examples of tests that are formed from a sequence of tables.

We often need to use several types of tables in such a test. For example, we may want to use an `ActionFixture` to make changes to a system under test and then use a `RowFixture` to check that a collection from the system under test is now as expected.

It is useful to include details about what's happening in the test. We show by example how comments can be added to a table sequence.

6.1   Chat Room Changes

We'll use a variant of the chat room examples from Section 4.2 on p. 26 and Section 5.1 on p. 31. The example here will illustrate a sequence of `ActionFixture` and `RowFixture` tables that test changes to a chat server, the system under test. The test sequence, reported in Figure 6.1, consists of six tables, as follows.

1. The first, `ActionFixture` table *start*s the system under test.

2. The second table, also an `ActionFixture`, connects the user anna, who creates a new chat room, lotr, and enters it. Note that this table has no *start* action because the system under test has already been started, in the first table.

3. The third table, also an `ActionFixture`, connects the user luke, who enters lotr, the current room.

4. The fourth is a `RowFixture` table that tests that there are two occupants of lotr, the only room.

5. The fifth is another `ActionFixture` table that disconnects the user anna.

6. The sixth is another `RowFixture` table that tests that there is one occupant left in the lotr room.

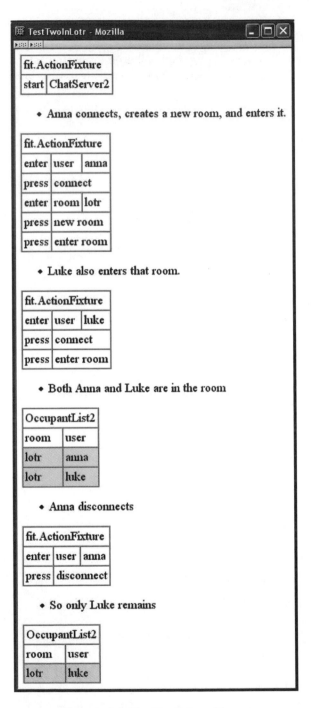

Figure 6.1 TestTwoInLotr Report

> **Note**
>
> The test writer and programmers need a shared agreement about what each table means, so that a programmer can write the fixture accordingly. As we'll see in Chapter 11, the table may be structured specifically to enable tests to be expressed clearly; this may require the programmer to create a new type of fixture to ensure that the tests may be run automatically against the system under test.
>
> We'll see in Part II that tests often evolve from a collaborative effort of businesspeople, testers, and programmers.

The textual comments between the tables reported in Figure 6.1 are helpful in explaining the steps in the test, as well as the overall intent of the test. Images, lists, and other information may also be included to aid comprehension and communication. These are all ignored by Fit, which simply interprets the tables as containing tests.

> **Tip**
>
> The first three tables in Figure 6.1 could have been combined into a single table. Instead, we have used three tables in order to separate and organize the actions of the two users.
>
> We'll see a similar use of separate tables to organize tests in the next section as well.

Another, related, test sequence is reported in Figure 6.2. The fifth table tests that there are no occupants of any rooms, and so it has no *expected* rows. This table is unusual in that it passes, but no green is reported.

The sixth table in Figure 6.2 is a `fit.Summary` table, which reports various test statistics about the previous tables in the test. The table does this by adding cells to the table; Figure 6.3 shows how the table is written in the original test.

> **Programmers:** The fixture code for the tests here is given in Section 24.1 on p. 203.

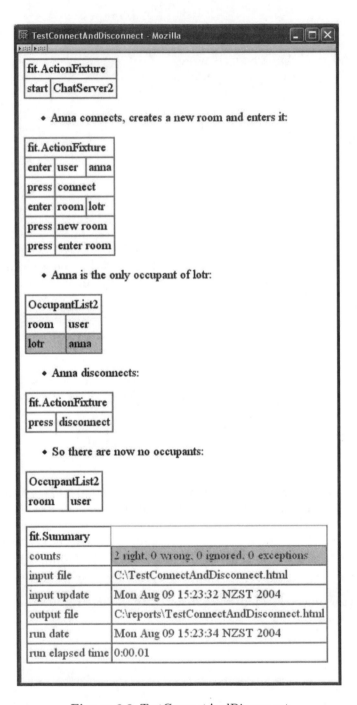

Figure 6.2 TestConnectAndDisconnect

fit.Summary

Figure 6.3 Fit Table to Give a Summary

6.2   Discount Group Changes

The business rule for determining the discount, based on the current discount groups, is as follows.

> Given a future value, an amount owing, and a purchase price, look through the discount groups from the first to the last. For the first discount group that matches, use the discount percentage of that group to calculate the discount on the purchase.
>
> Now a discount group matches if
>
> - The future value is the same as the future value of the group.
>
> - The amount owing is not greater than the maximum allowed for the group.
>
> - The purchase price is not less than the minimum price allowed for the group.
>
> If no discount group matches, the discount is 0 percent.

We use four Fit test tables, as shown in Figure 6.4. All are `ColumnFixture` tables that together test this business rule.

1. The first table configures the discount groups that are to be used in the subsequent tables of this test. The *calculated* column **add()** doesn't calculate anything; it is used simply to add the information in that row to the set of discount groups in the system under test.

2. The second table tests the available discount only for low *future value*. The first cell of the second *test row* is an *empty cell*, which is low by default. As with all `ColumnFixture` tables, the value of an *empty cell* is assumed to be the same as the previous nonempty cell in that column of the table. In the report that's generated, as shown in Figure 6.5, the current value is shown in gray in the cell that in Figure 6.4 was empty.

3. The third table tests the available discount only for medium *future value*. Like the previous table, it has empty cells in the first column.

4. The fourth table tests the available discount only for high *future value*.

As with the example in the previous section, in order to make the tests easier to read, we have chosen to separate tables that could be combined. The tests for the three cases for *future value* are provided in separate tables.

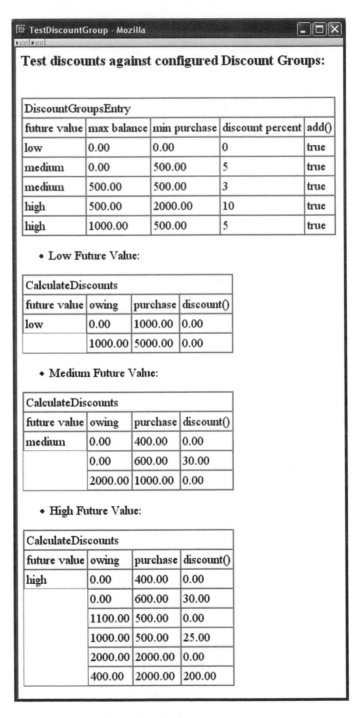

Figure 6.4   TestDiscountGroup

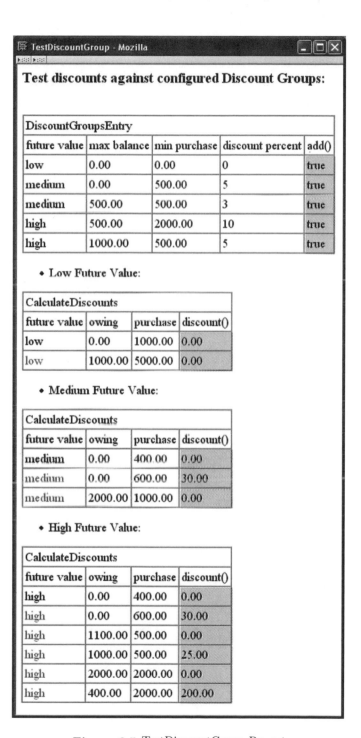

Figure 6.5 TestDiscountGroup Report

Questions & Answers

What happens if a cell in a `ColumnFixture` is empty but is the first one of the table?
It uses a default value, as defined in the fixture. For example, unless someone decides on a specific value by default, a number will be 0.

However, it's not a good idea to do this, because the initial value is hidden away; it's best to make it explicit in the first row of the table.

What if we want the text to be empty, such as when the address is not known?
Write "blank" in the cell instead; this is treated as empty text instead of as "the same as above."

Programmers: The fixture code for the tests here is given in Section 24.2 on p. 208.

Tip

We used an *add()* column to add a set of elements to a list, as shown in the first table in Figure 6.4. It's a common pattern to have setup tables to do this. In Chapter 11 we'll see the use of another type of table for adding elements, one that supports this pattern and avoids the need for the last column.

6.3 Summary

- Several types of tables are often needed in a sequence to define a single test.
- Our first example test uses an `ActionFixture` table and several `RowFixture` tables.
- The second example uses only `ColumnFixture` tables, with two fixtures.
- When a sequence of tables together make up a single test, they will all access the same system under test, or part of it, if they change its state.
- The first table in the sequence needs to be responsible for running the system under test. In Chapters 7 and 8 we'll see tools that support the sharing of common setup tables among tests.

6.4 Exercises

1. Using tables like those in Section 6.1, write a test that checks that there are no new rooms and no occupants when the chat server first starts.

2. Now write a test that checks that there are still no occupants of any rooms after anna has connected.

3. Write tests to confirm that only the user who creates a room may delete it. You will need to invent a new named button to *press*.

CHAPTER 7

Creating Tables and Running Fit

If you want to try using Fit right now, this chapter will help you get started. However, if you want to first know more about using Fit for testing, you may want to skip this chapter and the next one and come back to them later.

We cover how to create Fit tests in a spreadsheet and how to run Fit on them. We'll then see how to run collections of tests (test suites), organized in folders. We'll then cover how to create Fit tables with HTML (Hypertext Markup Language).

FitNesse is another approach to creating, editing, and running Fit tables, as covered in Chapter 8. Custom test data formats may also be handled, as discussed for programmers in Chapter 39.

We don't discuss installing Fit and related tools in this chapter. Setup information for programmers is covered in Chapter 26.

7.1 Using Spreadsheets for Tests

Fit tests can be easily created by using a spreadsheet. It can be convenient to use the spreadsheet to calculate some values, such as the *calculated* column values of a `ColumnFixture` table, instead of working them out by hand. To distinguish the Fit tables from other text within a spreadsheet, test tables have borders, as shown by the Excel spreadsheet `TestDiscountGroups.xls` in Figure 7.1.

Once you've edited a spreadsheet and saved it, you can run Fit on it to get a report. If you're not a programmer, ask a programmer to set things up for you (as discussed in Chapter 26).

The report in the `TestDiscountGroups.html` file results from running Fit on the spreadsheet in Figure 7.1. Double-click on this file to view it through a browser. For example, the report resulting from the test in the spreadsheet in Figure 7.1 is shown in Figure 7.2.

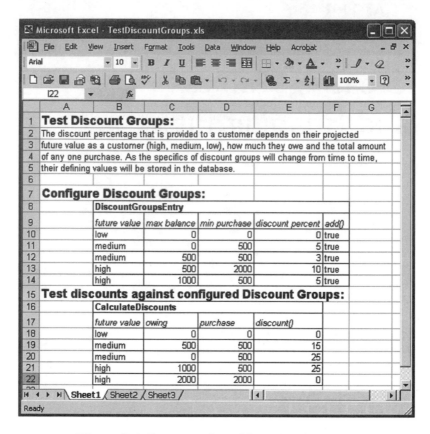

Figure 7.1 Creating a Spreadsheet File with Excel

After changing and saving the spreadsheet, you will need to run the tests again. Then click the *Refresh* button on your browser to see the latest report.

Questions & Answers

Can tables be placed anywhere on the spreadsheet?
Yes, although tables can't be placed side by side.

7.2   Organizing Tests in Test Suites

As the number of test files increases, we need a good way to organize them and a simple way to run them all. We can organize the Fit test files into folders, with related tests together. For example, in a chat server system, we could have folders for tests related to various important actions, as shown in Figure 7.3.

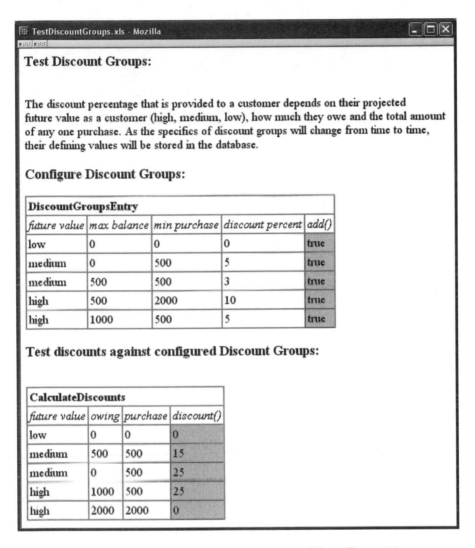

Figure **7.2** Report from the Spreadsheet File in Figure 7.1

You can then run Fit on the tests in a folder and in all subfolders. This makes it easy to run all the tests or a group of them, based on the folder structure. Running a suite of tests is much the same as running a single file. However, a `reportIndex.html` report file is generated. This report file summarizes the results of all the tests, providing links to the specific reports for each of the files.

As we'll see later, we often find that a group of tests all have the same setup tables. Including these tables in each of the files works fine, but it's a nuisance when we want to change the setup for them all. To avoid this duplication, a `SetUp.xls` file may be included in the folder structure. This file is automatically included before each test file in that folder, and in subfolders, before it is run.

Figure 7.3 Organizing Test Suites in Folders

Some groups of files may have corresponding tables at the end of each test, such as to shut down the system under test. In that case, a `TearDown.xls` may also be included in the folder structure. This file is automatically included after each test file before it is run.

Sometimes, only some of the tests within a test suite need to be run. Details are provided for programmers in Chapter 26 on how to manage the selection of the tests to be run.

7.3   Using HTML for Tests

Fit was originally designed to work with HTML files. HTML files can be edited with Mozilla, FrontPage, or DreamWeaver or an editor that can save to HTML, such as MSWord or MSExcel.

Figure 7.4 shows a test being edited with Mozilla. Figure 7.5 shows a test being edited with MSWord. (It needs to be saved as an HTML file.)

You can ornament your tables as you wish, as with spreadsheets, as most of the characteristics of an HTML table, such as the cell spacing or border size, are irrelevant to Fit. However, all tables are considered to be test tables by Fit, so you will get some odd reports if you use tables for other purposes. Other tagged formatting, such as formatted text, lists, images, and links, can be used both inside and around tables.[1]

Once the HTML is saved to a file, we can run Fit on it, using the same approach as in Section 7.1. Test suites, as described in Section 7.2, can include a mix of HTML

---

[1] However, it would be confusing to color cells in ways that conflict with the changes that Fit makes to tables in reports.

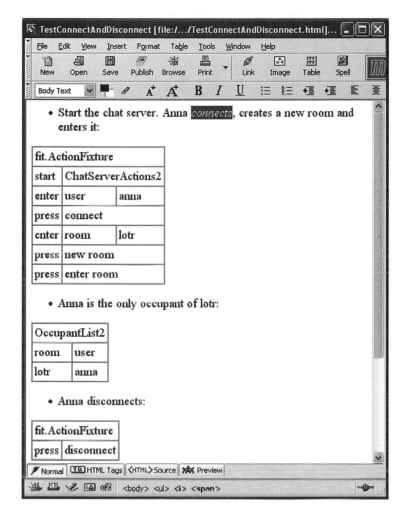

Figure 7.4 Creating an HTML Table with Mozilla Composer

files and spreadsheet files, and these files are reported in the same way. `SetUp.html` and `TearDown.html` files may also be provided, as alternatives to the spreadsheet equivalents.

Questions & Answers

What if the text in a cell is italicized with <i>12.00</i>?
Fit ignores the tags and uses the plaintext 12.00 from the cell.

Which HTML editor would you recommend?
FrontPage is very easy to use, and the HTML it creates is easy to edit directly as plaintext, if necessary. Mozilla also is good; it is free and runs everywhere.

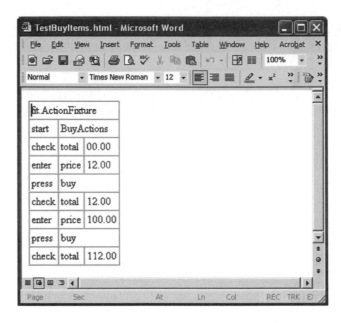

Figure 7.5 Editing an HTML File with MSWord

Other editors create masses of HTML for simple things. However, if you don't need to alter the HTML directly and you usually use MSWord for word processing, use it for editing your HTML.

What are the pros and cons of HTML versus spreadsheets?
The grid is already there with a spreadsheet, so it's easier to get started. However, if you have several tables in the spreadsheet, you end up having to resize the column widths to suit all the tables. This can look messy. HTML tables can be sized automatically and independently.

HTML also allows images and links to be used, which may be useful.

7.4   Summary

- We can edit a Fit table by using a spreadsheet or an HTML editor.

- Fit test results are reported in HTML.

- Groups of tests can be organized into folders and run as a test suite. This makes it easy to see whether any tests have changed to passing or are no longer passing. SetUp and TearDown files may be included, to be automatically incorporated into the tests.

7.5   Exercises

The following exercises assume that someone has set up the tools and application code to enable you to run Fit tests on a file or a set of files in a folder.

1. Get one of the early example test tables, such as **TestDiscount.xls** (as discussed in Section 3.1 on p. 13). Run the test.

2. Make some simple changes to the table so that passing tests now fail and vice versa. Run the test again.

3. Now make some simple changes to the table such as entering data in the wrong format, to see what happens when things don't work properly. This will make it easier, later, to work out what may have caused a problem when the tests don't run as you expected.

4. Now create a new file with a single table that uses the same fixture as in the previous exercises. Run it.

5. Now create a new file with one or more tables that use a new fixture, which doesn't yet exist. Run Fit on the table with the missing fixture code. It will give an error.

6. Set up a suite of tests and run Fit over them.

CHAPTER 8

Using FitNesse

FitNesse provides a convenient approach to creating, organizing, and running Fit tests. In this chapter, we show how to create Fit tables with FitNesse and how to run those tests. This chapter provides an overview of the important parts of FitNesse; we assume throughout that you will refer to the comprehensive FitNesse online user guide for further details.

8.1   Introduction

FitNesse allows you to view, change, and create Web pages containing documentation and test tables that are to be run by Fit. FitNesse makes it easy to access those pages through a Web browser and to share tables among many people working on a project.

In Chapter 7, we needed a spreadsheet or an HTML editor to change files, a double-click on a command file to run Fit, and a Web browser to view the Fit reports. By contrast, FitNesse enables the development and running of test suites through a single user interface (a Web browser).

> **Note**
>
> Micah D. Martin (micah@objectmentor.com) is the primary author and architect of FitNesse. Robert C. Martin (unclebob@objectmentor.com) is the number two man. Others who have contributed to FitNesse are Chris Beigay, Dan Flies, Steve Starkey, Paul Pagel, Kelly Harris, and Elmar Juergens.
>
> FitNesse builds on Fit, as developed by Ward Cunningham. FitNesse details and downloads are available at www.fitnesse.org.

8.2   Getting Started

A programmer will need to set up FitNesse and show you how to run it, as discussed in Chapter 27. It may well be useful to go over the following process with the programmers.

When you run your browser to connect to FitNesse, it shows the `FrontPage`. (You may need to log in first.) If that page has not been changed too much from the initial install, you will see several links to various pages in a `Table of Contents` table.

If you click the link FitNesse.UserGuide, you will see a new page for the FitNesse user guide. That page has a table of contents, with links to further pages. For example, the link WikiInstructions goes to a section of the guide that includes details of the markup language for bold text, headers, and so on. The manual is easy to follow, so we're going to focus now on what you need to do to start creating tables and running Fit tests.

Go back to the `FrontPage`, using the *Back* button on the browser or by clicking the FitNesse icon in the upper left of the page. Note the links at the top left of the page: Edit, Properties, Versions, and Search. Click Edit, and the unformatted text of the page is shown in an edit box. Add a wiki word—see the Note on page 60—such as TestMyTable, at the bottom of the edit page, as shown in Figure 8.1.

Ignore the other text on the page, but don't alter it; the markup used there is explained in the FitNesse user guide, which you may like to look at later. Click the *Save* button at the bottom of the page; you may need to scroll down to see it.

You should see the `FrontPage` afresh, but with your wiki word displayed with a following question mark (?)—for example, "TestMyTable?". If not, you've used the name of a page that already exists or is not a wiki word. So change it to something else by clicking *Edit* again, altering your wiki word, and clicking the *Save* button.

Click the ? of your wiki word, and you'll be taken to a new page for `TestMyTable`, ready for editing. Type in the following—a `ColumnFixture` table—with no leading spaces, and make sure that at least one blank line follows:

```
|eg.Division|
|numerator|denominator|quotient?|
|6|2|3|
```

FitNesse allows ? as an alternative to () in the calculated columns of a `ColumnFixture` table. Click the *Save* button at the bottom of the page, as before. Your new page is saved and displayed, as shown in Figure 8.2. Note that there is now a Test link at the top left of the page, below the image of the dial. If it's not there, see the Tips on page 59.

Click the Test link. A new page is displayed, showing the Fit report that results, as shown in Figure 8.3.

You may like to now edit your page and add extra rows to the table or experiment with adding text and markup to your pages. You will probably find it handy to see the user guide while you're editing pages. So start another browser window at the URL http://localhost and click FitNesse.UserGuide.

Figure 8.1 Editing a Page to Add a Wiki Word

Figure 8.2 TestMyTable

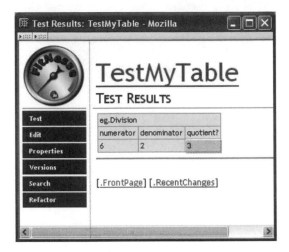

Figure 8.3 TestMyTable Report

> **Note**
>
> A wiki is a Web-based system that is accessed through a Web browser.
> Ward Cunningham's idea was to have a Web place where people could
> share information. For example, you may like to see the original wiki at
> http://c2.com/cgi/wiki.
>
> Each page of wiki has a title and contains text, images, and links, like an
> ordinary Web page. Unlike the usual Web page, however, a user can click an
> edit button and change the contents of that page. Some wiki systems limit
> who can make changes, based on their login.
>
> Any word in the text of a page that has a starting and an embedded
> uppercase letter is a *wiki word*: for example, FrontPage, FitNesse, and
> WorldWideWiki. When a wiki page is displayed with formatting—is not
> being edited—a wiki word is shown in one of two forms. If a page with
> that name exists, the name is shown as a link: underlined. If there is no page
> with that name, the name is displayed with a ? after the name, where the ?
> is a link to create and edit a new page with that name. This makes it trivial
> to make a new page; simply use the name in another page and click through
> to it.
>
> Simple markup is used for formatting headings, lists, and so on. This
> markup is less sophisticated than HTML because the main aim is to encour-
> age people to share information, not to have pretty pages.

> ## Tips
>
> If your page name doesn't start with "Test," the Test link won't be visible. You can still test it, but you need to first click Properties, tick the Test box at the top, and click the *Save* button.
>
> If you use a wiki word such as `ActionFixture`, inside your table, it will be shown with a ? character. To avoid this, place a ! just before the table. However, if you wish to format values in table cells, write it as `!-ActionFixture-!` so that it's not treated as a wiki word.

8.3 Organizing Tests with Subwikis

FitNesse, unlike many wikis, allows for a hierarchy of pages, analogous to the hierarchy of folders and files in a filing cabinet or a filing system, with pages playing both roles in FitNesse. These *subwikis* provide a convenient way to organize lots of tests, as well as to allow for separate software projects to be managed by the same FitNesse system.

As we saw in the previous section, we can add a new page at the same level as an existing page. We simply add a wiki word to that page, which creates the link, and then click the ? to edit and save the new page.

To add a subwiki, a new page *within* an existing page, we use a leading ^ in our wiki word. For example, to add a subwiki to our TestMyTable page, add ^WithinPage as a wiki word to that page and click its ? link. A new page is created within the current page, instead of at the same level. This can be seen from the title of the page, which includes the name of both the parent page and the new page: TestMyTable.WithinPage.

If we use an ordinary wiki word, such as SecondWithinPage, in our new WithinPage page and create it, SecondWithinPage will be located in the same subwiki. If we want to refer to the new SecondWithinPage page from a page not directly in that subwiki, we refer to it by its full name: .TestMyTable.SecondWithinPage.

To organize test pages, you may add subwikis within subwikis as deeply as you wish. For example, from the `FrontPage` of FitNesse, we could have a set of subwikis for each of the main areas of test for our application. Each of those areas could contain further subwikis containing individual pages of tests. Just as with folders and files, good naming of subwikis makes it easy to find specific tests.

Here are some quick pointers for organizing test pages; click the FitNesseUserGuide for further details.

- As tests evolve, we inevitably need to rename the corresponding pages. A FitNesse page can be renamed by clicking the *Refactor* button on the left-hand side of the page and filling in the new name in the **Rename this page** section.

- If a page has a lot of pages within it, it can be inconvenient to manage the list of them. Include the command !contents in the page, and FitNesse will generate a table of contents of all those pages in alphabetical order.

- If it is necessary to move a whole subwiki from one place in the FitNesse page hierarchy to another, it is not necessary to recreate all the pages. Click the Refactor button and fill in the new name in the **Move this page** section.

- By default, FitNesse uses the special pages .PageHeader and .PageFooter to display the header and footer information on other FitNesse pages. And PageHeader and PageFooter pages added within any subwiki in the page hierarchy are used instead in all pages within that subwiki.

8.4   Test Suites

FitNesse provides direct support for suites of test, a group of interrelated tests. If a page name starts with Suite, a Suite link appears in the left-hand side buttons when that page is showing. A page can also be turned into a suite by clicking Properties and ticking the Suite box.

When the Suite link is clicked, FitNesse runs Fit tests on that page and on all pages within it, to arbitrary nesting, in the subwiki page hierarchy and provides a report of all those test pages. For example, Figure 8.4 shows part of the report for the test suite used to test FitNesse itself.

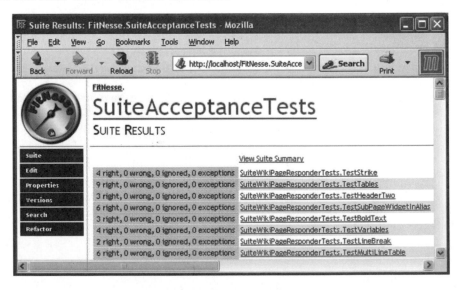

Figure 8.4 Suite Report for FitNesse Tests

A set of tests may have common initial and final tables. The pages SetUp and TearDown may hold tables that are run, respectively, before and after each test page. These tables are shown in every page where they apply, as well as in the report. (FitNesse looks up the page hierarchy from that test page and finds the closest `SetUp` and `TearDown` pages.)

The `SuiteSetUp` and `SuiteTearDown` pages are also provided to run before and after each test suite, in a comparable manner to `SetUp` and `TearDown` for test pages.

Questions & Answers

What happens if I start editing a page and someone else changes it while I'm doing so?

When you try to save your changes to the page, FitNesse warns you that the page has been changed meanwhile. That way, nothing is lost. FitNesse shows you the latest saved copy of the page, so that you can merge any changes with your own, if you wish. Or, you can decide to not go ahead with your changes.

8.5   Ranges of Values

There are a few small differences in the Fit fixtures in FitNesse. For example, `ColumnFixture` tables in FitNesse can check number ranges.

Sometimes, we want to check that a number is less than some specified value rather than that it is a specific value. For example, Figure 8.5 tests that stress tests involving various numbers of clients react within a specified maximum time.

StressTest		
clients	*max reaction time*	*within time()*
1	10	true
10	10	true
100	30	true
500	60	true

Figure 8.5 Checking Within Maximum

`ColumnFixture` provides a way to write this more directly, as shown in Figure 8.6. Instead of a number in the *calculated* column, we have a check that the result from the system under test with one client is less than 10 (`<10`).

StressTest	
clients	*reaction time()*
1	<10
10	<10
100	<30
500	<60

Figure 8.6 Checking Within Maximum with <

We can also compare <=10, >10 and >=10 and check that a *calculated* number is within a given range. For example, 3 < _ < 10 expects that the result in that cell, designated as _, is greater than 3 and less than 10.

8.6   Other Features

We have mentioned only some of the features of FitNesse. See the user manual for others, such as the following.

- Tables may be loaded from a spreadsheet.
- Markup may be used in table cells and is ignored by Fit, as is HTML formatting.
- TableWizard creates the start of a Fit table in a page, based on a menu selection, and is accessed through a menu at the bottom when editing a page.
- The !include command can be used to share common tables in pages without having to copy them.
- The report format can be changed. For example, this feature will be handy if you have trouble distinguishing the colors used or if you need larger text.

8.7   Summary

- FitNesse provides a wiki-based environment for creating and running Fit tables.
- FitNesse provides subwikis to organize the test pages in a hierarchy structure.
- FitNesse supports the running of multiple tests at once, with test suites.

8.8   Exercises

The following exercises assume that FitNesse has been installed.

1. Experiment with the markup of pages. See the user guide for details of the markup.

2. Experiment with adding pages at the same level, using wiki words without a leading ^ and within subwikis, using wiki words with a ^. See how full wiki words, with a leading ., and ordinary wiki words work from different pages within your page hierarchy.

3. Enter one of the early example test tables into FitNesse, such as TestDiscount, as discussed in Section 3.1 on p. 13. Ask for programmer support to set up your page to refer to the associated fixtures so that the tests can be carried out. Run the test.

4. Now make some simple changes to the table, such as entering data in the wrong format to see what happens under FitNesse when things don't work properly.

5. Create a new FitNesse page with a single table that uses the same fixture as in the previous exercises. Test it.

6. Now create a new FitNesse page with one or more tables that use a new fixture that doesn't yet exist. Test the table with the missing fixture code. It will give an error.

7. Experiment with a working table by adding and removing cells in rows of the table. Noting what happens when things go wrong will help when you later make mistakes with table layout of your real tests.

CHAPTER 9

Expecting Errors

In this chapter, we show how to use Fit tables to write tests in which errors are expected.

9.1 Expected Errors with Calculations

Sometimes, we want to test that the test data is rejected, as expected. For example, consider Figure 9.1, in which a negative *amount* is used in the first test row.

CalculateDiscount	
amount	*discount()*
-100.00	0.00
1200.00	60.00

Figure 9.1 Negative Amount

When this Fit table is run, we get the report (partly) shown in Figure 9.2, in which the program rejects the negative *amount*. The report also provides programmer-specific information about the error in the yellow-colored cell (see Plate 5), which we can ignore.

Assuming that our business rule stipulates that it doesn't make sense to calculate the discount on a negative amount, we'd expect to get an error in that first test row. We can express that expectation by using the special value *error* in the calculated column instead, as shown in the Fit test in Figure 9.3.

The *error* cell is colored green if an error occurred (an exception), as shown in Figure 9.4. Otherwise, it is colored red.

It makes sense to include the error case here because there is only one. (Fit will complain about any values that are not numbers.) However, many values in a table may not be valid, such as the dates entered by the user through the user interface. In that case, it makes sense to split the table into two: one for defining valid date values and one for defining the calculations on the valid dates. This topic is covered further in Chapter 18.

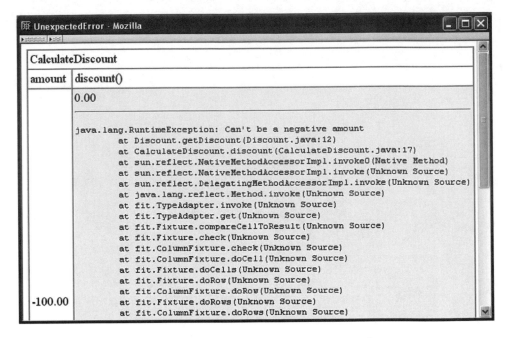

Figure 9.2 Negative Amount Is Rejected

CalculateDiscount	
amount	*discount()*
-100.00	**error**
1200.00	60.00

Figure 9.3 Use of *error* in ColumnFixture

Figure 9.4 Negative Amount in *error*, as Expected

9.2   Expected Errors with Actions

Errors may also arise in testing actions, as a supplied data value may be invalid. With `ActionFixture`, we can check for such errors in two ways. In Figure 9.5, we *check* the occupant count of a room that has not been created and expect an *error*.

fit.ActionFixture		
start	ChatServerActions2	
enter	room	lotr
check	occupant count	error

Figure 9.5 Use of *error* in `ActionFixture`

In Figure 9.6, a user cannot enter a room that has not been created. So we *check* that *room entered* is no to see that the *enter room* action was unsuccessful, as expected.

fit.ActionFixture		
start	ChatServerActions2	
enter	user	anna
press	connect	
enter	room	lotr
press	enter room	
check	room entered	no

Figure 9.6 Checking the Result after an Action in `ActionFixture`

9.3   Summary

Fit tests can explicitly test that the system under test gives an expected error.

- `ColumnFixture` tables can use the special value *error* for an expected error with a calculated value.

- `ActionFixture` tables can use the special value *error* for an expected error with a *check*ed value.

CHAPTER 10

FitLibrary Tables

We now consider a family of new fixtures, based on what we call flow, whereby a single fixture covers the actions in all tables of the test. We see that a sequence of Fit tables is organized differently, with only the first table having a fixture name.

We show how the two examples covered in Chapter 6 may be tested with these alternative fixtures. The following fixtures from the FitLibrary are covered:

- DoFixture, for testing actions
- SetUpFixture, for entering data at the start of a test
- CalculateFixture, for testing calculations
- ArrayFixture, for testing ordered lists
- SubsetFixture, for testing some elements of an unordered list

10.1   Flow-Style Actions with DoFixture

An alternative approach to writing tests for sequences of actions is to use a flow style in which we start with a **DoFixture** table. For example, the test reported in Figure 10.1 checks that on disconnecting, a user is no longer an occupant of a room. The *fixture* ChatStart is named in the first table. As this is a **DoFixture** table, it is the only one that needs a *fixture* name.

In the tables in Figure 10.1, the following sequence of steps is carried out.

1. The chat server, the system under test, is started.
2. A user connects to the chat server.
3. That user creates a room.
4. The user enters that room.
5. We check the single occupant in the lotr room.
6. The user disconnects.
7. We check that the room is empty.

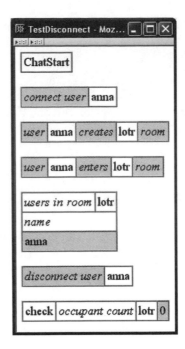

Figure 10.1 TestDisconnect

The names of the actions used in a table are chosen by the table writer to be clear about what is happening in the test.

Following are several differences between using flow style for action tests and `ActionFixture` tables.

- Only the first table in a flow-style sequence needs to have a fixture name, which is a `DoFixture`.

- In flow style, the name of an action, such as *connect user*, is made up by the test writer.

- A flow-style action is defined in a single row. For example, consider the second table of Figure 10.1. Instead of *enter*ing a *name* before *press*ing *connect*, as with an `ActionFixture`, we use a single action row, *connect user*, that includes the user name. This makes it easy to read the flow of the test, especially if actions have several data values.

- A flow-style action contains *keywords* in the first cell and in every second cell of the row thereafter. The keywords are shown in *italics* in Figure 10.1 and are colored green in the report; they may contain any characters. Such keywords allow us to be explicit about the role of the data values in the other cells. For example, the action row in the third table of Figure 10.1 includes the *keywords* *user*, *creates*, and *room*, which have been chosen to be clear about the role and order of the data values in the other cells of the action.

- Actions may be provided in separate tables but need not be. For example, the actions in tables 2, 3, and 4 of Figure 10.1 could be included together in a single table.

- Where a particular action may succeed or fail, **DoFixture** automatically marks the action accordingly in green or red in the report. All the actions in Figure 10.1 are of this form, except for the one in the last table. This avoids the need to explicitly check that an action has succeeded, making the test more succinct.

- A *check* action in flow style is applied to another action rather than to a single field, as with **ActionFixture**. For example, the last table in Figure 10.1 checks that the *occupant count* of the specified room is 0—empty.

- Instead of using a fixture name, an action in a flow-style table may select a particular fixture, determining how the rest of that table is to be used in testing. For example, in the fifth table, the action in the first row selects a **RowFixture** that is used to check the following rows against the occupants in the lotr room.

  Programmers: The fixture code for the tests here is given in Section 28.1 on p. 227.

Questions & Answers

Some action rows have a keyword in the last cell. Is that optional?
Yes, if it makes it easier to read the action, you can place a keyword at the end. It's also possible to have empty keyword cells, where no word is needed for readability; we'll see examples of such actions in Chapter 14.

Can the core fixtures, such as ColumnFixture, be used with DoFixture?
Yes, in two ways. In flow style, any table after the first can contain a fixture name. That table is handled in the normal way, as described in previous chapters. Subsequent tables are still in flow style.
    Also, an action in a **DoFixture** table can select any fixture, which is used to test the rest of that table. In Figure 10.1, this occurs in the fifth table where a **RowFixture** checks the users in the specified room.

Can a DoFixture table be used after core fixture tables?
Yes, but an explicit fixture name is needed in the first row of the table. Subsequent tables are not in flow style.

How do we know whether it's a DoFixture or a ColumnFixture table?
With a little experience, you can usually tell what type of table it is by the structure or contents of the rows and/or tables that follow or by understanding what the test is trying to do. Otherwise, you may need to ask the person who wrote the test or ask a programmer to find out by looking at the fixture code.

ColumnFixture and RowFixture tables have a regular structure, with rows of the same length and containing similar values. You can often tell that it's a ColumnFixture table by the header row, with one or more labels having () or ? after the name.

ActionFixture tables usually start with the fit.ActionFixture fixture. The rows that follow are of different lengths and contain the *enter*, *press*, and *check* actions.

DoFixture table rows vary in length and contain specific actions with names that should clarify what's going on in the test. Generally, several small tables are used in a sequence, sometimes with only one row in a table.

10.2   Expected Errors with DoFixture

With DoFixture, we can test directly whether an action has failed, as expected. For example, the tables reported in Figure 10.2 test that a room cannot be removed if somone is in it. In the fourth table, we check that the *remove* action does not succeed, by using the special action *reject* or, alternatively, *not* when it reads better, followed by the action concerned.

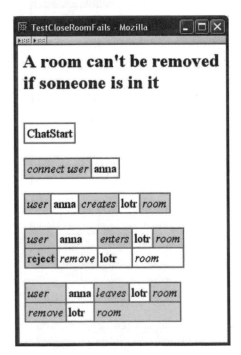

Figure 10.2 TestCloseRoomFails

Further capabilities of DoFixture are introduced in later chapters.

Programmers: The fixture code for the tests here is given in Section 28.2 on p. 231.

10.3   Actions on Domain Objects with DoFixture

As we've seen, the chat application has users and rooms, or what are called the *domain objects* of this system. Actions are carried out on those objects, such as when a user enters a room, as in the fourth table of Figure 10.1.

A DoFixture table may carry out a sequence of actions on a particular domain object that is selected from the system under test.[1] For example, the second table in Figure 10.3 includes an alternative approach to the user connecting, creating a room, and entering it. Rather than including the user name in each action, we have the first row, the **connect** action, provide access to the user, using another DoFixture. The rest of the rows of that table contain actions that apply to that user.

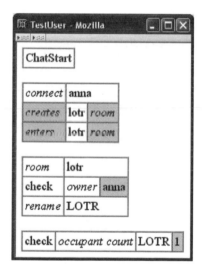

Figure 10.3 TestUser

The third table in Figure 10.3 acts on the room that is selected in the first row. The second row of that table checks the **owner** of the room—the user who created it—and the third row action renames the room.

---

[1] This is an advanced topic, which you may like to ignore for now.

In general, if a row selects an object through a `DoFixture`, the actions in the rest of the table apply to that object. This is similar to the way that `RowFixture` treats the remaining rows of the table as expected elements.

Questions & Answers

Can any row select an object?

Yes. So we could select a room in one row of a table, then select the owner of that room in a later row of the same table, and then act on that user.

10.4 Setup

We now switch to the second example in Chapter 6. The test in Figure 6.5 on p. 45 starts with a `ColumnFixture` table that enters data for the rest of the test; this table is shown again in Figure 10.4.

DiscountGroupsEntry				
future value	*max balance*	*min purchase*	*discount %*	*add()*
low	0.00	0.00	0	true
medium	0.00	500.00	5	true
medium	500.00	500.00	3	true
high	500.00	2000.00	10	true
high	1000.00	500.00	5	true

Figure 10.4 Setup Table Using `ColumnFixture`

Such data entry at the start of a test is a common pattern, as we'll see in Part II. However, Figure 10.4 makes use of a `ColumnFixture` table, which is better suited to testing calculations.

We can eliminate the last column, which is not calculating anything, by using a `SetUpFixture` table, as shown in the second (*set ups*) table in Figure 10.5. This enters the discount group data that is held in the remainder of that table. The later tables in Figure 10.5 are discussed in the following sections.

Tip

FitNesse provides a similar fixture to `SetUpFixture`; this fixture is `RowEntryFixture`.

Programmers: The fixture code for the tests here is given in Section 28.7 on p. 239.

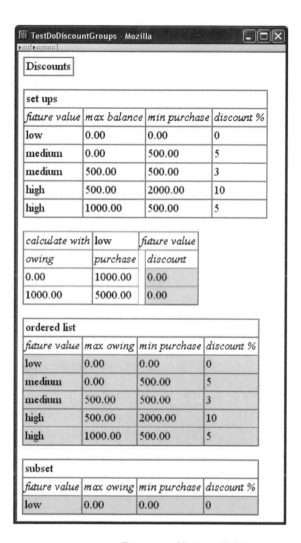

Figure 10.5 Discount: Various Tables

Questions & Answers

When do you use SetUpFixture *tables?*

We usually use them to get the system under test into a suitable state so that we can test some business process. Often, this means entering appropriate data, which we'd prefer to not do through long-winded workflow with actions, as they hide the fundamentals of the test. We cover this topic once we start looking at larger sets of tests, in Chapter 14.

We can also use a SetUpFixture table when several actions of the same form are carried out in sequence in the main part of the test.

10.5   `CalculateFixture` Tables

`ColumnFixture` uses special characters after a calculated field name in the header row. `CalculateFixture` is a simple alternative; it separates the *given* (to the left) and *calculated* columns (to the right) with an empty column.

This is shown in the third table in Figure 10.5. The action in the first row of that table selects a `CalculateFixture`, which is applied to the rest of the table. Rather than having a column with the value *low* repeated, as in Section 6.2 on p. 43, the `calculate with future value` action takes *low* as an argument and uses it in testing all the calculations in the rest of table.

`CalculateFixture` tables are helpful when the special table cell values used in `ColumnFixture`[2]—an empty cell, `error`, `blank`, and so on—get in the way of the tests you need to write. `CalculateFixture` assumes no special words but allows them to be defined by the fixture. This means, for example, that you could choose to use .. instead of an empty cell to mean *the same value as above in the table.*

10.6   Ordered List Tables

As we saw in Section 5.2 on p. 34, we can use `RowFixture` to test lists in which the order matters. We do this by including an extra column that gives the order of the rows.

Another approach is to use an `ArrayFixture`, which takes account of the order of the elements automatically. This is shown in the fourth table in Figure 10.5. The action `ordered list` selects an `ArrayFixture`, which checks that the expected and actual lists are the same, in the same order.

As with `RowFixture`, the header row labels four *expected* field values of each element in the list. Correct rows are colored green in the report.

Questions & Answers

What if the elements are out of order?
The differences are marked in the report of the table. Quite how they are marked will depend on how closely they match.

What if two rows in an ordered table are the same?
For the test to pass, there would need to be two matching rows in the same order in the actual list.

---

[2] As discussed in Section 9.1 on p. 67.

10.7   Testing Parts of a List

It can sometimes be inconvenient to test all the elements of a list; we may be interested in the values of only one or more specific elements. A `SubsetFixture` table allows us to check the elements of interest.

For example, the last table in Figure 10.5 simply tests that each of the rows corresponds to elements in the *actual* list from the system under test. This table uses a header row, just as with `RowFixture` and `ArrayFixture`. Any extras in the *actual* list are ignored and are not shown as *surplus*.

Questions & Answers

What if an expected row is missing with `SubsetFixture`?
It's handled the same as with `RowFixture`.

Note

The FitLibrary contains the fixtures introduced in this chapter, along with the `FolderRunner` for running test suites of HTML and spreadsheet files.

The FitLibrary was developed by Rick Mugridge and released through https://sourceForge.net/projects/fitlibrary in 2005.

10.8   Summary

We introduced some new fixtures, based on flow style.

- `DoFixture` tables check the actions in all the tables of the test. Actions may provide several values, separated by keyword cells. Actions are also used to provide fixtures for tests of calculations and lists.

- `SetUpFixture` tables are for data entry at the start of a test.

- `CalculateFixture` tables are a simple alternative to `ColumnFixture` for testing calculations.

- `ArrayFixture` tables test an ordered list.

- `SubsetFixture` tables test some of the elements of the list.

We make considerable use of these tables in Part II.

10.9   Exercises

Answers to selected exercises are available on the book Web site; see Appendix B for details.

1. Using `DoFixture` tables in flow style, write a new chat test: "Anna creates a second room and moves to it." As in the exercises in Chapter 4, you decide whether she is only in the latest room or is in both.

2. Write new tests for the chat server, such that each room is considered to have an *owner*, and only the owner may remove the room and only when it is empty.

3. Choose a simple sequence of steps in a business process that is relevant to you and write a test using flow-style fixtures.

4. From the exercises in Chapter 3, create a `CalculateFixture` table for this business rule:

   > We charge for time based on the charge rate of the consultant, in units of whole hours, and with a minimum charge of $5,000.

CHAPTER 11

A Variety of Tables

As we've seen in previous chapters, tables based on the standard fixtures are suitable for a wide range of Fit tests. However, it is not necessary to restrict yourself to those types of tables if the tests can be expressed better in a different way. In this chapter, we show three examples of tables that may encourage you to design new table structures for your purposes.

Custom table formats can simplify the process of creating and maintaining some types of tests. So feel free to invent a table structure that suits your needs. One aspect of the power of Fit is that it provides a very general approach to using tables for testing. It is not difficult for programmers to create custom fixtures for custom table formats. Of course, there is a tradeoff between the effort of those who create the test tables and those who write the fixtures; in general, it is worth putting programmer effort into the fixtures so that the Fit tables express the tests as clearly as possible.

11.1 Business Forms

It can be convenient to have a test that is similar in structure to a standard business form, such as an invoice. This reduces the gap between the business world and the tests, making it easier for businesspeople to write and to read the tests.

For example, Figure 11.1 shows a report for a Fit table that is based on an invoice. The number of rows in the table depends on the number of order items; here, there are two.

> **Programmers:** The fixture code for the tests here is given in Section 29.2 on p. 248.

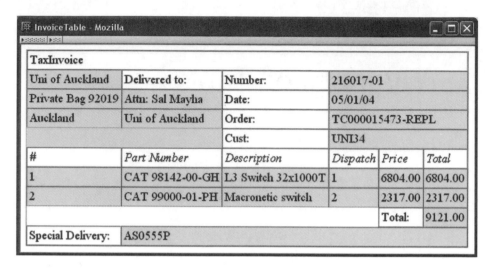

Figure 11.1 A Table Corresponding to an Invoice

Questions & Answers

What if much of the information on the form is fixed and irrelevant to the test, such as "Delivered to"?

Some of the fixed information, such as "Delivered to," is helpful in reading the test, so it is useful to include in the table. Having it laid out in a similar way to the printed form will mean that it's familiar and thus easy to read.

But there's no need to include information in the Fit table that is not needed to understand the rest of the contents of the form. For example, there would be no point in legal information about delivery that's printed at the bottom of the form.

11.2   Testing Associations

Sometimes, a test is easier to read with a picture than with text. For example, the table shown in Figure 11.2 tests the occupancy of various users in various rooms. The Fit fixture doesn't check the image itself but uses an internal format to make the check. If the test fails, a picture of the actual associations is provided (see also Plate 6).

Programmers: The fixture code for the tests here is given in Section 29.2 on p. 248.

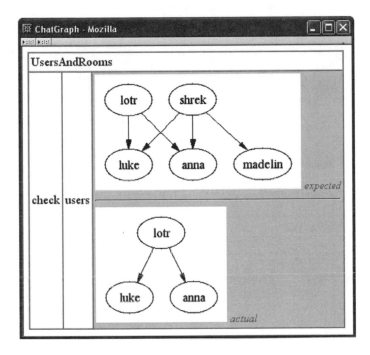

Figure 11.2 A Table Containing an Image

Questions & Answers

Could associations be used to show hierarchical information, such as a parts breakdown?
Yes, that would work well, as long as not too many parts are included.

What about something like a PERT chart?
Yes, that could also work well, as long as it's not too big.

11.3 Two-Dimensional Images

Rather than relying on text in Fit tables, it may be better to use images. When the test data is naturally graphical and in a two-dimensional grid format, images can be more direct in expressing the tests that are needed. **ImageFixture** tables allow this.

For example, Figure 11.3 shows part of the tests for a Sokoban[1] program: a

---

[1] Sokoban is a strategy game; the player moves a character around the grid in order to push all the boxes in the room into shelves in a goal area.

table with images in the cells instead of text. This format has been used to test
that the current board state of the Sokoban program is correct after several moves
have been made.

Programmers: The fixture code for the tests here is given in Section
29.3 on p. 251.

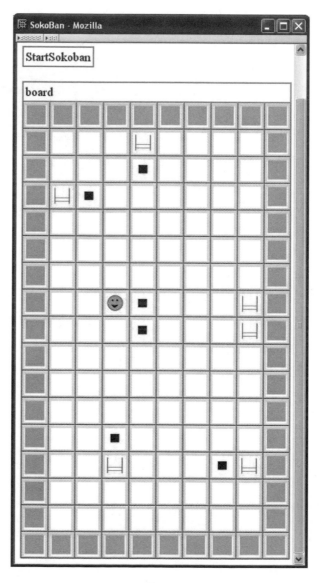

Figure 11.3 A Table of Images

11.4 Summary

- Fit is designed to encourage the design of table structures that work well in expressing specific tests.

- We have shown a variety of table structures to encourage you to find and invent table designs.

- Our first example showed how a business form can be laid out in a table and used as a test.

- The second example used graphics to show and test associations.

- The third example used a grid of simple images to test a game.

11.5 Exercises

1. Find a standard form that is used in your organization and that would serve well as a part of a Fit test for one of your computer systems. Express that form in a Fit table.

2. Consider whether there are examples of tests that are of a graphical nature, such as with associations, that occur naturally in your organization. Based on the second or third example, develop a suitable Fit test.

PART II

DEVELOPING TABLES FOR RentAPartySoftware

CHAPTER 12

Introducing Fit at RentAPartySoftware

For Part II of this book, we focus on how Fit tests are created and evolve and how they can be incorporated into the software development process of an organization. To make this concrete, and to consider the organizational issues that arise, we visit a small, fictitious software company, RentAPartySoftware (RPS). The people in RPS start with small changes to their tests, to improve communication and testing. We see how they work together to express their business rules as Fit tables. Over time, they end up making large, fruitful changes in the way they develop their software.

12.1   RentAPartySoftware

RPS produces *RentEz*, an application for managing the rental of party equipment, such as party tents. The application has been developed as a standalone, traditional desktop application. But that is no longer sufficient. Several RPS clients have multiple branches and want to run them as an integrated system. So RPS figured that a move to the Web would make sense and would also allow its clients' customers to make rental bookings over the Web. As one of the staff told us:

> "Some of our best clients have been slow to upgrade to newer versions of *RentEz* because of problems with quality. Lately, there have been more complaints about little problems in the software.
>
> "We've lost a few sales because we've been unable to add needed features in time. We used to make changes to *RentEz* quickly and well. But lately, everything seems to have slowed down."

The company has a good spirit. "People feel comfortable here." The company owner is enthusiastic and has close ties with his brother's party rental company, which was the prime mover for the software. People seem to get on well and be generally open to change. But the testers, who are blamed when things are delayed, are depressed and frustrated. "We feel second class and would like to have more influence on quality."

It's fascinating how much you get a sense for the people in a company after a few days: who makes things happen, the negative voice, the person who brings things together, the ones for and against change. They believe that they use a software development process, but it sure doesn't show.

Surprisingly, there wasn't too much resistance to change. RPS had been growing well, but its software was getting to the point where "we've lost control and are frightened of making big changes to it."

Questions & Answers

Is this information relevant to programmers too?
Yes, most certainly. Programmers and testers need to get experience with Fit before starting to help and then work with businesspeople on writing tests for their business rules.

Programmers will also need to write the fixtures to tie the tests to the system under test and so need to have a share in their meaning. Programmers also need to be involved in this process, using their abstraction skills at the right time.

12.2   Development Issues

Here are some of the *RentEz* issues that were raised by the developers at RPS.

- Some parts have had ongoing bugs, especially in the area related to charging.

- The developers seem to have a fear of changing the software and the database. "It's big and messy and needs rearchitecting."

- Their testing tools have been unsatisfactory.

- Delays in having problems fixed occur when the programmer responsible for that part is away.

- Problems with configuration on customer sites have occurred.

- All the documents are out of date.

- The testers are unhappy about the lack of time to test before new versions are shipped, especially with last-minute changes to the software.

- Little software problems have been fixed but mysteriously return later.

12.3   An Initial Plan

After discussions, it was agreed that using Fit to put customer tests in place would be a good step forward. This was a part of a larger process of introducing agile development techniques into RPS.

One of the more skeptical people had a good question: "How do we know if we've made an improvement?" This seemed a good time to consider the business goals. Here are some that were decided on, although no statistics have been kept for some of these goals.

- Have all customers eager to move to the latest version of *RentEz*, so as to cut the cost of maintaining several versions.
- Reduce the time taken to add new features, to help sales and to reduce costs.
- Improve the estimates of the effort to add possible new features.
- Improve current customer satisfaction.
- Reduce the number of complaints of problems with *RentEz*.

These goals turn into several more detailed goals for software development.

- Reduce the number of bugs reported from the field.
- Reduce the number of bugs yet to be fixed.
- Reduce the time spent in finding the cause of bugs and fixing them.
- Reduce the effort spent on developing extensions that require drastic rework.
- Reduce the overtime and the stress of last-minutes rushes to get software out, to avoid missing faults that are then picked up by the users.
- Focus the effort on the changes that help sell the product and are most beneficial to clients.

12.4 The Cast

Following are the people we meet at RentAPartySoftware:

- Mitra, a business analyst, who has a lot of experience with the product and has shown herself to be a clear thinker and communicator.
- Don, the most experienced tester, who has been with the company from the beginning. Some others see him as pedantic, but he is great at asking insightful questions and picking up problems large and small.
- Emily, the lead programmer, who has a depth of experience in software development and works well with people.
- Sarah, a younger tester who has recently joined the company, having had a little previous experience with agile testing.
- Neo, a programmer new to the company, who has had some previous experience with some of the Extreme Programming practices. His given name is Neil, but others noticed his superb online game-playing skills and gave him his nickname.

- Seth, a salesperson who gets involved in defining additions to *RentEz*. He has an uncanny ability to understand what customers need, even when they're unclear. He is also excellent at moving product.

- Tim and Fiona, who work for two rental companies that use *RentEz*. They became *RentEz* enthusiasts who are pleased to provide RentAPartySoftware with feedback on the product and its future direction.

12.5   The Rest of This Part

In Chapters 13–19, we look at the issues that arise when we develop Fit tables to aid communication and automated testing.

- In Chapter 13, we look at how to start incorporating Fit tests in the development process. We choose a first business rule to write tests for, based on calculations, and show how the tests aid communication.

- In Chapter 14, we see how Fit tables encourage dialogue in developing tests for business processes.

- In Chapter 15, we continue the development of the tests from Chapter 14 and show how tests that involve data and time can be written. We introduce some *bad-path* tests.

- In Chapter 16, we show how a large number of business process tests can be collapsed into a few calculate tests by focusing on the essential elements of the underlying business rule.

- In Chapter 17, we show how Fit tests can be used to define new business rules to be incorporated in a software system. In particular, we place Fit tests in the context of Extreme Programming.

- In Chapter 18, we discuss the design of Fit tables. We discuss several table *smells*: table problems that may need to be resolved through changes to the tables and/or their structure.

12.6   Summary

RPS is a reasonably typical small software development company. The employees have good morale but keep being pushed off balance by the actions of others and by their inability to make changes with confidence. They hope to achieve their business goals through changes to the way in which they develop their software. In the remainder of this part, we show how they start to incorporate Fit tests into their development process.

12.7 Exercises

1. Which of the issues in Section 12.2 apply to your organization?

2. Make a priority-ordered list of the issues that do apply. What factors helped you order them?

3. Are the uncertainties more about the market and what your product should do or more about the technology of platforms and tools for development?

4. What knowledge about your organization or its market are you missing?

5. How change resistant is your organization? Have you had lots of change forced on you? How much did you initiate? Which changes were successful? Why? Was the notion of *success* defined beforehand?

CHAPTER 13

Getting Started: Emily and Don's First Table

In this chapter, we look at the issues that arise when starting to use Fit tables with an existing application. What tests should be developed first? Who should start on these tests? How are tables designed? How many tables are needed? How much should the structure of tables reflect the current architecture of the application? Should the tests be comprehensive in small areas, or is it better to start with a broad brush stroke? We answer some of these questions in this chapter; others are tackled over the rest of this part.

> **Programmers:** The fixture code for the tests in this chapter is given in Chapter 31.

13.1 Introduction

It was Monday morning, after a week of training in Fit and agile processes. We met with Emily and Don[1] to start developing Fit tables for RPS.

They were enthusiastic about getting started and could set aside their normal work for a few days. They also had the respect of the management and their colleagues and had plenty of experience with the application. They were good choices to start getting real experience with Fit tables.

13.2 Choosing Where to Start

Emily and Don suggested several areas of their system to tackle first, based on a few guidelines that we had indicated. But none of those areas was simple enough for a first step. Then Don suggested *late returns:* "For example, a customer rents

---

[1] See Section 12.4 on p. 91 for an introduction to the cast.

a party tent overnight to be returned by 10 A.M., but doesn't return it until after lunch. The customer gets charged for being late."

The tests that Don had developed many months ago were now out of date. He'd tested through the GUI, and the GUI had changed. "I felt guilty about the tests being dated. But I'd been frustrated after changing the tests several times to match the revised GUI."

Emily agreed that this was a good area to pursue. "There have been ongoing problems in that area. A bug has just been reported, which is still to be dealt with. It looks rather like one that we've already fixed."

She wasn't very happy about her code: "There have been ongoing changes and it's a bit of a mess. And, I think, further changes are likely. Seth has been talking to a rental company that is very interested in *RentEz*. But that company handles late-return fees rather differently from our existing companies, so they'd need some changes to it."

We decided to proceed with *late returns*.

13.3   The Business Rule

Between them, Don and Emily worked out anew the business rules involved in *late returns*. After looking unsuccessfully for some old user documentation, Don looked over his old tests, and Emily refreshed her memory from the code. They figured that it would be good to get Seth to look over the tests once he had returned from his latest business trip.

This is the business rule they worked out, an hour later, according to Don.

A late fee may be charged if equipment is expected to be returned by a certain time. The fee depends on

- How long the item was rented for. There is usually one hour's grace. However, the longer the time, the longer the grace period.

- If the return is beyond the grace period, the late fee is based on either the extra time or the extra time minus the grace period. The choice of approach is defined in a database configuration table that's set up for a specific rental company and is not likely to change.

- Usually, the late fee is simply the extra time, as defined, charged at the usual rate for that item.

- However, when the item is in high demand, the grace period is reduced and an extra late fee is charged. This is especially important for rental items that have been booked out, as the rental company staff would need to source replacement equipment from elsewhere at some cost.

- The extra late fee may be associated with each rental item.

13.4   Starting Simple

"Is this starting to sound too complicated for a first step," wondered Emily, "with the configurations and all?" We said that it was worth pressing on, by tackling the tests in small steps.

We decided to simplify things so that we could make some progress. As things got clearer, we could add more aspects of the business rule. To start, we assumed a fixed grace period, assumed that all the extra time was to be charged, and ignored the high-demand part.

"How about this?" asked Don, who quickly drew the `ColumnFixture`[2] table shown in Figure 13.1 on the whiteboard.

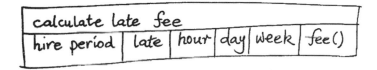

Figure 13.1 Don's First Table

After we had discussed making the labels in Figure 13.1 clearer, Don altered it, as shown in Figure 13.2. "Is this the right way to go?" he questioned. "Does the table have more information than necessary?"

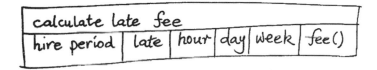

Figure 13.2 Don's Second Table

"We don't need to calculate the late fee in this table," Sarah suggested. "We can simply calculate the extra time period to be charged." We all agreed.

"Although," mentioned Emily, "this is moving away from how my code is organized." Figure 13.3 resulted.

Figure 13.3 Emily's Trimmed Table

---

[2] See Chapter 3 for an introduction to `ColumnFixture` tables.

"At this stage," Don pointed out, "we don't need the first column, either. Let's plug in a few quick tests." (See Figure 13.4.)

calculate late fee	
hours late	extra time()
0	0
0.9	0
1	1
9	9

Figure 13.4 Don's Added Tests

13.5 Adding the Grace Period

Then we tackled some more of the business rule. Emily suggested, "Let's show whether the grace period is included in the *extra time()*. We can handle that with ***count grace***, a *given* field." Emily sketched Figure 13.5 as a starting structure; this assumes a grace period of 1 hour.

calculate late extra		
hours late	count grace	extra time()
0	yes	0
0.9	no	0
1	yes	1
1	no	0
9	yes	9
9	no	8

Figure 13.5 Emily's Extension of the Tests with Grace Period

"Let's now sort out how the grace period is calculated, based on the rental period," suggested Don. He tried various ways of adding that to the current table. Then he realized, with a little prompting, "The grace period calculation would be best done independently." (We don't cover that here.) So that led to Figure 13.6, where the ***grace*** period is simply plugged in as a *given*.

calculate late extra			
hours late	grace	count grace	extra time()
0	1	yes	0
0.9	1	no	0
1	1	yes	1
1	1	no	0
9	1	yes	9
19	2	no	17

Figure 13.6 Don's Added Grace Period

13.6 Adding High-Demand Items

Now we could tackle the high-demand rental items. "We simply need another *given* column," Don pointed out. So he added the new ***high demand*** column, with all rows having a value of 0. He was about to add some more rows for when the ***high demand*** value is not zero; we suggested that they go into a second table.

"I'll change the name of the *calculated* field to ***extra hours()***," added Don. "And the test values in the second table should be changed too." This gave us Figures 13.7 and 13.8.

rent.CalculateLateHours				
hours late	*grace*	*count grace*	*high demand*	*extra hours()*
0	1	yes	0	0
0.9	1	no	0	0
1	1	yes	0	1
1	1	no	0	0
9	1	yes	0	9
19	2	no	0	17

Figure 13.7 High Demand Added

rent.CalculateLateHours				
hours late	*grace*	*count grace*	*high demand*	*extra hours()*
0	1	yes	10	0
0.9	1	no	10	0
1	1	yes	5	6
1	1	no	12	0
9	1	no	10	18
19	2	no	100	117

Figure 13.8 A Second Table, with High Demand More Than Zero

Questions & Answers

It wasn't easy to follow all the details of this lateness example.

That's OK; a lot of business-specific detail is involved here, which would take some time to fully understand. The first point of this example is to show the process of several people understanding *nontrivial* business rules through writing tests. The second point is how to focus on choosing a suitable area for writing the first tests, in order to gain experience.

Does it usually take this much back and forth to zoom in on suitable tests?

Yes, it can; this scenario is not at all unusual. It depends on the experience of the people, on how well they understand the business rules, and on the number of perspectives.

People are often surprised at how simple or how difficult it can be to express rules with suitable tests, owing to a fuzziness in thinking about the rules or conflicting values that underlie them. So you can't necessarily tell beforehand how long it will take. Different goals and points of view may need to be resolved in order to make progress.

Our business rules are poorly documented or are out of date. Someone proposing to change them doesn't take account of what we've learned in the past. Test tables would help there, even if they weren't automated.

Yes, you're right; the tests document the interesting cases. However, there is an underrated value in automating the tests: In building the system to satisfy the tests, programmers often find little inconsistencies between the different tests, and these are important to resolve.

The *system under test* tests the *tests* as much as the *tests* test the *system under test*. Together, they ensure that the documentation is kept up to date.

How do you handle a bug report once you introduce automated tests?

Write a Fit test for it and add it to the test suite. The test suite should be run regularly, at least once a day. And then, once it's fixed, the bug can't come back for long without being picked up by the test.

So far, we'd spent less than an hour on the tests, and we'd made good progress. We started to discuss the final step—how the grace period is calculated—but it was lunchtime. Emily and Don figured that they could do that by themselves after lunch, so we left them to it.

13.7   Reports

Emily developed the fixture code the next day and connected it to the application, as we discuss in Chapter 31. The report for the table in Figure 13.8 is shown in Figure 13.9.

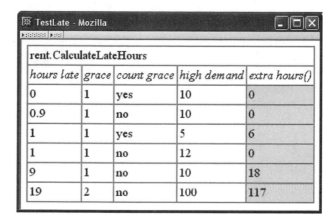

Figure 13.9 Report of Figure 13.8

13.8 Seth's Return

When Seth, from Sales, returned from his trip, he reviewed the Fit tables with Don and Emily. "I'm surprised at all the cases; I thought I really understood it." He had several questions about the test cases and suggested some other examples that highlighted test deficiencies, which turned out to be minor by the time they'd worked through them.

Seth had been talking to a potential buyer of *RentEz*. "Their business rules are at odds with our current approach to handling lateness. I've also brought back some complaints about excessive amounts being charged; I'll find the details and show you."

Seth, Don, and Emily agreed to meet later to discuss these issues and to reconsider the way that lateness may be handled for the next version of the software (see Chapter 16). Revising that could mean discussing and negotiating with those existing *RentEz* clients on a maintenance and upgrade contract.

Seth was pleased. "We now have a clear idea of the current business rule for handling lateness, which will make it easier to think about the future and reduce the likelihood of changes' having a bad impact on existing customers."

13.9 Summary

- It took some time to find a suitable area for writing the first Fit tables for the application.

- Emily and Don experienced working together, with some guidance, to develop tables step by step.

- When things seemed too complex, they tackled a part of the problem and evolved a simple table from there.

- It wasn't immediately obvious how to represent the business rule or even what the rule should be. The tables helped clarify what's needed, getting to its essence.

Emily and Don seemed to enjoy their experience. Here are some general characteristics that can help in choosing an early area for developing Fit tests:

- A part that needs attention because of past or current problems with errors
- Simple and clear business rules, with someone available to clarify any issues that may arise
- No tests or manual or automated tests that are difficult to read, too dependent on other tests, or are no longer valid
- People who are familiar with the business and with testing and are eager to participate and have time and support of management to do so

Having bright, enthusiastic, and respected people move first into the use of new tools and practices is essential. If they have a good experience, they'll soon be able to support and encourage others.

13.10   Exercises

1. Consider the tests in Figure 13.8. Write some tests that are likely to be useful additions.

2. Invent a business rule for the *calculated* grace period. Design a Fit table and add some tests.

3. Consider other possible table structures for Figure 13.8.

4. Select a business rule of relevance to you that involves calculations or decisions.

5. Work with one or two others to discuss the selected business rule as a Fit test.

6. What are the givens? What is being calculated?

7. If your business rule is at all complex, start with a small part of it and evolve the table step by step by adding more cases, as we showed in this chapter.

8. As your tables evolve, reconsider the vocabulary as you progress. Can it be made clearer?

9. Feel free to completely change things at any point; as you attempt to express the tests, you may find better ways to do so.

10. Try to use realistic examples, even if you have to simplify them initially.

11. You may find it useful to break the test into several tables.

12. Are you in fact tackling two or more related business rules? If so, split them.

CHAPTER 14

Testing a Business Process: Cash Rentals

In this chapter, we see how to handle various issues that arise in developing Fit tests for business processes:

- Having independent tests rather than combining them
- Managing setup that is common to several tests
- Finding good ways of managing contextual information, such as the current client

Once again, we see that Fit tables can encourage a dialogue about what needs to be expressed. A *vocabulary* evolves during this process, showing that communication is more than simply saying what is already understood.

Programmers: This is discussed further in Chapter 32 on p. 267.

14.1   Introduction

It's Wednesday, and Sarah, another tester, joined Emily and Don to develop Fit tests for actions that involve a sequence of steps in the use of *RentEz*. After choosing cash rental as a suitable area of use to gain experience in such tests, they began.

Don and the other testers had previously tested such actions through the GUI. "We'd developed automated test scripts to do this, but the GUI kept changing, and we were too busy to keep the tests up to date. After much frustration, we'd given up on the automated tests and had gone back to manual testing." Don smiled. "We're eager to find a way with Fit to avoid these problems."

We all agreed that the tests would be independent of the GUI but would address the important testing concerns. Instead of trying to write complete tests, Emily, Don, and Sarah wisely decided to ignore many of the issues until they'd made progress on the fundamentals. This is a good approach; otherwise, it can be difficult to make progress when too many issues are competing for attention.

Questions & Answers

But doesn't testing through the GUI ensure that the GUI itself works correctly as well?

Yes, that's true. However, as we'll see, there are many benefits to separating concerns, to focus on one sort of test at a time. With many testing issues in the business logic, it pays to get that sorted before automating GUI-specific testing.

14.2   Cash Rentals

To give us some background, Don took us through a few scenarios, using *RentEz*:

> A cash rental occurs when someone comes in to rent some party equipment, such as a coffee dispenser, for some time period. It's called "cash" if the client has not made a booking and will pay immediately rather than on account. A staff member at the rental company serves the client, recording the details, if necessary, as well as what the client wants to rent and for how long. A timed record is kept of what the client rented and when; that way, when the rental goods are returned, a check can be made as to whether the client owes more money or is due a refund of the deposit.

"For a start, we've decided to ignore several issues and details," said Don. These included

- The staff member's interacting with the client and entering details
- Much of the information kept about clients
- The clock time at the time of renting and when the rental goods were returned
- A client changes his or her mind at any stage about the rentals
- A client unable to pay after all, as his or her credit card limit is exceeded
- The consideration of only daily rental rates, not hourly and weekly rates
- The client's deposit on the rented goods, to cover damage and/or late return

Once it was clear that they were tackling a suitably sized problem, we left them to it for an hour or so. We returned to find them in the middle of an animated discussion about managing the tests for running totals for charges and deposit refunds.

They had written out several tests on the whiteboard and on three large sheets of paper stuck on the wall. "We've got some questions for you, including the best way of handling the hourly and weekly rental rates for RentalItems."

Emily had sketched three of the components of their system, as shown in Figure 14.1. "A Client may have several currently rented items. A Rental is an association between a Client and a RentalItem, with additional information, such as the number of RentalItems rented, the date/time the rental started, the period of the rental, and so on."

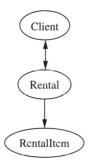

Figure 14.1 The Three Components

"We've decided to keep the identification of Clients and RentalItems simple at this stage," said Emily, as shown by one of their tests in Figure 14.2. They had used some initial tables in Figure 14.2 to provide some Client and RentalItem data (see the Tip on p. 107).

As Emily explained, the tables are as follows.

- An ActionFixture table[1] is used to start the system under test (setup).

- A ColumnFixture table[2] is used to define the items that may be rented (setup).

- A ColumnFixture table is used to define the clients that are known (setup)

- An ActionFixture table is used to rent two sets of rental items (action).

- A RowFixture table[3] checks that the rental has been recorded (check).

- An ActionFixture table is used to return most of the rental items (action).

- A RowFixture table checks that the outstanding rental is recorded (check).

Three roles are identified in these tables: *setup, action,* and *check.* Tables filling these roles occur in most action-based tests, in that order.

The first three setup tables were, more or less, included in all their tests. After discussion about the various tests they'd written, we all decided that several changes would be helpful, as we cover in the following sections.

- Have the first three tables in a SetUp, to be shared by all the tests. This would require some minor changes to the data values in one of the tests.

---

[1] See Chapter 4 for an introduction to ActionFixture tables.
[2] See Chapter 3 for an introduction to ColumnFixture tables.
[3] See Chapter 5 for an introduction to RowFixture tables.

fit.ActionFixture	
start	rent.Application

rent.RentalItems			
name	*count*	*cost per day*	*add()*
coffee dispenser	10	8.20	true
hot water dispenser	12	8.00	true

rent.Clients		
name	*phone*	*add()*
Joanna	373 7599	true

fit.ActionFixture		
enter	client name	Joanna
enter	item	coffee dispenser
enter	count	5
enter	days	1
press	hire	
check	cost	41.00
enter	item	hot water dispenser
enter	count	2
press	hire	
check	cost	16.00

rent.RentalList			
client	*rental item name*	*count*	*days*
Joanna	coffee dispenser	5	1
Joanna	hot water dispenser	2	1

fit.ActionFixture		
enter	client name	Joanna
enter	item	coffee dispenser
enter	count	4
press	return	
enter	item	hot water dispenser
enter	count	2
press	returns	

rent.RentalList			
client	*rental item name*	*count*	*days*
Joanna	coffee dispenser	1	1

Figure 14.2 Test Partial Returns

> **Tip**
>
> A useful technique is to have a compact way of setting up the initial data to use in a test. If that data had to be entered through tables that drive the usual workflow, several problems would arise.
>
> - It makes the test much longer, more difficult to read, and less clearly focused. The early setup distracts from the main point of the test.
> - If the workflow used to create Clients and RentalItems changes, all the tests that depend on that workflow must be changed.
>
> Yes, that does lead to a little more work for the programmers in creating extra fixtures that handle the setup. However, there are also benefits to this, as we'll see in Chapter 32.

- Change the names of the second and third tables to make their intent clear, and use a `SetUpFixture` fixture[4] to avoid the *add()* columns. This was better than adding comments to explain what the tables were for.
- Split the test into two, because it is testing two actions: rentals and returns.
- Use `DoFixture` tables[5] for the actions. Given all the information needed for the actions, this would make the tests more succinct.

14.3   Split and Restructure

The first step was to separate the setup of these tests; moving to a flow style with `DoFixture` has an impact on these tables. Figure 14.3 shows the common initial sequence of tables.

The second step was to separate the test in Figure 14.2 into two tests: one to test the rentals and the other to test that the partial returns had the right result. Figure 14.4 shows the first one. (We assume that the `SetUp` from Figure 14.3 will be included, either when using spreadsheets, as discussed in Section 7.1 or when using FitNesse, as discussed in Section 8.4 on p. 62).

Figure 14.5 shows the second test. Note that the extra `SetUp` table at the beginning is almost the same as the final check table in Figure 14.4.

---

[4] See Section 10.4 on p. 76 for an introduction to `SetUpFixture` tables.
[5] See Chapter 10 for an introduction to `DoFixture` tables.

rent.StartApplication		
enter rental items		
name	*count*	*$/day*
coffee dispenser	10	8.20
hot water dispenser	12	8.00
enter clients		
name	*phone*	
Joanna	373 7599	

Figure 14.3 Common SetUp Data for Tests

client	Joanna	*hires*	5	*of*	coffee dispenser	*for*	1	*days*
client	Joanna	*hires*	2	*of*	hot water dispenser	*for*	2	*days*
check	cost	16.00						

rental list			
client	*rental item*	*count*	*days*
Joanna	coffee dispenser	5	1
Joanna	hot water dispenser	2	2

Figure 14.4 Test Rental

rental entry			
client	*rental item*	*count*	*days*
Joanna	coffee dispenser	5	1
Joanna	hot water dispenser	2	2

client	Joanna	*returns*	4	*of*	coffee dispenser
client	Joanna	*returns*	2	*of*	hot water dispenser

rental list			
client	*rental item*	*count*	*days*
Joanna	coffee dispenser	1	1

Figure 14.5 Test Partial Return

Tip

It is only after writing several tests that their commonality becomes clear. It's often a mistake to focus on the SetUp too early, because you have to guess. As you develop the concrete examples, you can see what commonality arises naturally.

Questions & Answers

Shouldn't the tests be based more on the current implementation?
It's usually a mistake to do this too closely, because it tends to incorporate unessential details that are based on how the system happens to work rather than on the important business rules that underlie it.

Of course, it's also a mistake to invent a whole new system, so that the tests are useless for the current one. As tests are put in place and are run against the current system, they provide a solid foundation on which to ask what-if questions about the future development.

Doesn't that make it difficult to automate?
Not necessarily, as long as the essence of the tests matches the underlying system. The fixture code may need to do lots of work in order to keep the tests simple, but that's a good tradeoff, especially given that tools for managing Fit tests are still in their infancy, compared to programming tools.

What do you mean by "essence"?
In our current example, the Client, RentalItem, and so on, are essential to the business rule of renting some party items. How the Client information is presented on the GUI and how a particular client is chosen are not essential to the workflow; those elements could be changed without impacting the business process rule.

It's not easy to make decisions about the structure of tables, is it, given that they're rather "technical"?
Quite right; it's designing something, a way of "talking" about a part of the system under test. The skills of several people are likely to be needed to get the tables in the right shape with the right vocabulary. Once that's clearer, and businesspeople know what can be said with them, they can then use those structures to write more tests.

14.4 Which Client

"It's odd to have to mention the Client in every table," suggested Don. "In *RentEz*, a particular Client is selected and then any rentals, returns, and so on, are carried out within the context of that Client. This would be fine with one or two tests, but as we add more and more tests, there is much more incentive to be concise."

So Don altered the tests again to make the Client implicit after being selected. He decided to use an action in an extra table to select the current Client. This is shown in the revised SetUp tables in Figure 14.6.

The other tests were then altered to not mention the current Client, as shown in Figures 14.7 and 14.8. To be clear that only the Rentals shown in the last table of

rent.StartApplication		
enter rental items		
name	*count*	*$/day*
coffee dispenser	10	8.20
hot water dispenser	12	8.00

enter clients	
name	*phone*
Joanna	373 7599

client	Joanna

Figure 14.6 Changed SetUp to Select the Client

each test are for the specified Client (Joanna), Don changed that table to *rentals for client*.

He also changed the wording of the rentals and returns in the tables to read more easily; it's fine to have empty keywords. The *vocabulary* we use often changes like this as part of the ongoing dialogue and invention of a good way of expressing tests.

hire	5		coffee dispenser	*for*	1	*days*
hire	2		hot water dispenser	*for*	2	*days*
check	cost	16.00				

rentals for client	Joanna	
rental item	*count*	*days*
coffee dispenser	5	1
hot water dispenser	2	2

Figure 14.7 Changed Rental Test

rental entry		Joanna	
rental item		*count*	*days*
coffee dispenser		5	1
hot water dispenser		2	1
return	4	coffee dispenser	
return	2	hot water dispenser	

rentals for client	Joanna	
rental item	*count*	*days*
coffee dispenser	1	1

Figure 14.8 Changed Partial Return Test

The group had other work to attend to, so we agreed to continue with these tests the next day.

Questions & Answers

Why didn't you simply tell them how to do it from the start?
It's not necessarily that easy to design the tables for a set of tests in one go, and they knew about the business. Settling on a good vocabulary can take time. It's not until you're written several tests that you start to see the pattern of things that need to be said.

We all learned something by tackling these tests in this way. And this gives a realistic example of how your tests will evolve.

Does that mean that we may have to revise the vocabulary as the system changes?
Maybe. It depends on the sort of change. Some business changes will simply require you to extend your vocabulary for new tests for new parts of the system. Changes in the business rules may make different distinctions than before, which may require changes in vocabulary when you talk about those rules and thus changes in the vocabulary used in the tests. The tests lose value if they aren't current, and change is inevitable!

On the other hand, we want to avoid having to change our essential vocabulary just because the implementation has changed for nonbusiness reasons, such as in the database schema or the GUI. That's why the vocabulary of the tests needs to be oriented to the business, not the current implementation.

Tip

We're really eager to avoid unnecessary repetition in tests generally, not just in the SetUp. As the number of tests grows, the redundancy makes it

- Tedious to write the same stuff over and over
- Annoying when all the copies have to be changed, especially as it is so easy to miss changing some
- More difficult to read and check the tests

14.5   Summary

We have seen how to handle various issues that arise in developing Fit tests for business processes. One test was split into two independent tests. The group collected `SetUp` tables together to be used by several tests. We found a reasonable way of keeping track of the current client in our tests without excessive duplication.

The tests are still incomplete. We develop them further in the next chapter to take account of the issues that have been ignored initially, listed in Section 14.2.

By the end of this session, the group was feeling positive and had enjoyed the experience. Someone mentioned that it was nice to be able to ignore a lot of the details of the underlying system when writing the tests. However, Emily was a little bothered about the implications for the fixtures and *RentEz*, as the tests were rather different in structure from the application itself.

We have seen, again, how tables evolve as we come to grips with the business rules and associated shape and vocabulary of tables. The focus of table design has been on such business rules.

- The tests aim to communicate the business rules as clearly as possible, with a focus on the essential, ignoring incidental details of the implementation.

- This process often helps everyone's understanding of the essentials of the business rules.

- Tables filling the roles of *setup*, *action*, and *check* occur in most business process tests, in that order.

The vocabulary that we use in tests usually has to evolve through a dialogue between the businesspeople and the developers, making sure that the essence of what needs to be said can be expressed clearly. Instead of statements in English, we end up with statements that are in tables and whose precise meanings are shared. These meanings need to be incorporated by the programmers into the fixtures. We have more to say about the evolution of tables in Chapter 18.

Given the effort involved in getting the vocabulary right, it makes sense to start new developments with the test tables first and allow the system to follow. We discuss driving new developments with tables in Chapter 17.

14.6   Exercises

Here's a sequence of steps that you may like to try.

1. Choose a business area of interest to you that has a workflow component and that you'd like Fit tests for. We assume that a system already exists, but that's not necessary for these exercises.

2. Get together with a few others who share your interest, have a background that you may lack in the business, and have good testing skills or good abstraction skills, such as programmers.

3. Pick the smallest piece of that business workflow, and create or find an example. At this stage, don't try to create a Fit table. Focus on finding regular statements that you can make in English. (Those with an Extreme Programming background are advised to write stories.)

4. You may like to start writing these up on a whiteboard or on large sheets of paper, whatever you find works best. Don't use a computer to do this, because it will slow the process down and focus the attention on one person at the keyboard.

5. If too many things are going on at once, list them and decide which one to tackle first or next. It's easy enough to extend once you make progress on some of them.

6. After you've played with a few statements, try expressing them in Fit tables, using words from your statements as keywords in the actions.

7. Look for the usual three phases of the test: *setup, action,* and *check.*

8. If you find that your test is too long, consider breaking it up. Are several tests in there? Are you trying to deal with too many conditions too early? Simplify whenever you get stuck.

9. Keep the examples concrete and meaningful; that will make them much more useful, and you will make faster progress.

10. Don't spend too long on one example; trying several with some variation will give you a better sense of what needs to be expressed.

11. Don't spend too long at it; building shared understanding and vocabulary can be hard work, so stop for a break before you need it. When you start again, you may be surprised at how much your thinking has changed in the meantime, without effort.

12. If too many opinions conflict, try to focus on the examples that you can agree on; that gives you a basis for better discussing the differences later.

Don't be surprised that

- You're surprised at the outcome of this process, and you gain some insights.

- Everyone's views are slightly different.

- The people who use the system may well know more about it than their managers.

- The way the current system works does not match the business rule you've expressed.

- Some business rules are handled by the users in various "backdoor" ways because the system is incomplete or requires workarounds.

CHAPTER 15

Tests Involving the Date and Time

Our group continues to evolve the rental tests from the previous chapter, finding that it's good to use a common **SetUp** while avoiding unnecessary interactions between tests. The group finds that it's easy, after all, to write tests that depend on the date and time.

When tackling business transactions, the group makes such transactions explicit in the tests. Finally, the group develops *sad-path* tests, which check when things go wrong.

> **Programmers:** The fixture code for the tests in this chapter is given in Chapters 33 and 34.

15.1   Introduction

On Thursday, Emily, Don, and Sarah continued with the tests. Emily suggested that they start with deposits: "That seems simple and would be a good warmup before tackling date and time." Don agrees: "I'm not sure how to test when the system is affected by the date and time."

In the past, they hadn't automated time-based tests. "Doing the tests manually is no fun either," said Don, "as a test can't be completed until the right time has elapsed. Lots of careful checks are needed, which is time consuming. So after changes to *RentEz*, the tests were often not done and then often not as well as they could be."

We began with charging deposits.

15.2   Charging a Deposit

The general business rule here is as follows.

As well as the rental charge, a client pays a deposit before taking the rental items. When the client returns the items, the deposit is refunded if the items are in good condition and don't need replacement, fixing, or cleaning. Otherwise, a partial refund is made, or the client is asked to pay extra for the damage.

The group's first step was to add deposit information in the SetUp to the Hire-Items, as last shown in Figure 14.6 on p. 110. After some debate, Don made the deposit $0.00 for the two dispensers; that meant that the previous tests should still pass. As Don argued, "It would be great if we could add more data to the SetUp without breaking the old tests." The others agreed.

Don added cups as an item with a deposit and included the three rental rates: hourly, daily, and weekly, as shown in Figure 15.1.

rent.StartApplication					
enter rental items					
name	*count*	*$/hour*	*$/day*	*$/week*	*deposit*
coffee dispenser	10	1.50	8.20	60.00	0.00
hot water dispenser	12	1.50	8.00	50.00	0.00
cup	500	0.05	0.45	2.00	0.10

enter clients	
name	*phone*
Joanna	373 7599

client	Joanna

Figure 15.1 Extend the SetUp

Sarah wrote the test shown in Figure 15.2. She then questioned whether it made sense to have only a *weeks* column in those tables: "Will we need *hours*, *days*, and *weeks*?" "Let's wait until we add date/time processing and see what happens," Emily suggested.

rent	100		cup	*for*	2	*weeks*
check	cost	210.00				

rentals for client	Joanna	
rental item	*count*	*weeks*
cup	100	2

Figure 15.2 Rent with a Deposit

"This test is incomplete," Don then pointed out. "We should also check that there are 100 fewer cups in stock afterward." He extended Figure 15.2 to give Figure 15.3.

Immediately, Don was unhappy with that: "We need to check only the count." Emily added, "And we'd be better checking just the cups, not the other items. Otherwise, when we change the SetUp again, the last table (in Figure 15.3) will

rent	100		cup	*for*	2	*weeks*
check	cost	210.00				

rentals for client	Joanna	
rental item	*count*	*weeks*
cup	100	2

rental item list					
name	*count*	*$/hour*	*$/day*	*$/week*	*deposit*
coffee dispenser	10	1.50	8.20	60.00	0.00
hot water dispenser	12	1.50	8.00	50.00	0.00
cup	400	0.05	0.45	2.00	0.10

Figure 15.3 Rent with a Deposit with Extra Checking Table

fail." Don changed the table to give Figure 15.4, using a `SubsetFixture`.[1] He pointed out, "We'll need to have at least one test that checks that the other rental items are not altered at all."

rent	100		cup	*for*	2	*weeks*
check	cost	210.00				

rentals for client	Joanna	
rental item	*count*	*weeks*
cup	100	2

rental item subset list	
name	*count*
cup	400

Figure 15.4 Revised Last Table

"We need to write a test for returning the deposit when the rental items are returned," Emily noted. However, she realized, "We really haven't handled payments yet, let alone refunds. Let's leave that until after we do dates."

Questions & Answers

Do you tend to have lots of `SetUp`s or only one for all the tests?
For RentAPartySoftware, a common `SetUp` was used for almost all the tests. This avoided the need to make up new data for each test, which gets tedious, and it's difficult to remember the particular data. With common `SetUp`, we could keep a printed copy on hand.

I suppose the downside is that we may have had a little less variation in our tests than we'd have liked. No, maybe not, when I think about it some more.

---

[1] See Section 10.7 on p. 79 for an introduction to `SubsetFixture` tables.

In general, it depends on the system under test and how many distinct areas of the application there are. It may be that most tests share some common data, and then categories of tests share still more, so it's convenient to have automated support in gathering up the right SetUp to use for a particular test.

15.3   Dates

"We need an action that sets the date. Then we can control the time whenever we want," Sarah offered. After trying several action words, she suggested setting the date as shown in Figure 15.5.

time is now	2004/05/06 09:01

Figure 15.5 An Action to Set the Date

After Sarah added the time-change action to several tests, Emily suggested that she "put it at the end of the SetUp, as all tests will need date/time set." Sarah added that to Figure 15.1. She then changed the rental test in Figure 15.4 to become the test shown in Figure 15.6, having added in *hours* and *days* to the second table.

rent	100		*cup*	*for*	2	*weeks*			
check	cost	210.00							
rentals for client		Joanna							
rental item		*count*	*start date*			*hours*	*days*	*weeks*	
cup		100	2004/05/06 09:01			0	0	2	
rental item subset list									
name	*count*								
cup	400								

Figure 15.6 Test Rental with Dates

"Why not use an end date as well?" Don suggested. He changed the second table of the test, as shown in Figure 15.7.

rentals for client		Joanna	
rental item		*start date*	*end date*
rental item	*count*	*start date*	*end date*
cup	100	2004/05/06 09:01	2004/05/20 09:01

Figure 15.7 Revised Second Table of Test Rental with Dates

Questions & Answers

It's easy to write the test, but making it work is not so easy.

Yes, that's true, as we'll see in Chapter 34. But the payback from doing so is immense, as we can then write automated tests that pick up errors soon after they're made.

In the medium term, having test support and higher quality in the software can make a huge difference in the speed at which changes can be made. And being able to communicate about what's needed, using Fit tests to express that, is also so valuable; it helps to focus the effort where it's needed.

15.4   Business Transactions

It was time for Sarah, Emily, and Don to deal with the money, but they weren't sure of all the details. So Mitra, a business analyst, was asked to join the group to help with that and to gain experience with Fit tests.

As Mitra explained: "Customers may start saying what they want to rent, which is entered by the staff member serving them. But when they find that some item is not available, they may cancel everything. We have to ensure that they get the rental items if they want them, so we handle this with a business transaction." "And they can cancel part of it at any time," Don added. "So we need some way of handling that in our tests."

"For a transaction to be completed," Mitra continued, "customers have to have paid or had the amount added to their charge accounts. To cancel after they've paid, they have to first have that payment refunded, or it will be automatically removed as a charge on their accounts."

"So we need to be explicit about the transaction as a business object in our test," said Sarah, "so how about this for the action part of the test?" She sketched out the tables in Figure 15.8: "I've put all the actions to do with the transaction into a single table, as they operate within the context of that transaction."

begin transaction for client	Joanna				
rent	100		cup	for	2	weeks
check	total is $	210.00			
pay with cash $	210.00				
check	total is $	0.00			
complete transaction					

Figure 15.8 Test Rental Within a Transaction

Questions & Answers

What do you mean by "business object"?

In the business domain, that's something that is relevant to our system and that we want to be clear about. Obvious business objects are things like rental items, apartments, vehicles, and accounts. Less obvious are things like time periods and transactions. In RentEz, it doesn't seem as though transactions are to do with the large-scale business, but they certainly underlie much of the business workflow.

We introduced testing of such business objects in Section 10.3 on p. 75.

"There's no need to check the total before and after paying," Mitra recommended. "If the payment isn't for the full amount of the rental cost, the transaction cannot be completed. And the transaction mentions the customer, so there's no need to do that separately in the SetUp."

"We'll need to write some tests for the transaction failing to complete," added Don. "Let's leave that until later." (We cover that in the next section.)

Sarah changed the SetUp to include information about staff, as shown in Figure 15.9.

rent.StartApplication					
setup					
rental item name	*count*	*$/hour*	*$/day*	*$/week*	*deposit*
coffee dispenser	10	1.50	8.20	60.00	0.00
hot water dispenser	12	1.50	8.00	50.00	0.00
cup	500	0.05	0.45	2.00	0.10

setup	
client name	*phone*
Joanna	373 7599

setup	
staff name	*phone*
Bill	555 9876

time is now	2004/05/06 09:01

Figure 15.9 Revised SetUp

She then removed the amount checks from Figure 15.8, resulting in the test shown in Figure 15.10, which assumes the SetUp in Figure 15.9, as usual. The last table in Figure 15.10 was also changed by Don to include staff member Bill in the transaction.

begin transaction for client	Joanna	staff	Bill			
rent	100		cup	for	2	weeks
pay with cash $	210.00					
complete transaction						

rentals for client	Joanna		
rental item	count	start date	end date
cup	100	2004/05/06 09:01	2004/05/20 09:01

rental item subset	
name	count
cup	400

Figure 15.10 Revised Test Rental Within a Transaction

15.5   Sad Paths

Don was eager to focus on "when the transaction can't complete." In testing, this
is often called a *sad path* because it concerns what happens when things don't work
out well. After discussion and a few trials, the group came up with the first sad-path
test, as shown in Figure 15.11.

begin transaction for client	Joanna	staff	Bill			
rent	100		cup	for	2	weeks
reject	complete transaction					
pay with cash $	210.00					
complete transaction						

Figure 15.11 Testing a Transaction That Can't Complete

No payment has been made in the third row of Figure 15.11. So the `complete`
`transaction` in the third table must be rejected by the system under test. Once
the payment has been made in the fourth row, the transaction can be completed.

The group wrote 20 more sad-path tests for *complete* and *cancel* transactions,
including the one shown in Figure 15.12. A transaction can't be canceled until any
paid money is refunded.

begin transaction for client	Joanna	staff	Bill			
rent	100		cup	for	2	weeks
pay with cash $	410.00					
reject	cancel transaction					
refund cash $	410.00					
cancel transaction						

Figure 15.12 Testing a Transaction That Can't Be Canceled

Questions & Answers

But doesn't the test in Figure 15.11 consist of two tests?
Yes, you're right, with the first test simply checking that the `complete transaction`
was rejected. We also need to check that a previously rejected completion of a transaction can be completed later.

However, the test is so short that splitting it into two doesn't seem worthwhile,
especially as there are no other cases yet. There's usually a judgment call and often
a tradeoff in such decisions, and people differ in their approach to this issue.

15.6   Reports

By the following Wednesday, Mitra and Emily had finished developing the fixtures
for these tests, as discussed in Chapter 34. Everyone was eager to see the results.
The report for Figure 15.10 is shown in Figures 15.13 and 15.14.

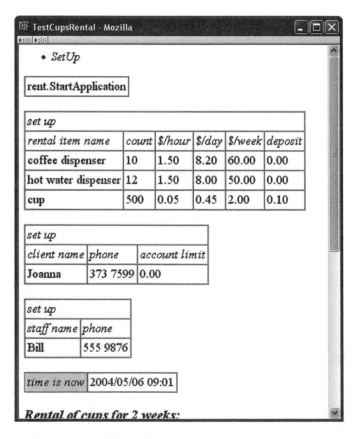

Figure 15.13 First Half of the Report for Figure 15.10

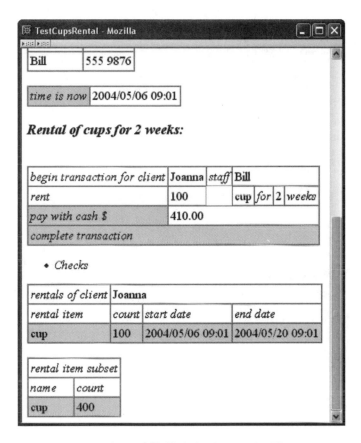

Figure 15.14 Second Half of the Report for Figure 15.10

Questions & Answers

Why are so many of the actions in Figures 15.13 and 15.14 green?
Because each of those actions may fail, under various circumstances; for example, a transaction can't be started with an unknown client or staff member.

(The fixture needs to be defined appropriately by a programmer to have this effect, as we discuss in Chapter 28.)

So why don't you explicitly check that they succeed?
We could do that. It's just a matter of personal style; the group preferred to keep the actions brief.

The report for Figure 15.12 is shown in Figure 15.15.

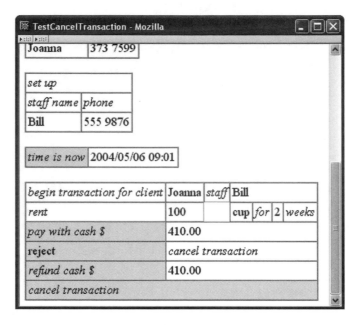

Figure 15.15 Part of the Report for Figure 15.12

15.7   Summary

- It's convenient to use a common SetUp for a set of tests. But as data is added to the SetUp, it's good to avoid breaking existing tests. We saw several ways of doing that.

- It's straightforward to write tests that set the date and time.

- It's useful to make business objects, such as business transactions, explicit in the tables in the tests. For example, user operations as a part of the transaction, such as making payments, are treated as actions in the *transaction* table in the test.

- We showed some examples of *sad-path* tests, which check when things go wrong.

15.8   Exercises

Write tests for the following situations.

1. A transaction may be canceled even when nothing has happened.

2. A transaction may be completed even when nothing has happened.

3. A partial payment may be made in a transaction, but the transaction cannot be completed until the rest of the payment is made.

4. A partial refund may be made in a transaction in which a payment has been made. The transaction cannot be canceled until the rest of the refund is made.

5. An overpayment is not permitted in a transaction.

6. An overrefund is not permitted in a transaction.

7. A negative payment, or refund, is not permitted.

8. A negative count, or time period, is not permitted in a *rent* action in a *transaction*.

CHAPTER 16

Transforming Workflow Tests into Calculation Tests

After writing several related workflow tests, we see an underlying pattern. Rather than repeatedly copying a test and making small variations, it pays to clarify the essential elements of the test.

We end up collapsing a large number of workflow tests into a few tables of calculation tests. We do this by cutting to the essential nature of the underlying business rules. As we'll see, it's not necessarily obvious from the start where we'll end up.

> **Programmers:** The fixture code for the tests in this chapter is given in Chapter 35.

16.1   Introduction

As we mentioned in Chapter 13, Seth wanted to revisit the business rules for late returns. But on Friday morning, Mitra, Emily, Sarah, and Seth had agreed with Don: "There are problems with both late and early returns. Let's focus on early returns next, as it's simpler." Sarah and Mitra had spent the morning writing lots of workflow tests for early returns, after some initial help.

We all got together that afternoon. Mitra and Sarah understood the issues better from having developed these examples. Mitra explained, "We realized that calculating refunds on early and late returns is not a matter of charging or refunding the difference." Consider her two scenarios.

1. In Figure 16.1, a deposit of $10 and a rental charge of $15 were paid on the cups, which were rented for 3 hours. When they were returned an hour early, the deposit was refunded, along with $5 for the reduced 1 hour of rental.

2. In Figure 16.2, however, the rental was for 1 day, with a deposit of $10 and a rental charge of $45. When the cups were returned an hour early, only the deposit was refunded. The rental charge for 23 hours is the same as the charge for a day because the daily cost of $45 is less than the $115 for 23 hours. As

rental entry	Joanna		
rental item	count	start date	end date
cup	100	2004/05/06 09:01	2004/05/06 12:01
time is now	2004/05/06 11:00		

begin transaction for client	Joanna	staff	Bill
return	100		cup
refund cash $	15.00		
complete transaction			

Figure 16.1 Refund When 1 Hour Early (Part of Test)

enter rentals	Joanna		
rental item	count	start date	end date
cup	100	2004/05/06 09:01	2004/05/07 09:01
time is now	2004/05/07 08:01		

begin transaction for client	Joanna	staff	Bill
return	100		cup
refund cash $	10.00		
complete transaction			

Figure 16.2 No Refund When 1 Hour Early (Part of Test)

there is no difference in charge between 23 hours and 24 hours, no refund is due.

Mitra and Sarah were unsure whether that was the best way to write the tests: "Perhaps there are ways to reduce the effort of writing all these tests, which are very similar."

"There's lots of cases," agreed Don. "We don't want to have develop lots more tests like this."

"So how can we avoid that?" asked Sarah. "I suppose that there is a lot of *noise* that is irrelevant to the main point in these tests."

"Yes," replied Don, "although we need some tests that show that the refunds and so on are made correctly within the workflow."

Emily summarized: "The specific client and the specific rental items are irrelevant. The deposit is irrelevant to the issue of refunds for early returns. We can ignore the staff member and maybe the count of items, too."

"So that leaves the paid-for period and the actual period," said Don.

"And the rental rates," added Emily. "How about something like this?"

16.2   Testing Calculations Instead

Emily sketched out the test shown in Figure 16.3. As Seth pointed out, "This could be used for late returns as well."

CalculateRefund							
per hour	per day	per week	pay from	pay to	returned	refund()	
0.05	0.45	2.00	2004/05/06 09:01	2004/05/06 12:01	2004/05/06 11:00	5.00	

Figure 16.3 Table for Early Returns

After adding some rows, Don suggested, "Why don't we simply write the hours, and so on, in directly? It's a pain working out the time differences from the dates." This led to the test shown in Figure 16.4. "The columns *hours1*, *days1*, and *weeks1* give the time period that was paid for, and *hours2*, and so on, give the time before returning the rental items."

CalculateRefund									
per hour	per day	per week	hours1	days1	weeks1	hours2	days2	weeks2	refund()
0.05	0.45	2.00	3	0	0	3	0	0	0.00
			3	0	0	2	0	0	5.00
			0	1	0	23	0	0	0.00
			0	1	0	0	1	0	0.00

Figure 16.4 Revised Table

"That makes the table very wide. We could get rid of the left three columns by providing them to the table as a whole," suggested Emily. This resulted in the test shown in Figure 16.5.

CalculateRefund	0.05	0.45	2.00			
hours1	days1	weeks1	hours2	days2	weeks2	refund()
3	0	0	3	0	0	0.00
3	0	0	2	0	0	5.00
0	1	0	23	0	0	0.00
0	1	0	0	1	0	0.00

Figure 16.5 Revised Table

Emily then suggested, "Let's split up the tables so we need to include only some columns; the rest we can assume to be 0. And let's be clear about what the rates are for in the first row. Let's use a DoFixture table to do that." This resulted in the tests shown in Figure 16.6.

Sarah then pointed out, "The refund calculation is one step removed from the underlying business rule: Which time period is fairer to use? To calculate the refund or the extra charge, we need to calculate the cost for the actual time period and subtract it from the original charge. So let's focus the test on the time periods." She then drew out some tables using this approach, as shown in Figure 16.7.

rent.CalculateRefund						
rate $	5.00	*/hour*	45.00	*/day*	200.00	*/week*
hours1	*hours2*	*refund()*				
3	3	0.00				
3	2	5.00				
5	1	20.00				
rate $	5.00	*/hour*	45.00	*/day*	200.00	*/week*
hours1	*days1*	*hours2*	*days2*	*refund()*		
0	1	0	1	0.00		
0	1	23	0	0.00		
0	2	0	1	45.00		
0	1	9	0	0.00		
0	1	8	0	5.00		
rate $	5.00	*/hour*	45.00	*/day*	200.00	*/week*
days1	*weeks1*	*days2*	*weeks2*	*refund()*		
0	1	0	1	0.00		
0	1	6	0	0.00		
0	2	0	1	200.00		

Figure 16.6 Split Tables

rent.CalculateCharge						
rates $	5.00	*per hour*	45.00	*per day*	200.00	*per week*
hours	*days*	*hours()*	*days()*			
0	1	0	1			
23	0	0	1			
rates $	1.00	*per hour*	45.00	*per day*	200.00	*per week*
hours	*days*	*hours()*	*days()*			
23	0	23	0			
rates $	5.00	*per hour*	45.00	*per day*	200.00	*per week*
hours	*days*	*weeks*	*days()*	*weeks()*		
0	4	0	4	0		
0	5	0	0	1		
0	6	0	0	1		

Figure 16.7 Fair Charge Tables

16.3 Using Durations

After looking at the new table briefly, Sarah then added, "It would be better to use durations in a cell, such as '1 day 2 hours,' instead of having separate columns for hours, days, and weeks. We should use such durations everywhere." The CalculateFixture tables[1] shown in Figure 16.8 resulted.

rent.CalculateFairCharge						
rates $	5.00	*per hour*	45.00	*per day*	200.00	*per week*
duration		*fair*				
1 day		1 day				
8 hours		8 hours				
9 hours		1 day				
23 hours		1 day				
3 days 4 hours		3 days 4 hours				
rates $	1.00	*per hour*	45.00	*per day*	200.00	*per week*
duration		*fair*				
23 hours		23 hours				
rates $	5.00	*per hour*	45.00	*per day*	200.00	*per week*
duration		*fair*				
4 days		4 days				
5 days		1 week				
6 days 5 hours		1 week				

Figure 16.8 Fair Charge Tables Using Durations

Don added, "That's a good start to early and late returns. We'll need to add a lot more tests later."

Questions & Answers

Instead of checking the days, weeks, and so on, couldn't the tests in Figure 16.7 check the charge, or cost of the rental?
Yes, that would be a reasonable way to do it. It means having to calculate the charge, so it's a little more work.

Why have people traditionally not written tests like this?
Because it appears to require access to the internals of the system under test. That's the easiest way to carry out such tests but not the only way. As we'll see in Chapter 35, the fixtures may run the tests by controlling the user interface.

---

[1] See Chapter 10 for an introduction to CalculateFixture tables.

Aren't they really tests that programmers should write, given that they are not end-to-end processing?

No, because they are concerns of the business. Although some people have a notion that acceptance testing is explicitly end to end, there doesn't seem to be any call for that to stop us.

In the early-return example here, and in many other cases, we find business rules that are at the heart of the process incorporated into software. Because they come from business policy, there needs to be clear communication between the businesspeople and the developers about such rules.

As we've seen, it's crucial that the tests be expressed as clearly as possible. To cut to their essence, it's necessary to peel away irrelevant detail.

16.4   Reports

The next day, Emily and Mitra had completed the fixtures for the tests in Figure 16.8, as shown in Figure 16.9 and discussed in Chapter 35. They had kept a

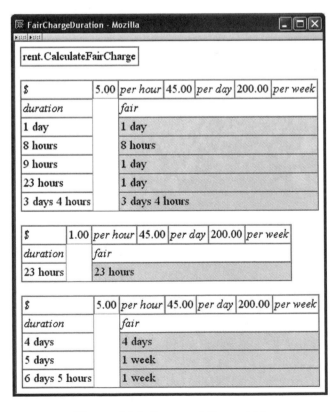

Figure 16.9 Report of Figure 16.8

few of the action-based tests to ensure that the fair charging was incorporated into the workflow (see Figure 16.10 for the report corresponding to Figure 16.2). They had also kept a subset of the tests in Figure 16.6 to test the actual refund (see Figure 16.11, which uses durations).

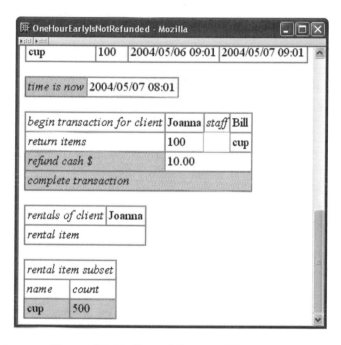

Figure 16.10 Part of Report of Figure 16.2

16.5 Summary

- Many people become disillustioned with automated testing because they write lots of workflow tests and then find them a pain to maintain.

- Maintenance problems can be a sign that business rules are not being expressed in the most direct way.

- Looking for the commonality in a set of related tests can point to the "noise," the test values that the business rule does not really depend on.

- By cutting to the essentials of the tests, we can reduce the effort of writing and maintaining them considerably. It's also easier to see what tests need to be added, such as within Figure 16.7.

- We have shown, step by step, how such Fit tables can evolve, based on calculations.

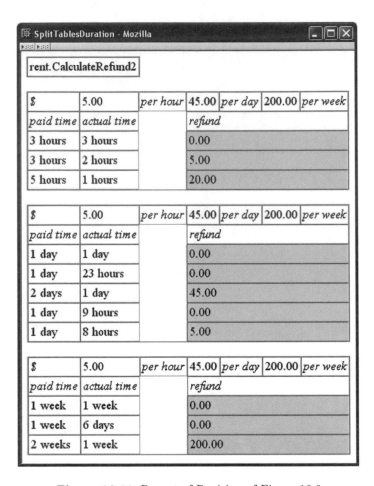

Figure 16.11 Report of Revision of Figure 16.6

16.6   Exercises

1. Write some further test rows based on Figure 16.7.

2. Write a new test table that includes days and weeks.

3. Design a variant of Figure 16.7 that calculates in terms of the charge rather than in terms of the actual time periods to be used in the charge.

4. Write late-return tests based on the format of Figure 16.7. Assume that the charges in the table are all that count and that negative quantities may be used in the calculated fields.

5. Consider whether there is any point in having a test table that includes hours, days, and weeks. If you think so, make up some tests that use it. (*Hint:* Think about what time period charge rates would make this so.)

6. Should we consider the case in which the hourly rate is greater than the daily rate? What assumptions and/or higher-level policies do you draw on? What tests may this thinking lead to?

7. Choose an area for which you have written, or could imagine writing, many workflow tests. Copying a workflow test repeatedly and making small changes to it is a good indication that there may be calculation-based tests waiting to get out. Look for such tests and extract them.

CHAPTER 17

Story Test-Driven Development with Fit

This is our first example in which Fit tables are used as *storytests*[1] to sort out what's needed anew in the system rather than testing what is already there. We'll see that the tables help formulate the requirements and then express, with concrete tests, the abstract design of extensions to the application. In turn, the tables help to communicate the ideas with several important clients to see whether new functionality will fulfill their needs.

17.1   Introduction

We catch up with RentAPartySoftware after a break of a few months. "Things are humming," Mitra exclaimed, "and we're seeing real benefits from the changes. We're all surprised at the improvement in quality, and we're getting fast at writing Fit tests for the current system and to drive new developments."

> **Tip**
>
> Writing Fit tests to communicate is a simpler and faster way to get feedback than to mock up a GUI to check out the ideas and much simpler than building a solution into the application for you to see and comment on.

"We've been adding tests in the areas that are changing and that are problematic," explained Don. "About 30 percent of the app is tested at this stage, and

---

[1] Joshua Kerievsky coined the terms *storytests* and *Story Test-Driven Development*. The latter is a core practice in Industrial XP. See http://industrialxp.org for further details.

almost no bugs have been reported for those areas. We've especially made progress in the charging area; the problems with early and late returns seem to be licked."

"The number of outstanding bugs has dropped right down," Don added, "and far fewer are being reported. A few bugs remain; the testers have not been able to duplicate reported problems."

"And," Seth reported, "We're seeing a pleasing increase in customer satisfaction."

RentAPartySoftware has been carrying out *agile software development* [Bec04], [Coc01], [Mar02], [SB02], [PP03], [Hig04], [Coc04], with *Extreme Programming*, for 6 weeks.

Note

The role of *Customer* is defined in *Extreme Programming*. The Customer role is responsible for setting the direction for the software development. This is filled by one or more people with a business perspective, such as business analysts. Mitra and Seth are the Customers on the development team at RentAPartySoftware.

In Extreme Programming, work is always done on the highest-priority additions to the software. Short, fixed-time *iterations* of, say, one or two weeks are used to evolve the software. At the start of each iteration, decisions are made by the *Customers* as to which functionality is to be added in that iteration.

These new functions are called *stories* in Extreme Programming. *Customers* create the stories, choose the highest-priority ones for the next iteration, and work with testers to write Fit tests for those stories. The tests help to define the requirements and are used to determine whether a story is implemented completely.

The short iterations mean that the Customers can try out the extended application with little delay. They can use it to assess the approach that's been taken in the software to respond to new opportunities and to solve important business issues. They have a system to play with to get feedback on their ideas and to refine their thinking. And, sometimes, this process inspires new ways of thinking about business problems and solutions.

The short iterations also force priority decisions to be made on a regular basis. Often, stories that are put forward earlier as "very important" are never selected, because feedback from the evolving system drives the development in unexpected but fruitful directions.

"Maybe a third of the stories that we wrote when we first started Extreme Programming have still not been selected," explained Mitra. "We've since realized that there are actually more important things to do."

Don proudly showed off a few of the 330 Fit tests (pages) that are in place now: "I'm delighted at the difference it makes to be writing Fit tests before the implementation, rather than afterward. Instead of pressure at the end, we can apply our skills at the start."

17.2 The Stories

As the Customers on the development team, Mitra and Seth, met the next morning to discuss the last of the new stories for the next iteration. The current iteration ended that day.

17.2.1 Previous Rentals Repeated

"The first story is crucial," Seth told us. "We have several requests for supporting repeated rentals from two of our major clients," said Seth. "What makes it especially urgent is that XYZ^2 allows for previous rentals by a customer to be repeated, which saves lots of customer-service time. There is pressure on us to match this in *RentEz*."

"That seems straightforward," replied Mitra. "Have you seen the *XYZ* rerent feature?"

"No, I haven't; it's probably better to come up with our own approach and not be influenced by what they do."

"Especially as we're sure to do miles better," laughed Mitra.

"The idea is that customers can say that they'd like the same rentals as last time," explained Seth. "Presumably, they may want to change the list," said Mitra. "Yes, the particular items and the numbers of them," replied Seth.

Mitra suggested a wording for the story and wrote it on an index card:

> RepeatRental. A customer wants the same rental as last time. The customer may change the various items and the numbers required.

"Yes, that's good," said Seth.

"We can flesh it out when we write the Fit tests, once we've sorted out the rest of the stories," Mitra concluded. "And it could be any prior rental."

17.2.2 Rental Calculations

After discussing other stories for an hour or so, Seth raised a topic for a fifth story. "Many people want to rent for a wedding, for example, but are not sure what quantities of things they need. Some rental companies provide rental lists for various numbers of guests. Others have spreadsheets to calculate the numbers of cups, and so on, based on the number of expected guests. But there's still a lot of data entry. It would be handy to have help in *RentEz* for calculating the numbers required."

"So why not have templates for various events? A template defines the numbers of each item as a proportion of the number of guests expected," replied Mitra. "Does *XYZ* allow that?"

---

[2] *XYZ* is a competitor rental application.

"Not as far as I know," said Seth. "What do you mean, *as a proportion?*"

"Well, here's an example. For every 50 people, you may need one coffee dispenser, so the proportion is 0.02."

"Oh, OK. So the template can be used for any number of people?"

"Yes," replied Mitra, "it would be like the spreadsheets that you mentioned but they would be built into *RentEz*. That would be quick."

Mitra wrote these new stories on two index cards, as follows.

> CreateRentalTemplate. A rental template defines a list of rental items. For each item, it specifies the proportion of that item per person.

> UseRentalTemplate. Given the number of guests, generate the rentals required.

"Can the numbers of items be changed once the template has generated the rentals?" asked Mitra.

"Yes, probably. Teetotallers wouldn't need some items for a party," Seth grinned.

"Let's not forget that we may need only one of an item, regardless of the number of people."

"Yes, usually only one microphone will be needed for a wedding," Seth replied.

17.3   The First Storytests

Sarah and Don got together with Mitra later that day, while Seth was on the phone, to create one or two Fit tests for each of the stories. Doing so would help refine their thinking about the stories. And the next day, when it would be time to choose the stories for the next iteration, these tests will help the developers estimate how long each story will take to implement.

17.3.1   Creating a Template

"So we've got several related stories," said Don. "Shall we start with creating a template from scratch?"

"Yes, OK," replied Mitra. "I imagine that a template is simply a list of rental items, with the proportions beside each one." She started to sketch it on the whiteboard, as shown in Figure 17.1.

create template			
add item	coffee dispenser	with multiplier	0.04
add item	hot water dispenser	with multiplier	0.04
add item	coffee table	" "	0.02
add item	cup	" "	1

Figure 17.1 Create a Template

"Do we assume that all the items will be rented for the same period?" asked Sarah.

"Yes," replied Mitra, "I imagine so. We need to allow for the return date to be changed on any rentals created from a template. Any of the information can be changed."

"Does the proportion have to be less than 1.0?" asked Sarah.

"No," replied Don, "more cups may be required than the number of guests."

"Wouldn't percentages be easier (4 percent instead of 0.04)?" asked Sarah. "It would be easier still if it were the number of people per item," suggested Don. "Also, we need to name the template." He altered the test, as shown in Figure 17.2.

create template	COFFEE BREAK			
item	Coffee dispenser	FOR	20	PEOPLE
item	hot water dispenser	FOR	20	PEOPLE
item	coffee table	FOR	40	PEOPLE
item	cup	FOR	1	PEOPLE

Figure 17.2 Create a Template, Altered

"That was pretty easy," said Mitra, "although we'll need to put it in the context of a transaction to complete it. What's next?"

17.3.2   Using a Template

They decided to work next on using a template. "That's much the same as renting," suggested Sarah, who sketched up the test shown in Figure 17.3.

begin transaction for client	Joanna	staff	Bill	
fill template	Coffee break	for	40	people for	1 day
pay with cash $	65.40			
Complete transaction				

rentals of client	Joanna		
rental item	Count	start date	end date
Coffee dispenser	2	2004/05/06 09:01	2004/05/07 09:01
hot water dispenser	2	"	"
Coffee table	1	"	"
cup	40	"	"

Figure 17.3 Use a Template

"We can alter that slightly for a booking," said Sarah, as she sketched out Figure 17.4.

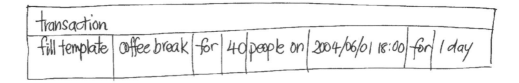

Figure 17.4 Use a Template for Booking

17.3.3   Using a Template Inside a Template

"The templates could have many items for a big event," Mitra mused. "Every time you serve coffee in an event, you'd need to repeat the data in Figure 17.2, as well as all the other things you'd need, such as milk, sugar, tea, and other drinks."

"One approach," suggested Sarah, "would be to allow for templates themselves to be used in templates.'

"How do you mean?" asked Don.

"Well, imagine that we're creating a template for a conference." said Sarah. "As well as including rental items in the list, such as audiovisual equipment, we could include a template for a *coffee break*, too. Of course, we'll need to ask Seth to discuss it with the people who really know how these things work."

She started to sketch out Figure 17.5. "Whoops, what do I put down for the number?"

Create template	conference		
template	Coffee break	for	..?

Figure 17.5 Using a Template Inside a Template

"Perhaps we don't need a number," suggested Don, "because the number of guests for the conference will be the same as the number for the coffee break."

"Let's leave it out then," added Mitra. "But what if we need coffee for the organizers of the conference? We may want to add those people."

"We could also allow a multiplier, I suppose." said Don. "But let's keep it simple for now, with no number."

"Yes," agreed Mitra, "it's better to start simple and extend it if—and when—there's a demand." She altered the last test, as shown in Figure 17.6.

Seth joined the group after he had talked to Tim and Fiona at the two rental companies about the current stories: "There is strong interest in having this in *RentEz*."

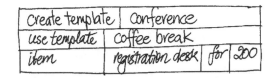

Figure 17.6 Using a Template Inside a Template, Revised

Mitra outlined their progress on the template idea and showed Seth the tests they'd developed.

"Your templates seem to do everything that's needed, and more," said Seth. "I like the template tests, although nested templates may be too complex."

"At least, people don't need to use them," said Mitra.

"We need to weigh the cost of this feature against the benefit," replied Seth. "Tim and Fiona like lots of things that they're not willing to pay for. I've told them that I'd show them the tests once they're completed, to get their feedback."

"I hope they like the templates," said Mitra.

"It's great that some of our customers really like being consulted early on about new developments," replied Seth. "When I talk them through the Fit examples, showing what we're planning, they often make excellent suggestions that are easy to incorporate. It also means that they know what's coming and can plan for it. They used to be so resistant to upgrades, but now they're enthusiastic. It's great having their confidence and enthusiasm again."

Questions & Answers

Is it usual to have two or more people working together? Doesn't this mean that more personnel time is used?

A range of skills is needed in all these activities: writing stories, writing tests, and developing software. Getting various perspectives at the start can be a much more effective use of time than having to do rework afterward, when problems are realized.

It can be efficient to have someone to bounce ideas off, to give another point of view, and to check that you've not made a simple mistake, such as forgetting an important case in a business rule.

17.4 The Planning Game

The next morning, the whole team got together for the planning game for the next iteration. Between them, Seth and Mitra introduced each of the new stories, as they placed the story cards on the table.

> **Note**
>
> The *planning game* is where the next iteration is planned. The Customers present a number of new stories, which are added to the old stories that haven't yet been chosen for implementation. The developers ask questions about each new story in order to estimate the time it will take to complete it.
>
> Once the new stories are estimated, the Customers pick sufficient stories from all the stories in order to fill up the time available in the next iteration, based on the story time estimates.
>
> Hence, both the estimated business value and the estimated development cost are taken into account in choosing the highest-value stories.

17.4.1 Previous Rentals Repeated

When the rerenting story was introduced and tabled, the testers and programmers had a few questions. "What happens if some of the rental items are not available?" asked Emily.

"I suppose, then, that the customer has a choice whether to cancel, just as with a single item," replied Mitra.

"Yes, it's not much different," agreed Seth.

"The customer may still want to rent everything else he or she needs," added Mitra. Don made a note of this test on an index card.

"Does this apply to bookings as well?" asked Sarah.

"That's a good idea," replied Seth. "Yes, it does," he added after a few moments. Don noted this on another card.

After some discussion among the programmers, Emily was ready to provide an estimate for the story. "It will take 5 days to do that, as it will require several changes to the GUI." She added that to the card.

The testers discussed the time they needed to allocate to writing the Fit tests. "Let's allow 1 day for that," Don suggested, "as I can imagine that there are several little cases." He started to write that on the card and then changed his mind and corrected it, "No, let's allow 2 days, as we often take about half the time of the programmers."

17.4.2 Templates

When the first template story was introduced some time later, there was lots of discussion about it. As Emily pointed out, "It's related to that earlier, rerenting story. Maybe they're trying to achieve the same thing."

"Possibly, in some cases," Seth answered, "but there would also be casual renters who want simple repeats."

"But if they keep rerenting and adjusting the numbers, it could indicate that a template is needed. How about generating a template from a previous rental?" asked Emily.

"Good idea," replied Mitra, "We'd simply need to know how many people were catered for."

"Of course," added Sarah, "the proportions would probably need adjusting."

"Yes, true," replied Mitra, "although that's needed anyway." With Seth's agreement, Mitra wrote a new story card:

> MakeTemplate. A template can be generated from a previous rental of several rental items. Given the number of guests, the template proportions are calculated automatically.

"Once we have lots of templates, we need a way of organizing them, so that they can be found," said Emily.

"In that case, we need another story," Mitra replied.

After further discussion, Mitra wrote another story card:

> FindTemplate. A template is found by name. It may be associated with a particular customer or may be for any customer.

"How many are there likely to be?" asked Sarah. "If there aren't many, we can simply list them. Otherwise, we may need something more sophisticated."

"Let's do the simplest for now," Seth suggested. "Once we've shown the new version to a few companies, we'll get feedback on what may be required. But they probably won't know until they try it out for a while."

17.4.3   CreateRentalTemplate

The group's attention then returned to the CreateRentalTemplate story. Emily was concerned about the calculations: "When we calculate the number of rental items, do we round up to the next highest whole number? For example, if there is a coffee dispenser for 20 people and there happen to be 30 guests, do we allocate one or two?"

"It will need to be two," replied Mitra, "so that there are sufficient numbers. The customer can always decide to reduce it to one."

"What if there are 21 people?" asked Emily.

"It's still two rentals," replied Mitra, "The principle still applies. We'll write a few tests that show this."

"We didn't work out what to do when a fixed number of rental items is needed, regardless of the number of guests," raised Seth.

"The simplest approach would be to say that the rental item is for 1,000,000 guests," suggested Sarah.

"Yes, that will do for now," agreed Mitra.

"It's also possible to have an item for less than one guest," introduced Don. "So the number could be, say 0.9."

"What does that mean, Don?" asked Emily.

"It means that more than one cup is needed per guest. For example, with 100 guests, we'd need 100 divided by 0.9 cups, which is roughly 110," replied Don. "So we'll need a Fit test that shows that, too," he said, as he picked up another card.

"Are the rental item numbers always based on the number of guests?" asked Sarah. "What about where the number of data projectors depends on the number of tracks of a conference?"

"Good point," replied Don. "We could have someone renting some things based on the number of guests and other things based on the number of tracks. That could mean distinguishing between people and tracks when the templates are created."

"Let's keep it simple for now," suggested Seth, "Let's see how well simple templates are used before we make it too sophisticated."

"OK," replied Don, "We'll write a story card for that as a reminder for later. Let's change the test to read better." The test in Figure 17.2 was revised, as shown in Figure 17.7.

Figure 17.7 Create a Template, Altered Again

The estimates were then made for the main story. "That'll take 7 days," Emily suggested, to general agreement. "And 3 test days," added Don.

17.4.4   Choosing Stories for the Iteration

Once all the stories had been discussed and estimated, Mitra and Seth started moving the cards into several groups on the table to help decide which were the highest priority (best cost/value ratio) and which of those would fit into the iteration period of 4 weeks. The rerenting and first two template stories were deemed to be of high priority and were included in the iteration.

Another story, on making regular bookings, was too big and wouldn't quite fit into the iteration, so it was split into two, and the two new stories were reestimated. The simpler one allowed for regular weekly bookings of the same rental items and was included, filling up the time of the iteration nicely.

It was agreed that Don and Sarah would work with Mitra and Seth to develop further Fit tests for the stories. They would call on the programmers to get involved once they started making progress.

"We'll do some spikes[3] on the template story and a few of the others over the next few days, so that will keep us busy," said Emily.

"And I'll have a chat with some of our clients to make sure we're on the right path," added Seth.

Questions & Answers

Does developing software in this way lead to a narrow focus rather than seeing the big picture?
There will be lots of discussion about the big picture as well and about the vision for the software and what it will achieve. The important thing is that the feedback from the evolving system helps us to revise that bigger picture to fit the reality that unfolds.

Setting priorities is very effective for using time wisely, and it's difficult to know what the best approach is overall without ongoing feedback.

As John Gall says, as quoted in [Boo94], "A complex system that works is invariably found to have evolved from a simple system that works.... A complex system designed from scratch never works and cannot be patched up to make it work" (p. 13).

Isn't it difficult to choose a few stories out of many?
It seems so, but Customers get good at it. Given that the iterations are only 4 weeks or so, it's not long before you can make your next choices.

If a software feature, which comes from a story, turns out to be not useful in practice, not a huge amount has been invested in it. This is much better than having to make decisions about the whole scope of a project before it starts, as the feedback comes far too late.

People are usually poor at estimating the time to implement software. What do you do about this?
Yes, that's true, particulary when they're asked to do so when much of the details of the requirements are unclear. The trick is to estimate in smaller chunks and to do it often. People get better at a task when they get regular, good, and immediate feedback.

17.5   Adding to the Storytests

Mitra and Don got together to write some further tests for the template stories. They quickly wrote the test shown in Figure 17.8, which allows for more than one item per guest.

---

[3] A *spike* is an experiment with the software, such as to find out the best way to do something.

create template	coffee break			
one	coffee dispenser	*for*	20	*people*
one	hot water dispenser	*for*	20	*people*
one	coffee table	*for*	40	*people*
one	cup	*for*	0.9	*people*

Figure 17.8 Template with Less than One Item

They then used that template, "coffee break," to test that the number of rental items was rounded up. Don calculated out loud: "With 21 guests, there will be 21 divided by 20, which is 1.05. We round that up to 2. With cups, there will be 21 divided by 0.9, which is 23.33. That rounds up to 24." This resulted in the test shown in Figure 17.9.

begin transaction for client	Joanna		*staff*	Bill		
fill template	coffee break	*for*	21	*people for*	1 day	
pay with cash $	65.40					
complete transaction						
rentals of client	Joanna					
rental item	*count*	*start date*		*end date*		
coffee dispenser	2	2004/05/06 09:01		2004/05/07 09:01		
hot water dispenser	2	2004/05/06 09:01		2004/05/07 09:01		
coffee table	1	2004/05/06 09:01		2004/05/07 09:01		
cup	24	2004/05/06 09:01		2004/05/07 09:01		

Figure 17.9 Template with Rounding

As these tests were completed, they were passed on to the programmers, who used them in the implementation of the new stories in *RentEz*. Further storytests were developed over the next 3 weeks and these included some `ColumnFixture` tables for testing rounding with a variety of examples.

17.6   Progress During the Iteration

Mitra is usually available to the developers at RentAPartySoftware to answer questions about the stories that they're implementing. She will sometimes ask Seth to join in on a conversation when he's available and she's not completely sure about what's needed.

One week after the planning game, Emily and Neo asked for Mitra's help. They had just completed the code to pass the test shown in part in Figure 17.10. This test makes a booking for some rental items for 1 day every week, starting on a given date.

"We've changed *RentEz* so that a customer can rent a mixture of single rental items and from templates," said Emily. "Do you want the same for bookings?" she asked.

> **Note**
>
> The description on a story card is short. Further discussion between the Customers and the programmers is required for the programmers to get into the details of a story, supported by the Fit tests.
>
> As an issue arises, the programmers ask the Customers questions about the story they (the programmers) are currently working on.

book	100		cup	*on*	2004/06/01 18:00	*for*	1 day	*every*	1 week

Figure 17.10 Regular Booking

"Yes, it does make sense to do that," replied Mitra "Will it take much extra effort?"

"No," answered Emily, "it'll be almost no more work, because of the way in which we've combined rental items and templates into *rentables* in the GUI."

Together, Mitra and Emily wrote the part of the test shown in Figure 17.11, in which the booking is based on the *coffee break* template.

book	coffee break	*for*	40	*on*	2004/06/01 18:00	*for*	1 day	*every*	1 week

Figure 17.11 Regular Template Booking

"What if the template is changed in the meantime?" asked Emily.

"Just apply the booking to the latest template," replied Mitra.

"OK, that will mean storing the booking of the template rather than calculating the numbers of rental items and storing the booking of those."

"Yes, given that the customer may later want to alter the number of people in the booking, that's the best approach," agreed Mitra.

"So let's complete the test to make it clear that the booking stores the template," suggested Emily.

As Mitra added, "We can show the next date and the rental period with the *from* and *to* dates. Those dates will be changed to be a week later, in this case, once the next booking is due."

The completed test, without the set up, is shown in Figure 17.12.

While Neo looked on, Mitra and Emily then wrote a separate test showing what happens when that booking becomes due. After Emily and Neo had extended *RentEz* to pass that test, Emily showed Mitra. The report is shown in Figure 17.13.

"We'll need to add a test involving a booking that has been made with a template and that has not yet been accepted," she added. "It needs to show that a change to the template affects the numbers of items when the booking is accepted. Let's do that later."

begin trans...	Joanna	*staff*	Bill		
book	coffee break	*for*	40	*on*	2004/06/01 18:00
		for	1 day	*every*	1 week
complete transaction					

booked template list	Joanna			
template	*people*	*from*	*to*	*repeat*
coffee break	40	2004/06/01 18:00	2004/06/02 18:00	1 week

Figure 17.12 Regular Template Booking

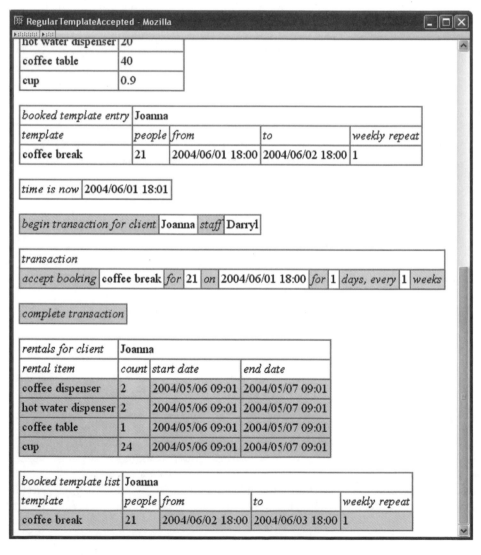

Figure 17.13 Fit Report for RegularTemplateAccepted

17.7   Exploratory Testing at Iteration End

At the end of the iteration, all the people involved in the development of *RentEz* met to carry out *exploratory testing* [Bac][Mar][KBN+02], an approach encouraged by the context-driven school of testing [Con].

Exploratory testing is nonautomated testing that is carried out to explore the quality of the system and to find out how well it achieves its goals. The tests are not preplanned but arise out of the exploration. They naturally go beyond the automated tests.

At RentAPartySoftware, *exploratory testing* was carried out socially, with an emphasis on creativity and fun: finding problems by "thinking outside the box." It was also a good way to celebrate and explore the results of the hard work of the finished iteration.

Questions & Answers

What happens if the development team goes faster or slower than expected?
During the iteration, stories or parts of stories—are added or removed by the Customers so that the iteration finishes on time. This encourages a focus on high value per cost and on getting clear feedback on story estimation.

What happens if a new story comes up during the iteration?
It is written on an index card for now. It may be chosen in the next iteration. Even if it seems important and should be done "right now," it's not long before the current iteration will complete.

As we saw in Section 17.6, the stories will be elaborated during discussions between the Customers and others on the team. It's a judgment call as to whether new ideas are a big enough change to be treated as a new story.

17.8   Summary

- Fit tests can dramatically improve the quality of existing software.

- But they can have a much greater impact when they are used to drive additions to existing systems or to drive new developments.

- In agile development, software evolves as the requirements are better understood and as external changes impact on what's needed. This evolution is managed through ongoing communication among all those involved and through feedback from using the current version of the system.

- In Extreme Programming, new functionality is based on stories, which are written by Customers and are scheduled into an iteration.

- One or two Fit tests are developed for each story to help clarify the story and aid developers in estimating the time needed to implement the story.

- The Customers choose stories for the next iteration, based on their business value and on the cost to implement them.

- Once the stories are scheduled for an iteration, the Customers and testers develop extra Fit tests to clarify the business rules associated with those stories.

- All the tests for a story are then used by the programmers to drive the implementation of that story.

- As questions arise, the programmers discuss the details underlying the story with the Customers, which may lead to additional Fit tests being written.

- A story is finished when all the associated tests pass and no outstanding issues remain.

- If the programmers go faster or slower than expected, stories may be added to or removed from the iteration, which is of a fixed time period.

- Exploratory testing at the end of an iteration can focus attention beyond the automated tests.

We have just skimmed the surface of applying agile software development techniques. There are many excellent books on agile development in general and on particular approaches, such as Extreme Programming [Bec04], [Coc01], [Mar02].

Questions & Answers

Is it better to write the tests before development? We write them in parallel.
It is better for the programmers to have at least one test to start with. Tests help them to see what the system should do. Tests extend the software just enough to pass the test, so that no work is being done on speculation, and all of it is tested.

Some teams think that it's necessary to wait until the software is developed before the tests are written. That's because they write tests that operate through the user interface. We've already seen all the problems that this approach causes.

It is essential that the tests be written first, which inevitably means that they have to be independent of the user interface. So it's lucky that that's the best way to write them, for many other reasons too.

But what if test generation is too slow?
That's one good reason to develop some tests along with the stories, before the planning game. This happens while the developers are working on the previous iteration. It may mean that some tests are written for stories that are never chosen.

But on the other hand, writing one or two tests for each story is helpful to the Customers, as it gets them thinking about some of the issues. The concrete examples in the tests are also helpful to the developers when they estimate the time for a story.

If the tests are still too slow in coming, you may need more skilled testers or need to make your tests more expressive. For example, writing lots of workflow tests can be slow and ineffective, as we showed in Chapter 16.

Do other tests often come out of discussions between the programmers and Customers during software development?
Yes, this happens all the time. As the programmers are getting into the details of the software, they have to think about issues that may have been missed by others. When they confirm what should happen, the best way to capture these new business rules is to write them as Fit tests.

17.9 Exercises

Consider the various planned extensions to your current software[4] that are or may be needed. Instead of planning to add tests for the changes after they've been done, try the following.

1. To work with you on this, ask someone who may be able to help more on the business perspective or on the testing aspects.

2. Choose an iteration time period and stick to it.

3. Together, write a story about each extension or a part of it. If the story is too big, break it into smaller parts.

4. For each story, write one or two Fit tests that you can use to decide whether the story has been implemented completely in software or in some other way. This may help refine the story.

5. Run the planning game. The people who will implement the changes are completely responsible for estimating the time/effort required.

6. Based on the estimates, choose the stories that will fit into the chosen time period.

7. As the changes are implemented, test for completion with the story tests.

8. At the end of the iteration, review how it went.

---

[4] You could also try this on a project that doesn't involve software. It will probably mean that you can't automate the tests, but everything else may well apply.

CHAPTER 18

Designing and Refactoring Tests to Communicate Ideas

We've seen the development of many Fit tests in the past few chapters. Now it's time to generalize from those examples and to consider some principles and practices to help with test design.

Tests help us think and to communicate about what's needed, so it's worth putting effort into making them work well. They also help to check that the system responds as we expect.

18.1 Principles of Test Design

In this chapter, we draw on three main principles of test design.

1. Tests are for communicating ideas.
2. Tests will change along with the business and the needs for the software.
3. Tests are automated to quickly show when we're done and to avoid errors from being introduced and going unnoticed.

Because a test is for communicating ideas, it needs to

*   Express business rules clearly, in the language of the businessperson
*   Be to the point and to avoid unnecessary detail
*   Be organized well, both internally and in relation to other tests
*   Focus on (part of) a single business rule
*   Evolve as understanding of that business rule evolves
*   Help evolution of such understanding

A set of tests needs to be comprehensive.

Because a test will change as the business and the software requirements change, it needs to

- Avoid overcommitment to details that are not essential to the specific business rule

- Be expressed in a nonredundant manner so that it's easier to change while keeping it consistent with related tests

- Focus on only one business issue, so that it is less vulnerable to change

Because a test is automated, it

- Needs to be independent of other tests, so that it can be run as a part of a test suite, in any order

- Needs to be self-sufficient, so that it can be run by itself

- Cannot sometimes pass and sometimes fail, depending on data or timing or other aspects outside the control of the test

See [MSA03] for a good introduction to test automation in the context of agile software development.

In the following sections, we discuss various approaches to the design of Fit tests. We also discuss various poor test designs, called *smells*, and what we can do about them. The idea of *smells* as a sign of trouble is a wonderful metaphor coined by Massimo Arnoldi and made popular by Martin Fowler et al. in [Fow99]. Smells are "indications that there is trouble that can be solved by refactoring" [Fow99, p. 75]. For our purposes, a *refactoring* of a Fit test or table is a change to the contents or structure of that table to improve the expressiveness or some other characteristic of that test.

As we see throughout this chapter, some smells are major and need to be dealt with as soon as possible. Other smells are minor and are simply an indication that something may need to be reconsidered.

18.2   Fit Tests for Business Rules

Fit tests are for communicating business rules. We have various ways to improve how we express those tests. We start with issues and approaches that apply generally, before tackling ones specific to particular table types.

18.2.1   Development of Tables

With simple business rules that are well understood, it may be easy to design Fit tables for expressing suitable tests in one go. Often, however, various issues have to be understood and dealt with, making it difficult to get under way on writing a test.

Let the tables evolve. Start with simple examples and gradually make them more complicated, as we have shown in earlier chapters. There's no need to make the examples comprehensive to start with; leave detail out until you've made progress and you're ready to tackle it.

Be prepared to change the names in header rows and actions as the table structure evolves. Short names may make sense to you at the time, but will you or others remember what they mean later? Choosing a name may not be easy but can aid in improving understanding.

Tables need to be clear. Can they be named well? Table smells may be the result of badly organized tests or may show that there is a problem in understanding what's required from the stories. Confusion in identifying or clarifying a business rule may be muddying the waters for the test that you're trying to write.

18.2.2 Meaningful Examples

As much as possible, use meaningful examples in tests. It will help everyone better understand how things are. Often, the subtleties of the real world may show us that our ideas about a business rule are too simple, forcing us to deal with all the relevant variations.

Because they often have an insufficient idea of the context in which the systems they build are used, programmers need all the help they can get. It's possible that tests may also be used to automatically generate online and offline user documentation, so it's handy if they're likely to be meaningful to the readers.

The use of meaningful examples is illustrated best in this book by the tests in the chapters in Part II.

18.2.3 Supporting Text

Use headers and comments to organize your test files and make them easier to read. Include descriptions of business rules with the tables or in related pages with FitNesse. Where they're useful, include images that help the reader understand a test and the underlying business rule.

The examples in this book tend to have little supporting text, owing to space limitations. The example test in Section 10.2 on p. 74 is clear in intent and reads easily.

18.2.4 Smell: Meaningless Numbers

Figure 18.1 illustrates this smell. In the first column, numbers are used instead of meaningful names for the three possible values: low, medium, and high, as used in Figure 5.7 on p. 34.

DiscountGroupList			
value	*max*	*min*	*%*
1	0.00	0.00	0
2	500.00	500.00	3
2	0.00	500.00	5
3	1000.00	500.00	5
3	2000.00	2000.00	10

Figure 18.1 Meaningless Numbers in First Column

Meaningless numbers in Fit tables are confusing and require that we repeatedly have to remember or look up what they mean. This makes the tables difficult to read and to check by hand.

18.2.5 Smell: Poor Names

Figure 18.1 also illustrates this smell. The header labels are not very useful: The *value* of what? The *max* of what? There's no point in expecting the reader to remember. The full labels, as used in Figure 5.7 on p. 34 are more useful: *future value*, *max owing*, *min purchase*, and *discount %*.[1]

Poorly named fixtures, test files or pages, header labels, or actions mean that we and others have to remember what they're about. Good names can be very helpful in reminding us of the purpose of a part of a test. They help us when we introduce a test to someone else. Using the appropriate business terminology can speed things up, as long as uses of a term are not contradictory.

It may seem easier to write a short name for an action because we know what that means now, while we're thinking about it. But consider the many times that someone will read the test or a related one in the future; make it meaningful now.

It may seem easier to not change a name as your thinking about it changes. But build your best approach to meaning into a name. Again, realize that the name is for communicating something, and we need to think of those readers in the future, including ourselves.

Confusion over names may be the result of a quick decision or may point to one or more underlying problems with a Fit test.

- It is not well understood.

- Points of view about it differ and need to be resolved.

- Several tests are combined, which is making it too big.

18.2.6 Smell: Brain Twisters

Look at the booking tests in Figures 18.2 and 18.3. The *from* and *to* values in Figure 18.2—2004/05/06 11:11 and 2004/05/07 09:11—differ by the amount of the *for* values—22 hours—in Figure 18.3. Which test is quicker and easier to read? When the time difference is important to the test, make the value obvious.

book	5		coffee pot	*from*	2004/05/13 11:01	*to*	2004/05/14 09:01

Figure 18.2 Brain Twister

book	5		coffee pot	*on*	2004/05/13 11:01	*for*	22 hours

Figure 18.3 Untwisted

---

[1] Even so, we have to assume some knowledge of the particular business area.

Keep the following points in mind. Is it difficult to determine whether a particular test is correct? Is there an easier way to express it so that you don't have to work it out? Express the tests as simply as possible, even if that's not the way it's likely to be handled through the user interface.

18.2.7 Smell: Unnecessary Detail

A test should focus on the essence of the business rule, avoiding unnecessary details. For example, because it was not relevant, Joanna's address was not included in any of the tests we saw in earlier chapters of this part. Verbosity in Fit tables simply hides the intent of the test.

The biggest smell arises when Fit tests for general business rules are expressed as operations through the user interface: "Select the Open menu item. Enter *Joanna* in this field."[2] There are likely to be many user interface operations that can be expressed succinctly as more abstract actions.

There is a synergy between this smell and the one in Section 18.6.3. Unnecessary detail causes problems when things inevitably change.

Questions & Answers

What if we want to test that the user interface operates correctly?
Let's say that you want to define important aspects of the user interface itself, such as whether a menu item is enabled, a dialog box is displayed as expected, or a link works on the Web.

Apply the general approach that we have used all along. Develop a test language that best describes what's important to you. For example, it may be convenient to use a RowFixture table to list all the GUI components that are currently enabled.

Don't be constrained by the language of specialized user interface fixtures that are available. The programmers can still make use of such fixtures in the fixtures they develop. It's important that they fulfill your need for expressiveness and conciseness in your Fit tests.

18.2.8 Smell: Tangled Tables

Tangled tables arise when a variety of interrelated tests are mixed together. You can suspect that a test is tangled when it is long and convoluted and/or many tests are similar but differ only in small details.

We avoided creating tangled tables in Section 13.5 on p. 98, when Don decided that "the grace period calculation would be best done independently." Instead, a grace period value was included in the late-return tables, and the calculation of an appropriate grace period, based on the rental period, was done elsewhere.

---

[2] Of course, Fit tests can be used to test the operation of that user interface, as distinct from testing the system under test *through* the user interface.

For a larger example, consider adding tests for bookings of rental items in the *RentEz* system that was covered over the past few chapters. In developing those tests, we find that several issues need to be clarified.

- What is a valid period of a booking, independent of the rental items? It can't be in the past. The start date must be before the end date. Are the start and end dates constrained to be at times when the rental company is open?

- For the rental items to be booked, are they available—not already booked— during all the required period? How much allowance should be made for other clients returning rental items late when they're required for a booking?

- What happens when a client asks for a booking that can't be satisfied?

- Are the charges for bookings the same as for immediate rental? When are the payments made?

- Can bookings be canceled or changed? What happens if a client turns up for the booked rental items but wants to rent only some of them now? Is a fee charged?

- Do some clients want regular bookings? How often: Every week? Every month? Every public holiday?

It is a trap to try and deal with all these issues at once in a set of tangled tests. It is essential to separate the business rules involved to be clear about them.

- We could use one `ColumnFixture` or `CalculateFixture` table to test the validity of date periods, independent of the holiday issue. Validation in general is usually best done in this way, separately from any workflow tests.

- Another test or group of tests could set up existing bookings with a `SetUpFixture` table and then check whether various new bookings can be accepted with a `ColumnFixture` or `CalculateFixture` table. There are many cases to check for here, as there are many ways in which existing and potential bookings can overlap.

- Separate `ActionFixture` or `DoFixture` tests will be needed to define what happens when a booking can/cannot be made.

- It should be straightforward to find out how charging is handled and to change that without having to change much else.

See Section 18.3.2 for one way to untangle tests.

18.2.9   Smell: Split Values

As we saw in Section 16.3 on p. 131, it was worthwhile handling time durations as single values in a cell instead of using several cells. For example, Figure 18.4 shows a table in which hours, days, and weeks are in separate columns. However, this makes it a little more difficult to read. More important, it requires that all columns be filled in, even if they're not relevant, such as 0 for most of the hour values in Figure 18.4.

$	5.00	*per hour*	45.00	*per day*	200.00	*per week*
hours	*days*	*weeks*	*days()*	*weeks()*		
0	4	0	4	0		
0	5	0	0	1		
5	6	0	0	1		

Figure 18.4 Split Values

Figure 18.5 shows a refactored table in which the duration of hours, days, and weeks is a single value.

$	5.00	*per hour*	45.00	*per day*	200.00	*per week*
duration		*fair*				
4 days		4 days				
5 days		1 week				
6 days 5 hours		1 week				

Figure 18.5 Duration as a Value

In general, consider whether a value that is split over several cells would be better expressed as a single value in a single cell. It can be false economy for programmers to avoid writing fixture code to handle such values or to improve the expressiveness of Fit tests in general. Putting a little effort into the fixtures can lead to better tests and to reductions in the efforts of the test writer and the reader.

18.2.10 Smell: Long Tables

If a table is very long, perhaps it can be made clearer by splitting it into several tables. There may be a way of organizing it so that the separate tables are meaningful units. We can then explain each of the tables with supporting text (Section 18.2.3).

18.2.11 Custom Tables

As we mentioned in Chapter 11, your tests may have a pattern that you're unable to exploit with the existing fixtures. It means that the tests are larger than they need to be, because they don't express things directly. People have a powerful visual ability that can quickly process and understand tests that show important associations spatially.

So go ahead and make up a custom table, and talk to the programmers about making a fixture for it. For a few examples, see Chapter 11.

18.3 Workflow Tests

We now focus on design ideas and smells that apply to action, or workflow, tests expressed with **ActionFixture** and **DoFixture**.

18.3.1   Smell: Missing Sad Paths in Actions

Do you have a `DoFixture` table action that is colored green? Do you also define what happens when the action is rejected? Do the various reasons for the rejection need to be spelled out independently?

We introduced the concept of sad paths in Section 15.5 on p. 121. To make the tests, and thus the application, comprehensive, spend some time on these sad paths in action tests.

It may be easier to tackle the sad paths once the good paths are done. However, if you're not sure whether a new story is a good idea, it may be best to ignore the sad paths of the tests for that story until you're more certain. If you have less interest in the unusual and little patience for the odd cases, you'll want to get testers to tackle those; they have experience in doing so.

18.3.2   Smell: Calculations Slow with Workflow

As we saw in Chapter 16, a large number of similar workflow, or action-based, tests may be radically reduced by clarifying the essential elements of the test, such as charging fairly for rentals. Instead of using many action tests, use a few tables of calculation tests for clarity, augmented with just a few action tests.

If you find yourself repeatedly making copies of an action-based test and making small changes, this smell may well apply, as well as if you notice that many existing tests are similar. To understand a particular business rule when tests have this smell, it's necessary to read through many tests to work out what is going on by considering the few differences. The rule is lost in all the details.

As we saw in Chapter 16, such tests can be refactored so that the essence of the various business rules can be expressed clearly and succinctly. Splitting the tests into those that are action based and those that are calculation based is the key (Section 18.2.8).

18.3.3   Smell: Long Action Tables

With long tables, it's more difficult to understand the test, because of all the details to follow. Consider splitting an action table into several, with each table grouping a few actions that belong together. Then support each of the tables with a little explanatory text (Section 18.2.3).

18.3.4   Smell: Unclear Workflow

Action-based tests usually have three parts.

1. *Setup:* Data is entered to put the system under test into a suitable state; for example, with some existing bookings. See Section 10.4 on p. 76 for more details of set up with `SetUpFixture`.

2. *State change:* An action is carried out, such as a new booking being made.

3. *Check:* The effects of the *state change*—or no change—are checked, such as the new booking's being accepted and recorded or rejected.

An action-based test may have a problem under the following conditions.

- All three parts don't seem to exist in the test.

- Any part seems incomplete. For example, are all the necessary conditions being checked in the *check* part?

- The role of parts of the test are unclear. However, a *state change* and *check* may sometimes occur in the same table or even in the same action. For example, we may define that a booking action is expected to be rejected.

18.3.5 Smell: Missing Tests

An action test may depend on a list of elements that have been set up, such as the single booked template entry in Section 17.6 on p. 148 and shown again in Figure 18.6.

booked template entry	Joanna			
template	people	from	to	repeat
coffee break	21	2004/06/01 18:00	2004/06/02 18:00	1 week

Figure 18.6 Setup of One Booked Template

If any of your tests are like that, have you assumed that the list has only one element? What if there are several elements? Or none?

Or have you assumed that the list always has several elements? What happens if it has only one element? Or no elements?

In general, have you written tests for all the important cases? If you leave one out, it may not be handled in the system under test.

18.3.6 Smell: Rambling Workflow

It can be difficult to track state changes in a long `ActionFixture`, especially when a *press* requires many previous *enters*, corresponding to a `DoFixture` action with several data values. For example, the test in Figure 18.7 is long and difficult to read because of all the fine detail. This test could be improved by splitting it into several tables and adding text comments between the tables about the current state (see Section 18.2.3).

Where it will help readability, consider changing `ActionFixture` tables to use `DoFixture`, as we showed in Section 14.3 on p. 107. Are there many repetitions of a particular sequence of *enter*, *enter*, *press* in `ActionFixture` tables or of a sequence of actions in `DoFixture` tables? It may be possible to express that sequence with a single `DoFixture` action more directly, by substituting the single action for the sequence. The fixture can do extra work automatically when the test is run.

transaction		
enter	count	3
enter	rental item	coffee urn
enter	hours	0
enter	days	2
enter	weeks	0
press	hire	
check	total	222.00
enter	count	4
enter	rental item	coffee urn
enter	hours	0
enter	days	3
enter	weeks	0
press	hire	
check	total	344.00
enter	count	7
enter	rental item	table
enter	hours	0
enter	days	3
enter	weeks	0
press	hire	
check	total	1568.00
enter	cash	3134.00
press	pay	

Figure 18.7 Rambling Table

18.3.7   Smell: Similar Setup

The first three tables of Figures 18.8 and 18.9 are the same.[3] We can extract those three tables into a SetUp file or FitNesse page, as shown in Figure 18.10, so it's common across the tests. This makes it less work to add further tests. And when reading those revised tests, we won't need to read the SetUp repeatedly.

chat server				
	anna	connects		
	anna	creates	lotr	room
	anna	removes	lotr	room
rooms list				
name				

Figure 18.8 Test Remove Succeeds

---

[3] This smell is related to the issues raised in Section 18.6.

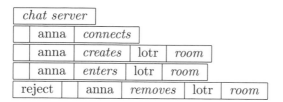

Figure 18.9 Test Remove Fails

Figure 18.10 Common Setup

18.3.8 Smell: Convoluted Setup

Sometimes, the setup for an action test may be rather convoluted because it requires
a series of actions to get the system under test into the right state for the essence
of the test. So rather than having extra details that distract from the important
part of the test, consider using `SetUpFixture` tables that more directly set up
the appropriate state. A secondary reason for using `SetUpFixture` tables is to be
explicit about the purpose of those tables in the overall test. (See Section 10.4 on
p. 76 for details of `SetUpFixture`.)

For example, consider the setup for testing bookings in the *RentEz* system. The
set up can enter the existing bookings without needing to include the transaction
and payment, as shown in Figure 18.11.

set up booked list	Joanna		
rental item	count	from	to
coffee dispenser	2	2004/06/01 18:00	2004/06/02 18:00
cup	40	2004/06/01 18:00	2004/06/02 18:00

Figure 18.11 Setup for Bookings

18.4 Calculation Tests

We now focus on design ideas and smells that apply to calculation tests expressed
with `ColumnFixture` and `CalculateFixture`.

18.4.1 Smell: Many Columns

A `ColumnFixture` or `CalculateFixture` with many columns may indicate that
something is wrong. Is there a tangle of tests here (see Section 18.2.8)? If so, can
they be split into separate tests with distinct tables?

Are there many repeats in a big table? If so, maybe they can be eliminated by breaking the table up into several smaller tables, with common column values expressed as arguments. For example, one such table from Section 16.3 on p. 131 is shown again as Figure 18.12.

rent.CalculateFairCharge						
rates $	5.00	per hour	45.00	per day	200.00	per week
duration		fair				
1 day		1 day				
8 hours		8 hours				
9 hours		1 day				
23 hours		1 day				
3 days 4 hours		3 days 4 hours				

Figure 18.12 Table with Arguments

18.4.2   Smell: Not Calculating

Consider the table shown again in Figure 18.13. This table is using the form of calculation tests, but the intent is to set up for an action test. It's clearer to use a SetUpFixture table, as shown in Section 10.4 on p. 76.

DiscountGroupsEntry				
future value	max balance	min purchase	discount percent	add()
low	0.00	0.00	0	true
medium	0.00	500.00	5	true
medium	500.00	500.00	3	true
high	500.00	2000.00	10	true
high	1000.00	500.00	5	true

Figure 18.13 Setup Table Using ColumnFixture

ColumnFixture tables can also be used for actions tests. For example, the ColumnFixture table in Figure 18.14 is testing that a rental return leads to the correct refund. The *returns()* column checks that the return succeeded; the *running total()* column checks the amount of the refund. This test can be expressed a little more clearly by using a DoFixture table without being confused as a calculation test.

hire.ChangeRentals				
rental item	count	days	returns()	running total()
coffee urn	5	1	true	-100.00
hot water urn	2	1	true	-140.00

Figure 18.14 A ColumnFixture Used for Action Tests

18.4.3 Smell: Many Rows

As we've already seen (Section 18.2.10), long tables may need to be organized into several tables to help the test reader and the writer. For example, in Section 13.6 on p. 99, we suggested that a separate table be used to define the late-return business rules when the *high demand* is not zero. Figure 18.12 shows one of several tables that define fair charging, based on time and the various charge rates.

In general, long tables can be split to create separate tables for the major cases. Order the rows in the tables clearly to make it easier to see the organization and easier to see whether cases are missing. Use blanks with `ColumnFixture` rather than repeating the same value down a column. Or use table arguments, as we saw in Section 18.4.1.

18.4.4 Smell: No Related Workflow

For any business logic that is tested as calculations, we'd expect to see two or more action-based tests to define what happens under the various circumstances. For example, if we have calculation tests that validate some data input, such as a date, we'd expect to see what happens in the workflow when it's valid and when it's not. For example, we have not shown any action tests for the late-returns tests covered in Chapter 13.

18.5 List Tests

We now focus on design ideas and smells that apply to list tests expressed with `RowFixture`, `ArrayFixture`, and `SubsetFixture`.

18.5.1 Smell: Too Many List Columns

Consider the Fit table shown in Figure 18.15, which is checking that the count of items is correct. Several columns are irrelevant to this test, adding unecessary and distracting detail. We can improve this table by eliminating the irrelevant columns, as shown in Figure 18.16.

rental items list					
name	count	hourly rate	daily rate	weekly rate	deposit
coffee urn	10	1.50	12.00	60.00	50.00
table	20	6.00	48.00	200.00	80.00
coffee pot	20	1.50	12.00	60.00	0.00
chair	20	6.00	48.00	200.00	0.00

Figure 18.15 Many List Rows

In general, if a Fit table for testing lists has many columns, consider whether all of them are relevant to the test. For example, you may decide to include just those columns that are expected to change or those that are expected to not change.

rental items list	
name	*count*
coffee urn	10
table	20
coffee pot	20
chair	20

Figure 18.16 Fewer Columns

18.5.2   Smell: Too Many List Rows

Suppose that we are interested only in the number of coffeee urns. Then the table in Figure 18.16, as discussed in Section 18.5.1, contains more detail than necessary. The SubsetFixture table shown in Figure 18.17 can then be used to focus on the number of that one rental item.

rental item subset	
name	*count*
coffee urn	10

Figure 18.17 Fewer Rows with SubsetFixture

Another approach to reducing irrelevant detail is to select some of the elements of the list. For example, the test in Figure 18.18 uses an argument, Joanna, to focus on a single client's rentals, avoiding the need to list the rentals of all clients.

rentals for client	Joanna		
rental item	*count*	*start date*	*end date*
cup	100	2004/05/06 09:01	2004/05/20 09:01

Figure 18.18 Fewer Rows, Using Arguments

18.6   Tests and Change

Inevitably, the Fit tests for a system will change as the business changes and as the needs of the business are better understood in relation to that system. Tests that are difficult to change will become a handicap, either slowing down development or becoming out of date and ignored.

Tests are difficult to change when they're not well organized or are difficult to understand. But the most common problem occurs when many similar changes need to be made to a large set of tests. It is very easy to miss one or two places where a change was required, leading to inconsistency between tests. We'd hope that such inconsistencies will be picked up when the tests are run against the revised system, but this is not guaranteed.

18.6.1   Redundancy

The need for many similar changes stems from *redundancy*, some of which results from unnecessary detail in tests. So one of the aims of table design is to reduce the redundancy in tests. However, we cannot eliminate it.

Redundancy arises when the same thing is said more than once. Such repetition makes for longer tests and more tests to change when the business rules change. But some redundancy is inevitable because we need to include the name of a client, for example, in many tests. Luckily, the approaches to managing change of Fit tables are mostly consistent with our communication aims.[4]

18.6.2   Smell: Duplication

If you find yourself copying several tables of one test to create a new test, you may be creating unnecessary duplication and thus redundancy. If you find that you're having to compare long tests with one another to determine the differences, those tests may contain redundancies.

Various specific smells were given earlier, along with approaches to avoiding such duplication:

- Unnecessary detail (Section 18.2.7)
- Tangled tables (Section 18.2.8)
- Long tables (Section 18.2.10)
- Laborious action-based tests for calculation (Section 18.3.2)
- Rambling workflow (Section 18.3.6)
- Similar Setup (Section 18.3.7)
- Convoluted Setup (Section 18.3.8)
- Many columns (Sections 18.4.1 and 18.5.1)
- Lots of rows (Sections 18.4.3 and 18.5.2)

18.6.3   Smell: Tests Changing Often

If the tests are changing more quickly than the needs of the system, a problem may exist. Maybe the tests include details about things that are still being decided—premature commitment. Or maybe the tests include too much irrelevant detail.

As we saw in Section 18.2.7, the biggest smell arises when Fit tests for general business rules are expressed as operations through the user interface. Of all the components of an application, the user interface is the one most likely to change.

In addition, if Fit tests are written early on in development, it will be unclear how the user interface will work. So rather than making premature commitments to something that's not essential to the business rule, leave that detail out. As we show programmers in Chapter 32, the fixtures for Fit tests for the tables in Chapter 14

---

[4] They differ in that eliminating too much redundancy will make tests more difficult to read.

may test the system under test through the user interface, without any need for that to be mentioned in the Fit tests themselves.

If we're testing too close to the GUI, we need to think about the actions that we want to carry out in a more abstract way. So rather than thinking about filling in a form, through several operations on the user interface, think about the fundamentals of the action. For example, the tests in Part II make no commitment to the user interface operations that may be carried out on the system.

18.7   Automation of Tests

Finally, our design of Fit tables has to take account of the way they are used as automated tests.

- Once the number of Fit tests grows, you'll need to organize them. You can save much time in finding and running tests, by organizing them into *test suites*. For example, organize related tests into a folder (Section 7.2) or a FitNesse subwiki (Section 8.3).

- Don't make assumptions about the order in which the tests will be run, as that order is sure to change one day to cause trouble. Each Fit test should stand alone and be able to run independently. Thus, each test usually needs to start from a known state.[5] We've seen in Section 10.4 on p. 76 and in Section 18.3.4 how we can use `SetUpFixture` tables to set up the state required.

- Provide useful feedback if a complex test fails, to help sort out whether the test or the system under test is at fault. For example, the FitNesse system comes with a set of acceptance tests, many of which provide feedback on the page that's being tested. `DoFixture` provides a *show* special action. (Programmers, see Section 28.6 on p. 237, for using it to display extra information within a test.)

18.8   Summary

Creating Fit tables is a creative, intellectual activity. It can be a process of invention and discovery, as concrete examples help clarify what is needed from a system.

Three principles of table design work together. Tests are for communicating ideas, especially when a test is written to help drive the development of a software system. Tests inevitably change as a system evolves, so we need to design Fit tables from the very start with that in mind. Tests are automated so that the developers know when they're done and know when something has been undone by mistake.

Tests need to be expressed clearly and succinctly. In the process of developing tests from concrete examples, a kind of language emerges: the vocabulary of header labels and actions that describe what's needed.

---

[5] Some calculation tests may be independent of the state of the system under test.

CHAPTER 19

Closing for Nonprogrammers

This chapter brings the first half of the book, for nonprogrammers, to an end. Now's a good time to review of the first half of the book, reflect, and consider the future.

Parts III, IV, and V assume a background in programming and focus on the development of fixtures that mediate between Fit tables and the system under test. Part III covers fixtures for the Fit tables in Part I. Part IV covers the development of fixtures for the tables in Part II. Part V focuses on custom development.

19.1   The Value of Fit Tables

Fit tables help solve three major problems in software development: communication, balance, and agility.

- Fit tables provide a way for people who want a system to communicate that need in a concrete way. As we've seen in Part II, it's usually best to let Fit tables evolve through using concrete examples of business rules. As the examples get more comprehensive or more complex, the language of the tests needs to evolve to find the best means of expression.

- Good Fit tests can mean that we spend less time unbalanced because of bugs that need to be fixed. Fit tests do this by reducing the number or severity of problems, catching them early, and making sure that they don't return. Better quality leads to improved customer satisfaction and lower costs in rework owing to errors and misunderstandings.

- Fit tables help keep the software in good shape so that changes can be made quickly and effectively to support business change.

19.2   Getting Fit at RentAPartySoftware

Fit tests were introduced at RPS along with agile software development. Several issues were raised at the beginning and some goals set. Let's review the progress after several months.

The issues were as follows.

- *Some parts have had ongoing bugs.* After focusing attention on these areas with Fit tests, Don felt that they were getting them under control. "Now we write a test for a bug before we try and fix it, improving our regression testing."

- *The developers fear changing the software and the database.* Once Fit tests were in place for parts of the system, Emily was pleased with progress on refactoring without fear. "Getting fast feedback on little, inevitable mistakes is so good. It's amazing to think how much debugging we used to do, without knowing better."

- *Their testing tools have been unsatisfactory.* Don is now at ease and fluent with Fit. "It takes a while to get into inventing and changing the language of the business rules—or tests. It's much more satisfying to write the tests as we work out what's needed, rather than afterward."

- *There are delays in having problems fixed when the programmer responsible for that part is away.* Neo sees this as less and less of a problem. "With the parts of the system that are changing, almost anyone can fix problems. Pair programming and no code ownership now work well. It took us some time to get used to making small changes and regular check-ins. Luckily, there are also far fewer problems in those parts of the system that are tested."

- *There have been problems with configuration on customer sites.* This issue still needs to be dealt with, but Don expects that automated tests for configuration will sort out much of this, as well as speed up any on-site time.

- *All the documents are out of date.* The old documents are still out of date. No one seems concerned about this. As Mitra commented, "Having the Fit tests up to date seems to be sufficient."

- *The testers are unhappy about the lack of time to test before new versions are shipped, especially with last-minute changes to the software.* Sarah had commented on how their whole approach to tests and testing has changed. "Rather than a scramble before delivery, the focus at that stage is now on exploratory testing. Having the tests up front frees the testers to add real value, rather than laboriously picking up trivial errors. It's great that the programmers are going well with unit tests."

- *Little software problems have been fixed but mysteriously return later.* Regression tests have helped sort that out.

Their goals were as follows.

- *Have all customers eager to move to the latest version of* RentEz, *so as to cut the cost of maintaining several versions.* Seth reported, "This is starting to happen. Several customers are now eager to get new releases."

- *Reduce the time taken to add new features, to help sales and to reduce costs.* Mitra had noticed that this was happening, "especially in the parts of the system that had been 'worked over.' I expect to see further improvements over time."

- *Improve the estimates of the effort to add possible new features.* As the planning game became second nature, Emily had tracked the vast improvement in the accuracy of estimates from the development team. As she commented, "It's amazing what good feedback can do!" This accuracy in turn helped Mitra and Seth make better decisions about what features to add next.

- *Improve current customer satisfaction and reduce the number of complaints of problems with* RentEz. "Several customers," reported Seth, "have commented on the higher quality of the latest release and our faster response to their needs. There have certainly been fewer compaints with that release than usual."

- *Reduce the number of bugs reported from the field and the number yet to be fixed.* Don reported, "The number of bug reports has dropped by half. The bugs outstanding have dropped right off, too."

- *Reduce the time spent in finding the cause of bugs and fixing them.* Neo reported, "Even when we take account of fewer bugs, we generally deal with them more quickly. Some parts of the system are problematic and need to be tested."

- *Reduce the effort spent on developing extensions that require drastic rework.* Mitra reported that where she and Seth had showed the Fit tests to customers, less rework seemed to be needed. "Where possible, we do the most important changes and get feedback if we can before proceeding. We pick up misunderstandings earlier than before."

- *Reduce the overtime and the stress of last-minute rushes to get software out.* Neo reported that "Extreme Programming, with an emphasis on doing the most important things first, is starting to have an impact here. With pair programming, it's more difficult to blob out. With test-driven development, we get excellent code coverage with our tests."

- *Focus the effort on the changes that help sell the product and are most beneficial to clients.* Seth admitted, "Yes, this focus has been a good one. It's not easy, however, to really understand potential benefit to our customers when they don't!"

PART III

INTRODUCING FIT FIXTURES

CHAPTER 20

Connecting Tables and Applications

A *fixture* acts as an intermediary between a Fit table and a system under test, carrying out the tests in the table, as illustrated in Figure 20.1.[1] For example, for each *expected* value in a row of a `ColumnFixture` table, the fixture will be called to carry out a test.

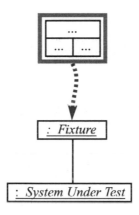

Figure 20.1 A Fixture as Intermediary

20.1   Writing Fixtures

In Chapters 21–23 we cover the basics of writing fixtures to bridge with a system under test for each of the three types of Fit tests: *calculations*, *workflow*, and *lists*. At this stage, we'll assume that it is easy to bridge from the tests into the system under test. Later, in Part IV, we look at the issues that arise in connecting tests to a system under test that was not developed to enable testing.

---

[1] The chapters in Part III assume a reading knowledge of Java or a similar object-oriented programming language.

The remaining chapters of Part III are as follows.

- Chapter 24 explains how to write several fixtures for a sequence of tables that need to coordinate in their use of a single system under test.

- Chapter 25 discusses how Fit handles the conversion of cell contents into values and vice versa with `TypeAdapter` and shows how user-defined and other types can be handled with Fit.

- Chapter 26 details the programmer specifics of installing and running Fit.

- Chapter 27 describes the programmer specifics of FitNesse.

- Chapter 28 outlines the development of fixtures for FitLibrary fixtures, as introduced in Chapter 10.

- Chapter 29 covers the custom table fixtures that were introduced in Chapter 11.

20.2   Fixtures and Traffic Lights

When it runs a table, Fit creates an object of the fixture class and passes control to that object, calling its method `doTable()`. The fixture carries out the tests, coloring the reported table so that we can tell which tests passed and which failed. As introduced in Section 3.2 on p. 14, the cell colors are as follows:

- *Green:* when an *expected* value matches the *actual* value from the system under test.

- *Red:* when a cell fails to meet expectations. Additional information may be provided: the actual value received, in a `ColumnFixture` or an `ActionFixture`; or the fact that a row was missing from the *actual* list, in the case of `RowFixture`.

- *Yellow:* when a value is of the wrong format, cells are missing, or an exception is thrown in the fixture or system under test.

- *Gray:* for a cell that was for some reason not processed.

Questions & Answers

What if the fixture class that is named in a table doesn't exist?
An *exception* is thrown and is reported in the first cell of the table.

How about testing other languages?
Besides Java, there are versions of Fit for several programming languages, including C#, Visual Basic.net, C++, Ruby, Python, and Smalltalk. In general, the same Fit table can be used with several programming languages, although the fixture code will be different.

CHAPTER 21

Column Fixtures

A fixture of type `ColumnFixture` defines how the specific *given* and *calculated* columns of a `ColumnFixture` table are mapped to the system under test. This information is used to run each of the tests in the table in turn. This chapter shows the fixtures for the Fit tables introduced in Chapter 3.

21.1 Fixture `CalculateDiscount`

Consider the discount tests from Section 3.1 on p. 13, shown again in Figure 21.1. The first row of the table names `CalculateDiscount`, the fixture that will be used to interpret the tests in the tables. This fixture is the name of a Java class or equivalent in other languages. The second, header, row of the table labels the *given* column *amount* and the *calculated* column *discount()*.

CalculateDiscount	
amount	*discount()*
0.00	0.00
100.00	0.00
999.00	0.00
1000.00	0.00
1010.00	50.50
1100.00	55.00
1200.00	60.00
2000.00	100.00

Figure 21.1 Fit Table for Testing Discount

The fixture code for this, in Java, is the class `CalculateDiscount`, shown in Listing 21.1. This class inherits its testing behavior from `fit.ColumnFixture`, its superclass. Corresponding to the *given* column, labeled *amount* in the table, is the `public` instance variable `amount` in the class (line 2 in Listing 21.1). Corresponding to the *calculated* column *discount()* is the `public` method `discount()` (line 5).

Listing 21.1 CalculateDiscount.java

```
1 public class CalculateDiscount extends fit.ColumnFixture {
2    public double amount;
3    private Discount application = new Discount();
4
5    public double discount() {
6       return application.getDiscount(amount);
7    }
8 }
```

> **Note**
>
> Fit fixtures don't follow the usual object-oriented convention of hiding
> instance variables, because the goal of fixtures is to mediate between the Fit
> tables and the system under test. The fixtures are not part of the application
> and are written to expose rather than to hide.

The instance variable `amount` is of the Java type `double`, a double-precision
floating-point number, so the values in the first column of the test rows need to be
`doubles`. As the method `discount()` returns a `double` value, the expected values in
the second column also need to be `doubles`. This fixture method calls the method
`discount()` of the system under test—of the class `Discount`, which we don't show.

When it runs this table, Fit creates a fixture object of the class `Calculate-`
`Discount`, as shown in Figure 21.2. Fit passes control to that object by calling its
method `doTable()`.

The `doTable()` code in `fit.ColumnFixture`, as inherited by `CalculateDiscount`,
reads the labels in the header row of the table to determine the order of the *given*
and *calculated* columns: *amount* and *discount()*. For the third row, the first test,
the code in `fit.ColumnFixture` carries out a sequence of steps. It

- Takes the text value 0.00 in the first cell and converts it to a `double`, the type
  of the instance variable `amount`.

- Assigns this `double` value to the instance variable `amount` of the fixture object.

- Calls the method `discount()` of the fixture object, getting the *calculated*
  result, a `double`. This fixture method calls the system under test, as shown
  in Figure 21.2.

- Takes the text value 0.00 from the second cell, the expected result, and
  converts it into a `double`, the return type of the method.

- Compares the actual `double` that was returned from the fixture method
  against the *expected* result. They are equal, so the second cell is colored green.[1]

---

[1] See Section 3.2 on p. 14 for details of the coloring scheme.

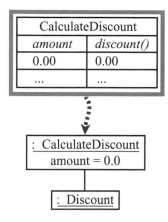

Figure 21.2 Fit Runs the Table

Code in `fit.ColumnFixture` processes each subsequent row of the table in the same way. With the fourth test row, row 6 of Figure 21.1, the *actual* and *expected* values don't match. So the cell is colored red, and the actual result, 50.0, as returned from the method call, is added to the cell in the report. When the rows of the table have all been completed, Fit produces the report as HTML, showing the results.

Note

The class `CalculateDiscount` simply defines the appropriate instance variables and methods, corresponding to the *given* and *calculated* columns. Its superclass, `fit.ColumnFixture`, does all the work.

Although the *amount* and *discount* are money, we have used type `double` in order to keep this first example simple. In Chapter 25, we show how to use a class `Money` for this.

Fit and `fit.ColumnFixture` use Java reflection to create an object of the fixture class, as well as to change instance variables and call methods of the fixture object. See class `Class` in Java for further details, if you're interested.

Questions & Answers

What does the () in the header mean?
The label of a *calculated* column has a suffix of () to signify that a method will be called. This method may simply calculate a value and return it, or it may carry out some action with side effects.

Do the *calculated* columns have to be after all the *given* columns?
No, not necessarily. The order matters, however, as the columns are processed from left to right, regardless.

What happens if the value in a cell cannot be treated as a `double`?
The cell is marked with yellow and an error message given.

What happens if a method to be called in the system under test takes several parameters?
In that case, more *given* columns and associated instance variables will be needed. We'll see that in the next example, in Section 21.2.

What if the two `doubles` are not quite the same?
They won't match. However, you can use `fit.ScientificDouble` instead; this checks the actual value against the expected value according to the precision of the expected value.

It's odd having a *public* instance variable in the fixture class.
Yes, we're usually encouraged to hide such implementation details. Here, however, the fixture class is simply acting as a bridge between the Fit table and the system under test, so different rules can apply. We'll see in Chapter 22 that `ActionFixture` takes a different approach to passing data from the table to the fixture.

Can Fit be used for other sorts of testing, such as response time?
Yes. You could have a *given* field with the maximum response time allowed, and a `boolean` *calculated* field for whether the response was within the time. Or, you could test that some *given* percentage of the responses were under the *given* time.

21.2   Extending Credit

The credit tests from Section 3.3 on p. 16 are shown again in Figure 21.3. Our fixture class is `CalculateCredit`, a `ColumnFixture`, as shown in Listing 21.2.

CalculateCredit				
months	*reliable*	*balance*	*allow credit()*	*credit limit()*
14	true	5000.00	true	1000.00
0	true	0.00	false	0.00
24	*false*	0.00	false	0.00
18	true	*6000.00*	false	0.00
12	true	5500.00	true	1000.00

Figure 21.3 Fit Table for Testing Credit

There are three *given* columns, so the class has three corresponding instance variables, which are declared on lines 2–4 in Listing 21.2. The two *calculated* columns, *allow credit()* and *credit limit()*, correspond to the two methods allowCredit() and creditLimit() on lines 7 and 10 in Listing 21.2. The simple translation here is defined by *camel casing*; see the Note below. The two methods each make use of the values in the instance variables to call methods in the system under test, of class Credit.

Listing 21.2 CalculateCredit.java

```
 1 public class CalculateCredit extends fit.ColumnFixture {
 2    public int months;
 3    public boolean reliable;
 4    public double balance;
 5    private Credit credit = new Credit();
 6
 7    public boolean allowCredit() {
 8        return credit.allowsCredit(months,reliable,balance);
 9    }
10    public double creditLimit() {
11        return credit.limit(months,reliable,balance);
12    }
13 }
```

> ## Note
>
> *Camel casing* handles spaces separating words in a ColumnFixture or RowFixture table label, as well as in the names of fields in *enter*, *press*, and *check* actions in ActionFixture tables. These spaces have to be removed to get a valid Java identifier.
>
> A sequence of space-separated words in the header is translated so that spaces are removed and the first letter of all words but the first is capitalized. For example, "allow credit" is translated into "allowCredit."
>
> An extended form, *extended camel casing*, handles arbitrary characters in labels and actions in FitLibrary fixture tables, as discussed in Chapter 28.

The operation is much the same as in the previous example, except that

- The first three columns are *given*. In running a test in a row, the values from each of these cells are assigned to each of the corresponding instance variables, working from left to right across the row.

- There are two *calculated* columns. The corresponding methods are called in turn, from left to right across the row, using the instance variable values assigned by the *given*s.

Questions & Answers

What if we want to test real numbers for equality?
Use class `eg.ScientificDouble`, available on the Fit Web site, at http://fit.c2.com.
This class tests that the actual value is equal to the expected value to the precision
of the expected value.

What if an instance variable or method is missing?
The fixture code throws an *exception* if an instance variable or method doesn't exist
or is not `public`, or if the *calculated* fixture method takes parameters.

21.3   Selecting a Phone Number

The test from Section 3.4 on p. 19 is shown again in Figure 21.4. Our fixture class
is `CalculateFirstPhoneNumber`, a `ColumnFixture`, as shown in Listing 21.3.

CalculateFirstPhoneNumber	
phones	*first()*
(209)373 7453, (209)373 7454	(209)373 7453

Figure 21.4 Fit Table for Testing First Phone

There is one *given* column, so the class has a corresponding instance variable,
which is an array. There is one *calculated* column, corresponding to the method
`first()`.

Listing 21.3 **CalculateFirstPhoneNumber.java**
```
public class CalculateFirstPhoneNumber extends fit.ColumnFixture {
   private Client client = new Client();

   public String[] phones;

   public String first() {
      client.setPhones(phones);
      return client.firstPhone();
   }
}
```

21.4 ColumnFixture **in General**

We can now state the operation of `ColumnFixture` in more general terms. When it runs a table, Fit creates an object of the fixture class named in the first row, calling the method `doTable()` of that fixture object.

For a `ColumnFixture` type of table, `doTable()` in `fit.ColumnFixture` reads the labels in the header row of the table to determine the order of the columns. For each cell in the header row, working from left to right, `doTable()` determines the type of column label for that cell and creates a suitable object of class `TypeAdapter`[2] for that column. For a *given* label:

- The `TypeAdapter` uses the label to find the corresponding instance variable of the fixture object and thus its type.

- However, if the instance variable is missing or is not `public`, an *exception* is thrown and is reported in the cell.

For a *calculated* label:

- The `TypeAdapter` uses the label to find the corresponding method of the fixture object and thus its *return* type.

- However, if the method is missing, is not `public`, or takes arguments, this is reported in the cell.

Below the header row, working down each test row, and for each cell, working from left to right, it uses the `TypeAdapter` for that column.

- For a *given* label, it uses the `TypeAdapter` to convert the value in the cell and assign it to the instance variable of the fixture object.

- For a *calculated* label, it uses the `TypeAdapter` to (1) call the method of the fixture object, getting the result; (2) take the expected text value from the cell and convert it into a value of the *return* type; and (3) compare the value that was returned from the method against the expected result. If they match, the cell is colored green. If they do not match, the cell is colored red, and the actual result is added to the cell in the report. However, any exception thrown by the method call is reported in the cell.

Questions & Answers

What if a cell is empty?

If a *given* cell is empty, the current value of the corresponding instance variable is reported in that cell. If it's a *calculated* cell, the value returned by the corresponding method is reported.

---

[2] `TypeAdapter` is discussed further in Chapter 25.

But what if the *given* value was intended to be the empty string?
Use the special word *blank* for this case. However, if this also clashes, you'd need to choose a special `String` value to represent an empty string, such as `((EMPTY))`. Then test for that value in the fixture code, and use an empty `String` instead in any calls into the system under test.

Alternatively, you could use `CalculateFixture`, which doesn't necessarily process empty cells in a special way. `CalculateFixture` is discussed in Section 28.8 on p. 242.

21.5   Summary

- A fixture acts as a bridge between a Fit table and a system under test.

- We aim to keep fixtures as simple as possible, with minimal knowledge encoded in them of how the system under test works.

- A fixture for a table of type `ColumnFixture` is a subclass of `fit.Column-Fixture`, which defines (1) a `public` instance variable for each *given* column that is labeled in the header row of a table; (2) a `public` method for each *calculated* column in the table. Usually, this method will use the instance variable values to make a call into the system under test. The result of this fixture method is compared against the *expected* value in the *calculated* column.

- *Camel casing* removes spaces from a label to create a valid Java identifier.

21.6   Exercises

1. Experiment with changing the supplied example fixture classes and corresponding tables. Note the errors that result from a mismatch between the table and the fixture.

2. What happens if instance variables and methods in the `ColumnFixture` subclass are not referred to in the table?

3. What happens if a `void` method is provided in the fixture for a *calculated* column?

4. Write simple tables and corresponding fixtures for some of the tables in the exercises in Chapter 3.

5. Write a table that encodes spaces specially as `((SPACE))`. Develop the corresponding `ColumnFixture` fixture class to handle spaces correctly to and from the system under test.

CHAPTER 22

Action Fixtures

An `ActionFixture` table tests that a series of actions carried out on an application work as expected. An `ActionFixture` fixture *starts* a named class by creating the *actor*, an object of that class. Subsequent actions are made through method calls on that separate *actor* object. This chapter shows the fixtures for the Fit tables introduced in Chapter 4.

22.1 Buying Items

Consider again the summing line items tests from Section 4.1 on p. 23, as shown in Figure 22.1.

fit.ActionFixture		
start	BuyActions	
check	total	00.00
enter	price	12.00
press	buy	
check	total	12.00
enter	price	100.00
press	buy	
check	total	112.00

Figure 22.1 Fit Table for Testing Line Items

When it runs this table, Fit creates an object of the `ActionFixture` class and calls its method `doTable()`, as shown in Figure 22.2. This method interprets the actions, working down each row of the table in turn.

- The *start* action in the second row of Figure 22.1 creates an object of the named class `BuyActions`, as shown in Figure 22.3. This is the *actor*; its class is shown in Listing 22.1. It starts the system under test, `LineItems`, as shown in Figure 22.4.

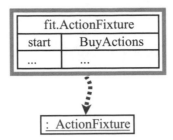

Figure 22.2 Fit Runs the Table

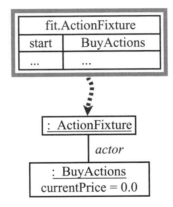

Figure 22.3 `ActionFixture` *starts* the *Actor*

Listing 22.1 BuyActions.java

```java
public class BuyActions extends fit.Fixture {
   private LineItems lineItems = new LineItems();
   private double currentPrice = 0.0;

   public void price(double currentPrice) {
      this.currentPrice = currentPrice;
   }
   public void buy() {
      lineItems.buyFor(currentPrice);
   }
   public double total() {
      return lineItems.totalIs();
   }
}
```

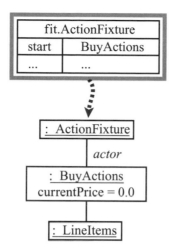

Figure 22.4 The *Actor* Calls the System Under Test

- The *check* (total) action in the third row calls the named method `total()` of the actor, which returns a `double`. This value matches the *expected* value, 0.00, in the third cell of the row, so it is marked with green.

- The *enter* (price) action in the fourth row calls the named method `price()` of the *actor*, passing to it the value 12.00 given in the third cell of the row. The value is used in the next action.

- The *press* (buy) action in the fifth row calls the named method `buy()` of the *actor*. This calls a method in the system under test, passing as a parameter the `price` that had just been *enter*ed.

- The *check* (total) action in the sixth row calls the named method `total()` of the *actor*. The returned value matches the *expected* value, 12.00, which is marked with green in the report, as shown in Figure 4.2 on p. 24.

- And so on.

Questions & Answers

What if the `price()` method returned a value?

It doesn't matter whether a method corresponding to a *press* returns a value; the value is ignored by `ActionFixture`.

22.2   Changing State of Chat Room

The chat room tests, from Section 4.2 on p. 26, are shown again in Figure 22.5.
The fixture code for this is shown in Listing 22.2.

fit.ActionFixture		
start	ChatServerActions	
enter	user	anna
press	connect	
enter	room	lotr
press	new room	
press	enter room	
enter	user	luke
press	connect	
press	enter room	
check	occupant count	2

Figure 22.5 Fit Table for Testing Chat Room Changes

Listing 22.2 **ChatServerActions.java**

```java
public class ChatServerActions extends fit.Fixture {
   private ChatRoom chat = new ChatRoom();
   private String userName = "";
   private String roomName = "";

   public void user(String userName) {
      this.userName = userName;
   }
   public void connect() {
      chat.connectUser(userName);
   }
   public void room(String roomName) {
      this.roomName = roomName;
   }
   public void newRoom() {
      chat.userCreatesRoom(userName, roomName);
   }
   public void enterRoom() {
      chat.userEntersRoom(userName,roomName);
   }
   public int occupantCount() {
      return chat.occupants(roomName);
   }
}
```

The operation of `ActionFixture` on this table is much the same as in the previous example. Each of the actions in the rows of the table is carried out in turn, starting with the second row.

- The *start* action in the second row of this table creates an object of the named class `ChatServerActions`. This is the *actor*, which in turn starts the system under test by creating a `ChatRoom` object, as shown in the code in Listing 22.2.

- The *enter* (user) action in the third row calls the named method `user()` of the *actor*, passing to it the `String` value anna given in the third cell. This sets up the fixture value in *userName* for the next action.

- The *press* (connect) action in the fourth row calls the named method `connect()` of the *actor*. This in turn calls the method `connect()` of the system under test, passing the current *userName* as parameter.

- The *enter* (room) action in the fifth row calls the named method `room()` of the *actor*, passing to it the value lotr given in the third cell. This sets up the fixture value in *roomName* for the following action.

- The *press* (new room) action in the sixth row calls the named method `newRoom()` of the *actor*. This in turn calls the method `userCreatesRoom()` in the system under test, passing the current *userName* and *roomName* as parameters. The method name in the table is in *camel casing* (see the Note), so *new room* is treated as the method name `newRoom()`.

- The *press* (enter room) action in the seventh row calls the named method `enterRoom()` of the *actor*. This in turn calls the method `enterRoom()` in the system under test, passing the current *userName* and *roomName* as parameters.

- And so on.

The final row of the table has the action *check*, which calls `occcupantCount()` of the *actor* and checks that the returned value is 2.

The actions *enter*, *press*, and *check* require that a `public` method with the right arguments and an appropriate return type exist in the *actor*.

Note

Camel casing, as introduced in the Note on 183, is used to remove spaces in the names in the *enter*, *press*, and *check* actions in `ActionFixture` tables in order to produce a valid Java identifier.

22.3   `ActionFixture` in General

For each row of the table, the text in the first cell is one of the following actions:

- `start`
    - Treat the text in the second cell as a class name.
    - Create an object of that class, called the *actor*, which is used in subsequent actions, until another `start`.
    - However, if the class does not exist or is not a subclass of `fit.Fixture`, throw an *exception*.

- `enter`
    - Take the text in the second cell as the name of a method, such as E.
    - Find the corresponding method in the current *actor* with one parameter, such as `public void E(T t)`.
    - Determine T, the type of the single parameter of method E.
    - Convert the text in the third cell into a value of type T.
    - Call the method E with that value.
    - However, if the method does not exist or cannot be called or the cell contents can't be converted to a value of type T, throw an exception.

- `press`
    - The text in the second cell names a method, such as P.
    - Find the corresponding method in the current *actor* with no parameter, such as `public void P()`.
    - Call the method P.
    - However, if the method does not exist or cannot be called, throw an exception.

- `check`
    - The text in the second cell names a method, such as C.
    - Find the corresponding method in the current *actor* with no parameter but that returns a value, such as `public T C()`.
    - Determine T, the return type of the *check* method.
    - Take the text in the third cell and convert it to an *expected* value of type T.
    - Call the method C and compare the result with the *expected* value. If it matches, mark the third cell with green. If not, mark that cell with red and the *actual* value returned by the method.
    - However, if the method does not exist or cannot be called or the result cell contents can't be converted to a value of type T, throw an exception.

- Otherwise, an exception is thrown.

ActionFixture Row:	*Corresponding Actor Method:*
enter │ E │ t	public void E(T t)
press │ P	public void P()
check │ C │ t	public T C()

Figure 22.6 Methods Corresponding to Each of the Actions

We summarize the way that actions are mapped to methods in the actor in Figure 22.6, in which the cells marked with t must contain a value of the type T for the corresponding actor method.

Questions & Answers

Why does the *actor* have to be a subclass of fit.Fixture?
As we'll see in Chapter 25, that's so that extra information can be given for parsing values of user-defined classes in table cells.

Why do you say "current" *actor*?
It's possible to dynamically switch the *actor* of an ActionFixture table.

What happens when the system under test uses a database?
As we'll see in Chapter 33, we have to either: (1) set the (test) database to a known state before running each test or (2) have the system under test not use the database during testing but something else. Either way, the system under test has to be configured with testing in mind. Luckily, that has other valuable consequences when we build systems with testing support right from the start. Again, this is an important topic that we will carefully take up later.

Won't the database slow down the tests?
Yes, that's why we avoid using a database during much of the testing. Yep, that sounds weird, but we hope to convince you otherwise—later, in Chapter 33.

22.4   Summary

- A fixture for an ActionFixture table uses an *actor* that is *start*ed as one of the actions of the table.

- The other actions that apply are *enter*, *press*, and *check*. These actions are mapped into corresponding methods in the *actor*.

Questions & Answers

Is Fit really relevant to programmers?
Yes, most definitely. We need a concrete way of discussing what's needed with the businesspeople. We need to write the fixtures. We need to know when we're done. And we need to know the detail of what's required.

For program-level tests that are inherently tabular, Fit tables may be more convenient than using a unit testing framework, such as JUnit. ColumnFixture and RowFixture tables are more likely to be useful for such tests than are ActionFixture tables.

How do you test through the GUI?
Avoid testing the application explicitly through the GUI. The GUI is likely to change more often than the application and so makes the tests vulnerable to change. Such tests tend to be more detailed as well. We'll say more about this in Chapter 32, when we show how a fixture may test through the GUI until the system under test has been changed to allow tests to be made directly.

So what do you test in the GUI?
You test that the GUI itself is acting appropriately; for example, that menu items are disabled and enabled correctly, that a button click acts on the currently selected item, and so on.

Can Fit be used for performance and stress testing?
Yes, certainly.

22.5   Exercises

1. For the ActionFixture tables that you created for exercise 3 in Chapter 4, write the corresponding fixture.

CHAPTER 23

List Fixtures

RowFixture tables test that the *expected* elements of a list match the *actual* list, or result of a query or search, in the application under test, regardless of order. A fixture of type RowFixture simply provides the appropriate list of elements from the system under test, as well as the type of those elements. This chapter shows the fixtures for the Fit tables introduced in Chapter 5.

23.1 Testing Unordered Lists

Let's now return to the chat room occupant test from Section 5.1 on p. 31, as shown again in Figure 23.1. This is a RowFixture table, with the header row labeling the fields that make up the elements of the list.

OccupantList	
user	*room*
anna	lotr
luke	lotr

Figure 23.1 Fit Table for Testing Occupants

The application has a list of rooms, each of which has a list of users occupying that room. The fixture code needs to collect the data from the system under test and create a local collection specifically for RowFixture to use in matching against the rows of the table. Figure 23.2 shows this, with the Room and User objects from the system under test at the bottom and the Occupancy objects created from them by the fixture to the right.

The fixture code is shown in Listing 23.1. As a subclass of fit.RowFixture, OccupantList defines the two methods query() and getTargetClass(). The method query() returns an array of elements of the actual collection; the method getTargetClass() returns the class of the elements of the array. The method query() of the fixture (line 4 in Listing 23.1) assembles the elements of the *actual* list from the List of Room supplied by the ChatServer, the system under test.

The appropriate data is assembled into an array of Occupancy in the query() method in Listing 23.1. As shown in Listing 23.2, the target class is Occupancy,

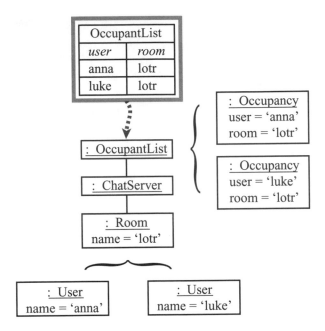

Figure 23.2 Fit Runs the Table

Listing 23.1 **OccupantList.java**

```
 1 public class OccupantList extends fit.RowFixture {
 2    private ChatServer chat = new ChatServer();
 3
 4    public Object[] query() throws Exception {
 5      List occupancies = new ArrayList();
 6      for (Iterator it = chat.getRooms(); it.hasNext(); ) {
 7        Room room = (Room)it.next();
 8        collectOccupants(occupancies, room);
 9      }
10      return occupancies.toArray();
11    }
12    public Class getTargetClass() {
13      return Occupancy.class;
14    }
15    private void collectOccupants(List occupancies, Room room) {
16      for (Iterator it = room.users(); it.hasNext(); ) {
17        User user = (User)it.next();
18        Occupancy occupant = new Occupancy(room.getName(),
19                                           user.getName());
20        occupancies.add(occupant);
21      }
22    }
23 }
```

which has `public` instance variables for `user` and `room`, corresponding to the labels in the header row in Figure 23.1.

Listing 23.2 Occupancy.java

```java
public class Occupancy {
  public String room, user;

  public Occupancy(String roomName, String userName) {
     this.room = roomName;
     this.user = userName;
  }
}
```

Inherited by `OccupantList`, the `doTable()` code in `fit.RowFixture` has four major steps to carry out:

1. Call the method `getTargetClass()` of the fixture to determine the class of the elements of the *actual* list (`Occupancy`)

2. Gather up the *expected* list from the table

3. Call the method `query()` of the fixture to gather up the *actual* list, which is assembled in this case with data from `Room` and `User` objects in the system under test

4. Compare the actual and expected lists and mark both the test rows green to show that the *actual* list matches the two *expected* elements

Questions & Answers

Can RowFixture test an array of int?
No, it can handle only an array of `Object`. The fixture could wrap up an array of `int` into an array of objects, where each object has a single `public` instance variable of type `int`. An easier alternative would be to handle it as a list of values in a single cell, as shown in Section 3.4 on p. 19.

Why does query() have throws Exception?
In general, the method in the `RowFixture` subclass may fail with an *exception* for some reason, such as when connecting to a database.

23.2   Testing Ordered Lists

We now look at the fixture for the discount group test from Section 5.2 on p. 34, as shown again in Figure 23.3. In this case, we make use of *order*, an extra column in the table.

DiscountGroupOrderedList				
order	future value	max owing	min purchase	discount percent
1	low	0.00	0.00	0
2	low	0.00	2000.00	3
3	medium	500.00	600.00	3
4	medium	0.00	500.00	5
5	high	2000.00	2000.00	10

Figure 23.3 RowFixture Table That Tests the Order Explicitly

The fixture class DiscountGroupOrderedList is shown in Listing 23.3. As a subclass of fit.RowFixture, this class defines the methods query() and getTargetClass().

Listing 23.3 DiscountGroupOrderedList.java

```
 1 public class DiscountGroupOrderedList extends fit.RowFixture {
 2    public Class getTargetClass() {
 3      return OrderedDiscountGroup.class;
 4    }
 5    public Object[] query() throws Exception {
 6      DiscountGroup[] groups = DiscountGroup.getElements();
 7      OrderedDiscountGroup[] ordered =
 8            new OrderedDiscountGroup[groups.length];
 9      for (int i = 0; i < groups.length; i++) {
10        DiscountGroup g = groups[i];
11        ordered[i] = new OrderedDiscountGroup(i+1,
12              g.getFutureValue(),g.getMaxOwing(),
13              g.getMinPurchase(),g.getDiscountPercent());
14      }
15      return ordered;
16    }
17 }
```

Method getTargetClass() of the fixture (line 2 in Listing 23.3) returns the class of the elements of the list, OrderedDiscountGroup. RowFixture uses the returned Class to check that instance variables correspond to each of the header labels in Figure 23.3.

The method query() of the fixture (line 5 in Listing 23.3) gets the elements of the *actual* list by calling a method in DiscountGroup. These elements are then mapped into elements of a temporary array of class OrderedDiscountGroup, with the order added, as shown in Listing 23.4.

Figure 23.4 shows some of the objects concerned when Fit runs this table. Inherited by DiscountGroupOrderedList, the doTable() method of RowFixture carries out four major steps:

1. Determines the class of the elements of the *actual* list (OrderedDiscountGroup) by calling the method getTargetClass() of the fixture.

Listing 23.4 OrderedDiscountGroup.java

```java
public class OrderedDiscountGroup {
  public int order;
  public double maxOwing, minPurchase;
  public String futureValue;
  public double discountPercent;

  public OrderedDiscountGroup(int order, String futureValue,
                   double maxOwing, double minPurchase,
                 double discountPercent) {
    this.futureValue = futureValue;
    this.order = order;
    this.maxOwing = maxOwing;
    this.minPurchase = minPurchase;
    this.discountPercent = discountPercent;
  }
}
```

DiscountGroupOrderedList				
order	*future value*	*max owing*	*min purchase*	*discount percent*
0	low	0.00	0.00	0
...	...	...	...	...

: OrderedDiscountGroup
order = 1
maxOwing = 0.00
minPurchase = 0.00
futureValue = 'low'
description = '...'
discountPercent = 0

: DiscountGroupOrderedList

: OrderedDiscountGroup
order = 5
maxOwing = 2000.00
minPurchase = 2000.00
futureValue = 'high'
description = '...'
discountPercent = 10

: DiscountGroup

Figure 23.4 Fit Runs the Table

2. Gathers up the *expected* list from the table, using the header row to determine the order of the *expected* fields in each element of the list.

3. Gathers up the *actual* list from the system under test by calling the method `query()` of the fixture.

4. Compares the actual and expected lists and marks the cells of report rows that match, those that don't quite match, *expected* rows that are *missing*, and *unexpected* rows that are *surplus*. Surplus rows are those that do not appear in the *actual* list.

Before it gathers up the *expected* elements from the table in Figure 23.3, `RowFixture` uses the five labels in the header row of the table. Each of these labels corresponds to an instance variable in `OrderedDiscountGroup`, the class returned by `getTargetClass()` of the fixture.

The first label is *order*, which corresponds to the `public` instance variable `order` in class `OrderedDiscountGroup`. This instance variable is an `int`, so `RowFixture` uses the text in the first cell of each of the *expected* rows as an `int`. The other columns correspond to instance variables of type `String` and `double`, so some of the element values in these columns need to be converted before the comparisons can be made.

To compare the *actual* and *expected* lists, `RowFixture` attempts to match each *expected* row against an *actual* row, based on the table labels. The fixture starts with the leftmost column of the table and works across the cells in the row as a match is made.

Questions & Answers

What if a table row is too short or too long?
An error is given if a row is too short. If it's too long, the extra cells are ignored.

Does the *future value* have to be a `String` in the system under test?
No. It could be stored as an `int` and converted to a `String` in the fixture to make the tests readable. It's much the same issue as with a user interface: presenting data clearly.

What if there are thousands of elements?
For most testing purposes, we'd try to keep the number of test cases down. Stress testing with large numbers is a different matter.

What if the order of the `DiscountGroups` didn't matter? Would we still have to make a copy of the elements with `OrderedDiscountGroup`?
Yes, we would with `RowFixture`, which requires access to `public` instance variables. As discussed in Section 28.3 on p. 232, however, a copy would not be needed with `SetFixture`, which handles property getter methods as well as `public` instance variables.

23.3   Testing a List with Parameters

Let's now return to the example from Section 5.1 on p. 31 of testing the occupants of a specific chat room, as shown again in Figure 23.5. This is a `RowFixture` table, with the parameter *lotr* provided in the first row.

OccupantListInRoom	lotr
user	
anna	
luke	

Figure 23.5 Table for Testing the Occupants of a Selected Room

The fixture code for this is shown in Listing 23.5. The parameters provided in the first row of any table, after the fixture name, are accessed in the fixture code through the instance variable `args`, which is a `String[]`. The crucial difference from the code shown in Listing 23.1 is that here, the `query()` method uses `args[0]` to select a single room by name. Note that we use the Occupancy, from Listing 23.2, again in Listing 23.5, even though the *room* is irrelevant here.

Listing 23.5 OccupantListInRoom.java

```java
public class OccupantListInRoom extends fit.RowFixture {
  private ChatServer chat = new ChatServer();

  public Object[] query() throws Exception {
    List occupancies = new ArrayList();
    collectOccupants(occupancies,chat.room(args[0]));
    return occupancies.toArray();
  }
  public Class getTargotClass() {
    return Occupancy.class;
  }
  private void collectOccupants(List occupancies, Room room) {
    for (Iterator it = room.users(); it.hasNext(); ) {
      User user = (User)it.next();
      Occupancy occupant = new Occupancy(room.getName(),
                                         user.getName());
      occupancies.add(occupant);
    }
  }
}
```

23.4   Summary

- We have explored the use of `RowFixture` for testing lists, both ordered and unordered.

- A fixture for a table of type `RowFixture` is a `fit.RowFixture` subclass that provides the *actual* list of elements from the system under test, along with the class of those elements.

- `RowFixture` compares the *expected* and *actual* elements and reports on those *expected* elements that partially match, those that are *missing* from the *actual* list, and those elements that are *surplus*, or not expected.

- The *actual* list may need to be assembled from objects from the system under test.

Questions & Answers

What would happen if the *future value* of the first row of Figure 23.3 were changed from *low* to *slow*?
When it attempts to match that row against an *actual* element, `RowFixture` starts from the leftmost column and works to the right. Because that *futureValue* doesn't match any element, the row is treated as "missing." The corresponding *actual* element is then marked as "surplus" in the report.

Why can't the element type be worked out automatically by the fixture?
It could be, although there may not be a common superclass of all those objects. But a fixture like `RowFixture` could process each of the elements individually.

What if the elements don't share a superclass?
In that case, the actual common superclass is `Object`, which has no instance variables. One approach would be to use separate tables, each with its own fixture; each fixture would have to filter out the elements of the right class to assemble a suitable array for the table concerned.

    Another approach is for a fixture to handle the differences between objects in the actual collection and expect that a cell is empty if there is no corresponding instance variable. This approach is taken with `ArrayFixture` and related FitLibrary fixtures, as we see in Section 28.9 on p. 243.

23.5   Exercises

1. Write fixture classes for the tables you created in exercises 3 and 6 in Chapter 5.

CHAPTER 24

Fixtures for Sequences of Tables

As we saw in Chapter 6, a single Fit table may not be sufficient to define a test, and we often need to use several types of table. Usually, `ActionFixture` tables have side effects on the system under test, so the underlying fixtures for the tables in a workflow test need to be organized so that they all access the same system under test.

In this chapter, we show, step by step, how fixture objects are created. We show several ways in which the fixtures underlying the tables of a single test can be coordinated.

24.1 Chat Room Fixtures

We now look at the fixtures underlying the tables in Section 6.1 on p. 39. These fixtures are similar to the ones given in Section 22.2 on p. 190 and Section 23.1 on p. 195, except that they are organized to reference the same system under test.

It is useful to understand the steps that are carried out when a sequence of tables is used. We look at the first six tables of the second example test in Section 6.1, shown again in Figure 24.1.

When it is run by Fit, the first Fit table in Figure 24.1 creates an `ActionFixture` object, shown as af1 to the left in Figure 24.2. The first action of the first table is a *start*, which creates the *actor*, shown as the `ChatServer2` object in Figure 24.2.

Class `ChatServer2` is shown in Listing 24.1.[1] Its constructor is called when the *actor* object is created, which in turn creates the system under test—an object of class `ChatRoom`—as shown at the bottom of Figure 24.2.

---

[1] This is almost the same as `ChatServer` in Section 22.2 on p. 190 but accesses the system under test through a `static` variable.

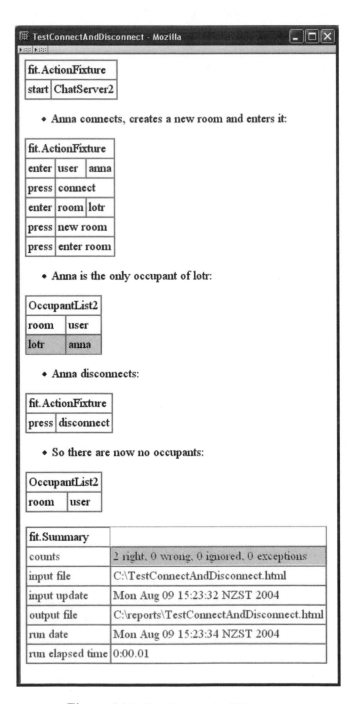

Figure 24.1 TestConnectAndDisconnect

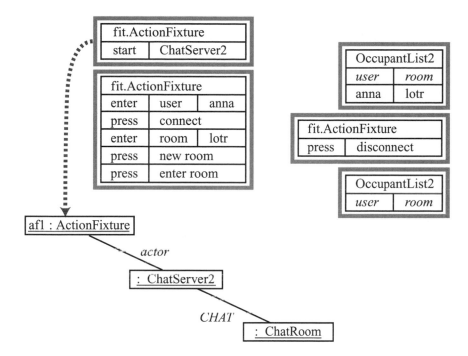

Figure 24.2 Fit Runs the First Table

The constructor of **ChatServer2** saves a reference to the system under test in the **static** variable CHAT. Subsequent actions through the fixture **ChatServer2**, in tables 2 and 4, both act through this **static** variable (from af2 and af3) on the single system under test,[2] as shown in Figure 24.3.

When it runs the third table in Figure 24.1, Fit creates ol1, a fixture object of class **OccupantList2**, as shown under the third table in Figure 24.3. This object checks that the rows in the table match the elements in the collection supplied by the **RowFixture** fixture class **OccupantList2**. The object accesses the system under test via the **public** static variable CHAT of class **ChatServer2**. Much the same happens when Fit runs the fifth table, as shown in Figure 24.3.

---

[2] That's why it's important that only the first **ActionFixture** table in this sequence has a *start* action.

Listing 24.1 **ChatServer2.java**

```java
public class ChatServer2 extends fit.Fixture {
  public static chat.ChatRoom CHAT;
  private String userName = "";
  private String roomName = "";

  public ChatServer2() {
    CHAT = new ChatRoom();
  }
  public void user(String userName) {
    this.userName = userName;
  }
  public void connect() {
    CHAT.connectUser(userName);
  }
  public void room(String roomName) {
    this.roomName = roomName;
  }
  public void newRoom() {
    roomCreatedOK = CHAT.userCreatesRoom(userName, roomName);
  }
  public void enterRoom() {
    roomEnteredOK = CHAT.userEntersRoom(userName,roomName);
  }
  public int occupantCount() {
    return CHAT.occupants(roomName);
  }
  public void disconnect() {
    CHAT.disconnectUser(userName);
  }
}
```

The code for OccupantList2, shown in Listing 24.2, provides a collection of class Occupancy2, as shown in Listing 24.3. The collection comes from the current system under test, which is accessed through the **static** variable CHAT of class ChatServer2.[3]

Questions & Answers

What happens if the first table of Figure 24.1 is removed?
An exception will be thrown because the system under test hasn't been started. This is a minor weakness of the preceding approach. We'll see a better way in the next example.

---

[3] Otherwise, OccupancyList2 is the same as OccupancyList in Section 23.1 on p. 195.

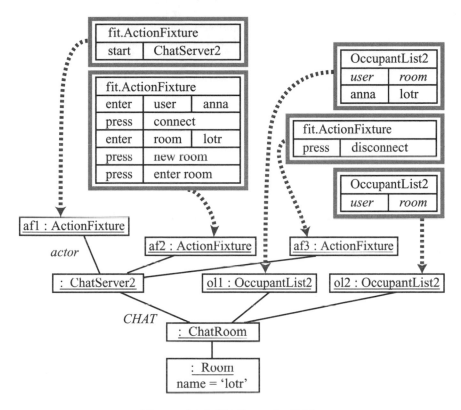

Figure 24.3 Fit Runs the Tables

Note

A **static** variable of a class is shared by all instances—objects—of that class. The variable can be accessed directly in any of the code of the class. If the variable is **public**, it can also be accessed from outside the class. For example, class **OccupantList2** in Listing 24.2 accesses the **static** variable CHAT in class **ChatServer2** through the expression **ChatServer2.CHAT**.

Listing 24.2 **OccupantList2.java**

```
public class OccupantList2 extends fit.RowFixture {
  public Object[] query() throws Exception {
    List occupancies = new ArrayList();
    for (Iterator it = ChatServer2.CHAT.getRooms();
                    it.hasNext(); ) {
      Room room = (Room)it.next();
      collectOccupants(occupancies,room);
    }
    return occupancies.toArray();
  }
  public Class getTargetClass() {
    return Occupancy2.class;
  }
  private void collectOccupants(List occupancies, Room room) {
    for (Iterator it = room.users(); it.hasNext(); ) {
      User user = (User)it.next();
      Occupancy2 occupant = new Occupancy2(room.getName(),
                                           user.getName());
      occupancies.add(occupant);
    }
  }
}
```

Listing 24.3 **Occupancy2.java**

```
public class Occupancy2 {
  public String room, user;

  public Occupancy2(String room, String user) {
    this.room = room;
    this.user = user;
  }
}
```

24.2   Discount Group Fixtures

We now look at the fixtures underlying the tables in Section 6.2 on p. 43. Figure 24.4 shows the tables and objects. The example test is shown again in Figure 24.5.

Listing 24.4 shows the fixture code for the first table of Figure 24.5. The code makes use of a **static** variable **APP** so that the fixture objects for each of the tables can access the same system under test. Whenever the system under test is needed

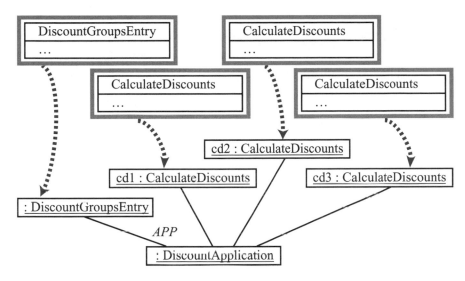

Figure 24.4 Fit Runs the TestDiscountGroup Tables

in the fixture, a call is made to the **static** method **getApp()**, which returns the **DiscountApplication** object, which is created once, when it is first needed.

The method **add()** of class **DiscountGroupsEntry**, as shown in Listing 24.4, is called in turn for each row of the first table. The code simply simply calls the **addDiscountGroup()** method of the system under test and returns **true** to show that the addition was successful.

Listing 24.5 shows the fixture code for the other tables. This fixture class accesses the system under test through the **static** variable of class **SetDiscountGroups**.

Questions & Answers

Could **DiscountGroupsEntry** and **CalculateDiscounts** be combined?
Yes, into a single class in this case, given that they're both **ColumnFixtures**. It's still necessary to use a **static** variable, because a fixture object is created for each table.

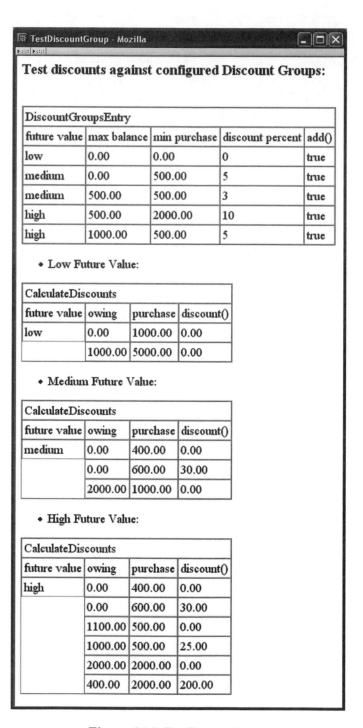

Test discounts against configured Discount Groups:

DiscountGroupsEntry				
future value	max balance	min purchase	discount percent	add()
low	0.00	0.00	0	true
medium	0.00	500.00	5	true
medium	500.00	500.00	3	true
high	500.00	2000.00	10	true
high	1000.00	500.00	5	true

- Low Future Value:

CalculateDiscounts			
future value	owing	purchase	discount()
low	0.00	1000.00	0.00
	1000.00	5000.00	0.00

- Medium Future Value:

CalculateDiscounts			
future value	owing	purchase	discount()
medium	0.00	400.00	0.00
	0.00	600.00	30.00
	2000.00	1000.00	0.00

- High Future Value:

CalculateDiscounts			
future value	owing	purchase	discount()
high	0.00	400.00	0.00
	0.00	600.00	30.00
	1100.00	500.00	0.00
	1000.00	500.00	25.00
	2000.00	2000.00	0.00
	400.00	2000.00	200.00

Figure 24.5 TestDiscountGroup

Listing 24.4 DiscountGroupsEntry.java

```java
public class DiscountGroupsEntry extends fit.ColumnFixture {
  public double maxBalance, minPurchase;
  public String futureValue, description = "";
  public double discountPercent;

  private static DiscountApplication APP;

  public boolean add() {
    getApp().addDiscountGroup(futureValue,maxBalance,
                      minPurchase,discountPercent);
    return true;
  }
  public static DiscountApplication getApp() {
    if (APP == null)
      APP = new DiscountApplication();
    return APP;
  }
}
```

Listing 24.5 CalculateDiscounts.java

```java
public class CalculateDiscounts extends fit.ColumnFixture {
  public String futureValue;
  public double owing, purchase;

  public double discount() {
    return DiscountGroupsEntry.getApp().discount(
              futureValue,owing,purchase);
  }
}
```

24.3 Summary

- Several types of tables are often needed in a sequence to define a single test.

- When a sequence of tables together make up a single test, they need to all access the same system under test.

- Because a new fixture object is created for each table, we make use of `static` variables to provide the interconnection.

- The first table in the sequence needs to be responsible for creating the system under test.

24.4   Exercises

1. Update the fixture `ChatServer2` to handle the new *press* action introduced in exercise 3 of Chapter 6.

2. Combine the two fixtures in Section 24.2 into a single class.

CHAPTER 25

Using Other Values in Tables

Until now, we have taken for granted that Fit will handle the values that we use in table cells. However, Fit handles only some of the standard Java types, including the ones that we have been using so far, such as `String`, `int`, and `double`. Now it's time to see how to use other values in tables with Fit fixtures.

We begin with a brief discussion of how Fit handles the standard types with `TypeAdapters`. We then look at how fixtures can handle other value types in tables. We illustrate with an example that uses `Money` values.

25.1 Standard Values

When it interprets a table, a Fit fixture checks the types of the instance variables and methods involved, using reflection. For example, for each label in a header row, `ColumnFixture` checks in the fixture object for the corresponding variable or method.

For each `public` instance variable, method parameter, and method return value that's used in a table, Fit creates an appropriately typed `TypeAdaptor` object. For a `public` instance variable, a `TypeAdapter` is first passed an object from which it accesses the appropriate `public` instance variable; that object is a fixture object for `ColumnFixture` and any object, in an array, for `RowFixture`.

A `TypeAdapter` object is able to

- Accept a textual version of the *expected* value, such as 2.3, and convert it to a value of the underlying type. This is used

    - To assign a value to an instance variable by a `ColumnFixture`

    - To compare it with an *actual* value by many of the fixtures

    - As a method parameter, with an *enter* by an `ActionFixture`

- Take the *actual* value from an instance variable or method call of a given object and compare it to the *expected* value. This is used when checking the value of

    - A *calculated* field by a `ColumnFixture`

- An instance variable or method call by a `RowFixture`

- A method call with a *check* by an `ActionFixture`

• Produce a textual version of a value, to be used in reporting differences between *expected* and *actual* values.

Fit has `TypeAdapter`s for all the primitive Java types and their corresponding wrapper classes, such as class `Double` for a `double`, so that these can all be used as values in tables. There are also `TypeAdapter`s for the classes `String`, `Date`, and `ScientificDouble`[1] and for arrays of any of these classes or of the primitive types. An array value is a comma-separated list of values, such as 1, 2, 3, as shown in Section 3.4 on p. 19.

That's all we need to know about `TypeAdapter`s for this chapter. Some of the other functionality of `TypeAdapter` is covered in Section 37.6 on p. 311.

25.2   Values of Money

We will now look in detail at how values of `Money` can be used in Fit tables. In the process, we will show how the fixture needs to deal with the conversion and comparison issues as discussed in the previous section. Specifically, we need to specify how `String` values will be converted to objects of that type, and vice versa, and how two values of that type will be checked to see whether they are equal.

Consider the altered discount tests shown in Figure 25.1. Here, we require that the money values be shown with a leading $ and exactly two decimal places of precision.

CalculateDiscountMoney	
amount	*discount()*
$999.99	$0.00
$1000.00	$0.00
$1000.01	$50.00
$1001.33	$50.07
$1010.00	$50.50
$1100.00	$55.00
$1200.00	$60.00
$2000.00	$100.00

Figure 25.1 Revised Table for Testing Discount

---

[1] A `Number` class that is provided with Fit.

The fixture code for this is the class **TestDiscount**, as shown in Listing 25.1. The **public** instance variable **amount** is of type **Money**, which Fit does not handle automatically.

To handle conversion from the textual form of the value to a corresponding object—here, of **Money**—the fixture defines the method **parse()**. This method overrides the default method in class **Fixture** to specify how to convert a textual value, from a table cell, into an object of the right class. This method is called whenever a **TypeAdapter** is needed by a fixture, such as when a **ColumnFixture** is processing the labels in the header of the table.

The **parse()** method in class **TestDiscount**, as shown in Listing 25.1, checks whether the type is **Money**. If so, the method calls the **static** method **parse()** of class **Money**. Otherwise, the superclass method is called to handle it.

Listing 25.1 TestDiscount.java

```java
public class TestDiscount extends fit.ColumnFixture {
    public Money amount;
    private Discount application = new Discount();

    public Money discount() {
        return application.discount(amount);
    }

    public Object parse(String s, Class type) throws Exception {
        if (type == Money.class)
            return Money.parse(s);
        return super.parse(s, type);
    }
}
```

As Fit needs to report unexpected values, a **String** value from our **Money** object is needed. The standard method **toString()**, as defined in class **Object**, is used for this purpose.

As Fit fixtures need to make comparisons, we need a way to test whether the expected and actual values, or objects, are the same. Fit relies on the standard method **equals()** to do this.

The relevant part of our application class **Money** is shown in Listing 25.2. The **static** method **parse()** takes a **String** and converts it to an object of **Money**. The method **toString()** provides a **String** value. The **equals()** method checks whether two **Money** objects are the same; it is called by Fit with the *expected* and *actual* values after they have been converted to objects.

Listing 25.2 Money.java

```java
public class Money {
  private long cents;

  public Money(long cents) {
    this.cents = cents;
  }
  public boolean equals(Object other) {
    return other instanceof Money &&
       ((Money)other).cents == cents;
  }
  public int hashCode() {
    return (int)cents;
  }
  public String toString() {
    String centString = ""+cents%100;
    if (centString.length() == 1)
      centString += "0";
    return "$"+cents/100+"."+centString;
  }
  public static Money parse(String s) {
    if (s.charAt(0) != '$')
      throw new RuntimeException("Invalid money");
    int dot = s.indexOf(".");
    if (dot < 0 || dot != s.length() - 3)
      throw new RuntimeException("Invalid money");
    String scent = s.substring(1);
    double amount = Double.valueOf(scent).doubleValue()*100;
    return new Money((long)amount);
  }
  // ...
}
```

Questions & Answers

Where does `parse()` go with an `ActionFixture`?
It goes in the *actor* class. That's why *actor*s have to be `Fixture`s.

What about with standard Java classes, such as `Point`?
The same approach applies; you override the `parse()` of the fixture concerned
to specify the text-to-object conversion. An example of formatting `Date` in a
specialized way is provided in Section 34.4 on p. 292.

It's likely that the class will have suitable `toString()` and `equals()` methods.
If not, you'd need to wrap them up in another object that provides the behavior
you require. This is a way, for example, to make comparisons case insensitive.

What if many fixtures need to use our own classes? Won't there be lots of duplication?

In that case, use the subclassing approach to eliminate unnecessary duplication. Define your own `ColumnFixture` and `RowFixture` subclasses that include the needed `parse()` method. Then create subclasses of those classes for your specific fixtures.

For `ActionFixture`, define your own subclass of `Fixture` with the needed `parse()` method, and make all your *actor* classes subclass that class.

Isn't there a better way?
See the next section.

25.3   Values in FitNesse and the Flow Fixtures

The FitNesse version of Fit checks whether the class of the value concerned has a `static` method `parse()` that takes a `String` and returns an object of that class. Fit uses this method if it exists.

In that case, because class `Money` has the appropriate `parse()` method, the `parse()` method in Listing 25.1 is not needed. This approach is also used with the FitLibrary fixtures, as discussed in Section 28.11 on p. 245.

25.4   Summary

Other values may be used in Fit tables, but we need to provide the following extra information about the associated class:

- How to convert from a `String` to an object of the given class. This conversion is defined by the `parse()` method in the fixture. The method will usually pass control to a `static` method of the class, such as `parse()` in `Money`.

- How to create a `String` from an object of our class. This operation is defined by the `toString()` of the class.

- How to compare two objects of our class for equality. This operation is defined by the `equals()` of the class.

25.5   Exercises

1. Design a Fit test that makes use of a `Point` value in table cells, such as (100,200).

2. Implement the fixture for this table, overriding the `parse()` method to handle the conversion of a `String` to a `Point` object.

3. Decide whether the `Point` class defines a suitable `toString()` method.

4. If not, you'll need to introduce an intermediate (adapter) class to manage the conversion of a `Point` to a `String`.

5. In your application, now choose a class that has specialized values that would be handy to use in the cells of Fit tests. Carry out the preceding steps for your class.

CHAPTER 26

Installing and Running Fit

As we saw in Chapter 7, Fit can run tests and suites of tests created in an Excel spreadsheet or in HTML. In this chapter, we briefly cover the installation of Fit and show how to make it easy for nonprogrammers to edit, organize, and run their tests.

26.1 Installing Fit and FitLibrary

Download Fit For Java from http://fit.c2.com. Unzip the Fit zip file; inside the *Release* folder is the latest JAR (Java Archive) file, `fit.jar`. Download `FitLibrary.jar` from http://sourceforge.net/projects/fitlibrary.

26.2 Running Fit on Folders

The simplest approach to running Fit on the .XLS and .HTML files in a folder is to use the following command in that folder[1]:

```
java -cp javafit1.1.jar fitlibrary.jar;poi.jar;code
fit.runner.FolderRunner
```

This example command assumes that the JAR files are in the current folder and that the code for all the fixtures and the system under test are in the `code` folder. The `FolderRunner` runs Fit over all .XLS and .HTML files in the folder, and all subfolders, producing a test suite report in the file `reportIndex.html`.

To specify other folder locations for the test files and for where the reports are to be written, include the two file names in the command:

```
java -cp javafit1.1.jar fitlibrary.jar;poi.jar;code
fit.runner.FolderRunner Tests Reports
```

---

[1] This may change, so see the FitLibrary documentation.

As it runs the tests in a folder, `FolderRunner` looks for `SetUp.xls` and then `SetUp.html` files in that folder, in that order, to prepend to the start of each test file. Likewise, `FolderRunner` looks for `TearDown.xls` and then `TearDown.html` files in that folder, in that order, to append to the end of each test file.

> **Note**
>
> `FolderRunner` depends on `Poi`, an open source system for reading and writing Excel files. Poi is available from jakarta.apache.org/poi.
>   As `Poi` is still under development, you may find that it cannot read some Excel files.

26.3   Running Fit on HTML Files

You can instead use `FileRunner` to run Fit on a single HTML file. For example, here's a command to run the tests within a file `Test.html` to produce a report in `Report.html`:

```
java -classpath fit.jar;. fit.FileRunner Test.html Report.html
```

The `eg.AllFiles` fixture provides another way to run selected HTML test files. For example, it may be useful to run some tests to quickly check that nothing major has been broken after a change has been made to the system under test. See the Fit Web site for details.

26.4   Running Tests During the Build

In order to test as a part of the build cycle, use Ant to run all the tests in your test suite after compiling the code. Details of Ant tasks to do this are available on the Fit Web site.

26.5   Other Ways to Run Tests

Following are other approaches to running Fit tables.

- FitNesse, as introduced in Chapter 8, with technical information provided in Chapter 27.
- When testing a Web server, it can be convenient to include extra servlets, or java ServerPages (JSPs), that run the tests on the server itself and provide the Fit report as a result.

- Ward's Wiki Runner. See the Fit Web site at http://fit.c2.com for details of wiki tables and Wiki Runner. See [LC01] for details of wiki.

- Using other test formats. Other test formats can be converted into HTML first or directly into the internal format, **Parse**. We leave the details of the latter for programmers until Chapter 39.

26.6 Summary

- Running Fit depends on the input format, HTML or XLS, and whether a test suite is being used.

- Running the tests can be incorporated into the regular build.

- Other input formats are possible, as discussed in Chapter 39.

CHAPTER 27

Installing FitNesse

As we saw in Chapter 8, FitNesse is a wiki-based system for creating, organizing, and running Fit tests. FitNesse is based on a Web server, making it easy to share Fit test tables among many people working on a project. FitNesse converts the page into HTML before passing it to Fit for running and displays the report generated by Fit through the browser.

In this chapter, we discuss how to install FitNesse and support nonprogrammers. We show how to use virtual wiki pages with FitNesse to allow developers to access Fit tables from a shared server and test them against code on their own machines.

27.1 Installation

Here are brief technical details.

- You need Java system 1.4.0 or higher to run FitNesse, even if you plan to run your tests with a different programming language.

- Go to www.fitnesse.org to download the system as a zip file.

- Unzip the file and double-click `run.bat`—or `run.sh` if you're on Linux or Unix—in the main folder of the FitNesse system to run it on your machine.

- FitNesse runs as a server that can be accessed through a browser at the URL http://localhost: a standard HTTP port on your own machine.

- You may choose to run FitNesse on another port.

- You can decide whether to require login to FitNesse. See the online manual that's included with FitNesse for details.

27.2 Locating the Code

In order for FitNesse to run tests from your pages, you need to specify the location of the code for the fixtures and for the system under test. You do this with `path` commands of the following form, which specify the location of Java class files and JAR files:

```
!path Examples/EquipmentRental/build
!path c:\lib\junit.jar
```

To allow several projects to coexist in a FitNesse wiki, different paths may be provided in different subwikis. Simply add your specific paths to a page within your subwiki. Before running a test on a page, FitNesse looks for paths up the page hierarchy and accumulates all the paths it finds.

27.3   Larger-Scale Use with Virtual Wiki

FitNesse pages are available through the Web, providing easy access to the tests by all developers on a project. Multiple developers can work in parallel, each running the Fit tests from a common FitNesse server against the code that's being developed on their own machines.

Each developer runs a FitNesse system on his or her own machine and refers to subwikis on the FitNesse server running on a common machine. This allows the developers to define their own paths to access the code they are working on. Changes to those tests can be made by anyone with appropriate access rights to the tables on a single server; the tests are automatically available to all developers through the virtual wiki. (This is analogous to file sharing across the network.)

A virtual wiki link from a page on the local machine is made by clicking the *Properties* button for that page and entering a suitable URL in the *VirtualWiki URL* field. Thereafter, accesses to that local page reference the corresponding subwiki on the common machine. To see what pages are available from the virtual wiki, you will need to put !contents on the local page that refers to the page on the server.

27.4   Debugging FitNesse Tests

Given that FitNesse runs as a Web server, it is not so easy to debug fixtures. The simplest, most direct approach is to display diagnostics with System.out.println(). These diagnostics can be accessed through a link at the bottom of the report page that's generated when the test is run.

If you need to run a debugger, use Fit directly. To use Fit with a FitNesse page, take the source of the HTML that FitNesse generates for the browser. Discard the extra level of table that's used to organize the whole page, and use what remains with Fit.

If the test tables have identified some problems within the application, it will be simpler to use JUnit to help track down the problem. You can use a debugger with that. And this will encourage you to create suitable JUnit tests into the heart of the application.

Questions & Answers

When should we use Fit tables and when JUnit tests?
Usually, Fit tables are used for testing the business rules and the use of the system. Ideally, someone who knows what's needed, such as a business analyst, writes these tests, in collaboration with testers and other developers. Usually, JUnit tests are written by developers and testers to test and to drive the development of the inner parts of the software.

Sometimes, each may be used in the other role. For example, Fit tables may be used for programmer testing when the amount of tabular test data is easier to manage in Fit tables than by using JUnit.

Are there any differences in the way Fit and FitNesse handle tests?
There are some small differences; tables are written in a different way in FitNesse, which converts a wiki page into HTML before running Fit. FitNesse passes on to Fit any HTML that you put in table cells, such as <BR>; this can be used to better format the report or to signify line breaks to the fixture, for example.

Is there a way to have FitNesse run Fit tests automatically as a part of a build?
Yes. See the FitNesse manual for details.

27.5 Summary

- FitNesse provides a wiki-based environment for creating and running Fit tables.

- Several developers can share tests from a common FitNesse server and also run those tests against the code that they have under development.

FitNesse continues to evolve, so check its Web site at www.fitnesse.org for the latest. For help with FitNesse, and information about further developments, join the FitNesse yahoo newsgroup at www.yahoo.com, or send e-mail to the developers (see Section 8.1 on p. 57).

27.6 Exercises

Nonprogrammers may need your help in getting started with FitNesse. They may also need your advice about using test suites and other FitNesse features.

1. Install FitNesse on your machine and carry out some of the exercises from
    Chapter 8.

2. Enter one of the early example test tables into FitNesse, such as `TestDiscount`,
    as discussed in Section 3.1 on p. 13. Enter the `path` to refer to the associated
    fixture code, downloaded as cited in Appendix B. Run the test.

3. Install and run FitNesse on a central server. Enter test pages on that server.
    Now run FitNesse on your local machine to access pages off the server through
    virtual wiki. Define appropriate paths to your fixture and application code on
    your own machine.

CHAPTER 28

FitLibrary Fixtures

As we saw in Chapter 10, if the first table of a sequence is a DoFixture, subsequent tables with actions don't need to include a fixture name. We also introduced several new fixtures for testing lists, as well as CalculateFixture and SetUpFixture, new fixtures for testing calculations and for handling setup respectively. In this chapter, we cover writing fixtures for the examples in Chapter 10 and explain the operation of the FitLibrary fixtures.

28.1   Flow-Style Actions with DoFixture

The first test for the chat server from Section 10.1 on p. 71 is shown again in Figure 28.1. Fit interprets the sequence of tables in the following steps.

1. For the first table a fixture object of class ChatStart is created, as usual. This class is shown in Listing 28.1. As this class is a DoFixture, this first fixture object is involved in the interpretation of the rest of the tables in the file or page. We call this fixture object the *flow fixture object*.

2. The action in the second table results in a call to the method connectUser() of the flow fixture object. This in turn calls a method in the system under test. As the method returns true, the action is colored green.

3. The action in the third table results in a call to the method userCreatesRoom() of the flow fixture object.

4. The action in the fourth table results in a call to the method userEntersRoom() of the flow fixture object.

5. The first action in the fifth table, *users in room* results in a call to the method usersInRoom() of the flow fixture object. This returns a Fixture, a RowFixture, that Fit uses to interpret the rest of the table. This is discussed in more detail later in this chapter.

6. The action in the sixth table results in a call to the method disconnectUser() of the flow fixture object. As this returns true, the action is colored green.

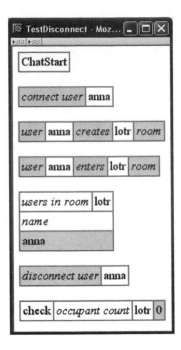

Figure 28.1 TestDisconnect

7. The action in the final table results in a call to the method `occupantCount()` of the flow fixture object, with the argument lotr. The result of this call is then checked against the expected value, 0, in the last cell of the row. As this value is correct, the cell containing the expected value is colored green.

As we've seen, the method `usersInRoom()` in Listing 28.1 returns a `Fixture`, which Fit then uses to interpret the rest of that table. Because it is called in the flow fixture object, this method has access to `ChatRoom`, the system under test, as an instance variable,[1] as well as the parameter, `roomName`. Together, these are used to create a copy of the users for `RowFixture` to use through the class `ParamRowFixture`. The copy is made to provide `name` as a `public` instance variable so that `RowFixture` can access it.

The class `UserCopy` is shown in Listing 28.2. This class simply makes the user `name` available to `RowFixture` as a `public` instance variable, which is not the case in the class `User` in the system under test.

The class `ParamRowFixture` is shown in Listing 28.3. This class simply stores the target class and collection and provides them through the two methods required by `RowFixture`.

---

[1] So the flow fixture object avoids the need to use `public` `static` variables as global variables to share access to the system under test among fixture objects.

Listing 28.1 **ChatStart.java**

```java
public class ChatStart extends DoFixture {
   private ChatRoom chat = new ChatRoom();

   public boolean connectUser(String userName) {
      return chat.connectUser(userName);
   }
   public boolean userCreatesRoom(String userName, String roomName) {
      return chat.userCreatesRoom(userName,roomName);
   }
   public boolean userEntersRoom(String userName, String roomName) {
      return chat.userEntersRoom(userName,roomName);
   }
   public Fixture usersInRoom(String roomName) {
      Set users = chat.usersInRoom(roomName);
      Object[] collection = new Object[users.size()];
      int i = 0;
      for (Iterator it = users.iterator(); it.hasNext(); ) {
         User user = (User)it.next();
         collection[i++] = new UserCopy(user.getName());
      }
      return new ParamRowFixture(collection,UserCopy.class);
   }
   public boolean disconnectUser(String userName) {
      return chat.disconnectUser(userName);
   }
   public int occupantCount(String roomName) {
      return chat.occupants(roomName);
   }
}
```

Listing 28.2 **UserCopy.java**

```java
public class UserCopy {
   public String name;

   public UserCopy(String name) {
      this.name = name;
   }
}
```

Listing 28.3 **ParamRowFixture.java**

```java
public class ParamRowFixture extends fit.RowFixture {
   private Object[] collection;
   private Class targetClass;

   public ParamRowFixture(Object[] collection, Class targetClass) {
      this.collection = collection;
      this.targetClass = targetClass;
   }
   public Object[] query() throws Exception {
      return collection;
   }
   public Class getTargetClass() {
      return targetClass;
   }
}
```

Questions & Answers

Is there a way to avoid having to copy the User data into UserCopy?
Yes, if **name** was made a **public** instance variable in the class **User**, it wouldn't be necessary to make a copy. Instead, the collection of users returned from chat.usersInRoom() could be passed directly to the **ParamRowFixture** in the method usersInRoom() in Listing 28.1. We can avoid copying such data with SetFixture, a new fixture, because it also handles properties, as we discuss in Section 28.2.

The interaction of the fixtures and the first five tables is illustrated in Figure 28.2. Fit creates the object of class **ChatStart** for the first table. As this is a **DoFixture** object, it interprets subsequent tables as the flow fixture object. The second table contains a single row, which is an action, so the method connectUser() is called in the flow fixture object.

The actions in the third and fourth tables are treated in the same way. The method for the action in the first row of the fifth table returns a fixture, which interprets the rest of the table. The **ParamRowFixture** object refers to an actual collection with a single element in it, the **UserCopy** for anna.

In the next two sections, we progress through several reductions of the **ChatStart** code, making use of the automatic capabilities of **DoFixture**.

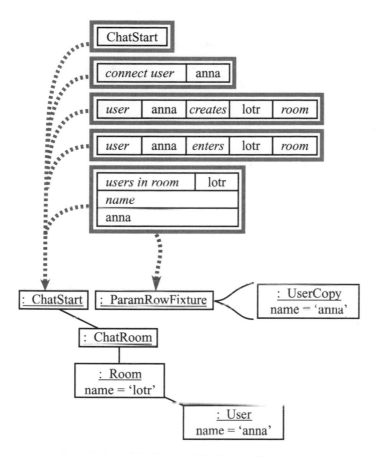

Figure 28.2 Fit Runs the First Five TestDisconnect Tables

28.2   DoFixtures as Adapters

Note that many of the methods in ChatStart in Listing 28.1 simply call a method of the same name and with the same arguments in the system under test. With DoFixture, such adapter methods can be removed.

In the revised class ChatStart, as shown in Listing 28.4, we have eliminated many of the methods.[2] The constructor calls the superclass method setSystemUnderTest(), passing a reference to the system under test. When the picture has no method that corresponds to an action in a table, the fixture calls the corresponding method in the specified system under test directly.

For example, the action in the second table of Figure 28.1 is mapped to the method connectUser(). As this method is not defined in the ChatStart flow fixture object, the method connectUser() in the system under test is called instead. On

---

[2] The changed method usersInRoom() is discussed in the next section.

Listing 28.4 **ChatStart.java (version 2)**

```java
public class ChatStart extends DoFixture {
  private ChatRoom chat = new ChatRoom();

  public ChatStart() {
      setSystemUnderTest(chat);
  }
  public int occupantCount(String roomName) {
    return chat.occupants(roomName);
  }
  public SetFixture usersInRoom(String roomName) {
    return new SetFixture(chat.usersInRoom(roomName));
  }
}
```

the other hand the fixture method `occupantCount()` for the action in the last table is still needed, as it calls a method of a different name in the system under test.

28.3   Using `SetFixture`

Let's now consider the revised method `usersInRoom()` in Listing 28.4. This method instead makes use of `SetFixture`, a new fixture for testing unordered lists. This fixture reports in the same way as `RowFixture` but is more flexible. We can supply the actual collection as an argument to the constructor of `SetFixture` rather than having to subclass it.

`SetFixture` treats a header label as the name of a property if there is no instance variable of that name. Hence, it will call the method `getName()` of `User` objects.

The interaction of the fixtures and the first five tables is illustrated in Figure 28.3. The collection supplied to the `SetFixture` object has a single `User` element.

If a method call for an action in a flow fixture object returns a `Set`, `DoFixture` automatically creates a `SetFixture` with it and returns that fixture. Hence, we can remove the method `usersInRoom()` in Listing 28.4. Then, when the action *users in room* is carried out, it leads to a call of the method `usersInRoom()` in the system under test. Because this returns a `Set`, `DoFixture` automatically creates a `SetFixture`, which is used to interpret the rest of the table.

Further details of `SetFixture`, and related list fixtures, are given in Section 28.9.

28.4   Expected Errors with `DoFixture`

Consider now the test from Section 10.2 on p. 74, shown again in Figure 28.4. The second row of the fourth table tests that the action to remove a room is rejected.

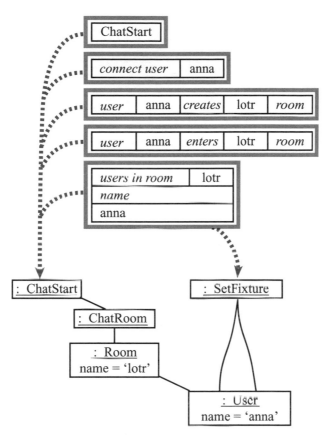

Figure 28.3 TestDisconnect with SetFigure

The *reject* special action calls the method `removeRoom()` in the system under test. The method `removeRoom()` returns `false` in this case, as it's not possible to remove a room if users are in it. Hence, the *reject* succeeds.

Questions & Answers

Can the fourth table in Figure 28.4 be split into two rows?
Yes, as both actions apply to the flow fixture object.

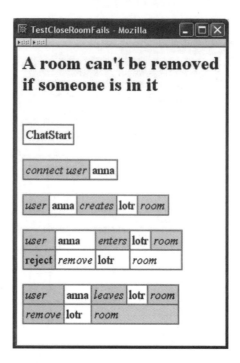

Figure 28.4 TestCloseRoomFails

28.5   Actions on Domain Objects with DoFixture

Consider now the test from Section 10.3 on p. 75, shown again in Figure 28.5. The action in the first row of the second table selects a User, with the actions in the rest of the table being applied to that User.

As we see in the extended fixture class in Listing 28.5, the method connect() carries out the connection action and then returns a UserFixture to interpret the rest of the table. The class UserFixture is a DoFixture, as shown in Listing 28.6. It has methods corresponding to the two actions in the second and third rows of the second table in Figure 28.5.

The *room* action in the first row of the third table of Figure 28.5 selects a room. The method room() in ChatStart is called, which creates a new DoFixture with the Room as argument. The two action rows that follow call through that new DoFixture to the underlying Room object.

In general, if a method call for an action returns an Object, which is not a Collection, Iterator, or an array, DoFixture automatically creates a new DoFixture with it and returns that. Hence, the method room() can be removed from ChatStart. Then the method room() in the ChatRoom, the system under test, will be called instead. This returns an object of class Room, which is automatically wrapped with another DoFixture, and that is returned to interpret the rest of the table. The final, slimmed-down ChatStart class for all these tests is shown in Listing 28.7.

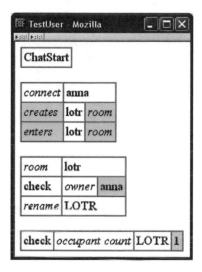

Figure 28.5 TestUser

Listing 28.5 **ChatStart.java (version 3)**

```java
public class ChatStart extends DoFixture {
   private ChatRoom chat = new ChatRoom();

   public ChatStart() {
      setSystemUnderTest(chat);
   }
   public int occupantCount(String roomName) {
      return chat.occupants(roomName);
   }
   public UserFixture connect(String userName) {
      if (chat.connectUser(userName))
         return new UserFixture(chat, chat.user(userName));
      throw new RuntimeException("Duplicate user");
   }
   public DoFixture room(String roomName) {
      return new DoFixture(chat.room(roomName));
   }
}
```

Listing 28.6 UserFixture.java

```java
public class UserFixture extends DoFixture {
  private ChatRoom chat;
  private User user;

  public UserFixture(ChatRoom chat, User user) {
    this.chat = chat;
    this.user = user;
  }
  public boolean createsRoom(String roomName) {
    chat.createRoom(roomName,user);
    return true;
  }
  public boolean entersRoom(String roomName) {
    return chat.userEntersRoom(user.getName(),roomName);
  }
}
```

Listing 28.7 ChatStart.java (version 4)

```java
public class ChatStart extends DoFixture {
  private ChatRoom chat = new ChatRoom();

  public ChatStart() {
    setSystemUnderTest(chat);
  }
  public int occupantCount(String roomName) {
    return chat.occupants(roomName);
  }
  public UserFixture connect(String userName) {
    if (chat.connectUser(userName))
      return new UserFixture(chat, chat.user(userName));
    throw new RuntimeException("Duplicate user");
  }
}
```

Questions & Answers

So, presumably, the second table of Figure 28.5 couldn't be split?
That's right. If the second action were in a row by itself, it wouldn't work, because it would then be applied to the flow fixture object. If we added a first row to that new table to *connect* anna, it would fail because anna would already be connected.

Are there any disadvantages in not having simple adapter methods in a DoFixture? Yes. If a programmer renames a method in an application class that is accessed directly from a Fit table action, the Fit test will be broken. The programmer may not realize this until the Fit tests are run but can then simply add an adapter method to map from the name in the Fit table action to the name of the method in the application class.

When looking at a DoFixture class, it's not obvious which actions it really supports; it is necessary to look at the Fit tables and/or the associated system under test. The latter is similar to the need to look at its superclasses to understand the behavior of a class.

28.6   DoFixture in General

When it is a DoFixture, the fixture object of the first table interprets the rest of the tables in a special way. For each table, it considers the first row as follows.

- If the row contains an action, a call is made to the corresponding method in the flow fixture object or system under test and any result returned.

    If the method returns a **boolean**, the following apply.

    - If the value is **true**, the action is colored green in the table.

    - If the result is **false**, the action is colored red.

  Otherwise, if an exception is thrown, the action is colored yellow, with an error message.

- If the row contains one of the following special actions, no result is returned.

    - **check** compares the expected value in the last cell of the row against the result of the action in the rest of the row. As with the *check* in **ActionFixture**, the cell containing the expected result is colored red, green, or yellow, depending on the match. Unlike *check* in **ActionFixture**, "error" is not supported as an expected result; the special action **reject** is used instead.

    - **reject** carries out the action in the rest of the row. If the action would have been colored green, the *reject* cell is colored red. If the action would have been colored red or yellow, the *reject* cell is colored green.

    - **not** is the same as **reject**.

    - **note** ignores the rest of the row. This action is for including comments in **DoFixture** tables.

    - **show** carries out the action in the rest of the row, showing the result of the action in a cell that's added to the row. If the result contains HTML, it will rendered as HTML in the report.

– calculate returns a CalculateFixture applied to the same system under test as the current DoFixture.

- The row refers to a property of the flow fixture object or of the system under test. This property is accessed through its getter method, such as getName(), and any result returned. If the result is a boolean, coloring occurs as for actions.

- The row contains the name of a fixture. An object of that class is returned. This means that a DoFixture table may be used to start a sequence of tables that are interpreted in the usual manner.

The interpretation of the rest of the table depends on the result returned from processing the previous row.

- If there is no result or if the result is a primitive value, such as an int, the current DoFixture object handles the rest of the table. This will usually be the flow fixture object but may be a new DoFixture that was introduced in a previous row of the same table.

- If a Set is to be returned, it is wrapped in a SetFixture, which is returned instead.

- If any other Collection or a Map, Iterator, or Object[] is to be returned, it is wrapped in an ArrayFixture, which is returned instead.

- If any other Object is to be returned, it is wrapped in a DoFixture, which is returned instead.

- If a fixture is returned, it is used to interpret the rest of the table. However, the next table is interpreted independently, using the flow fixture object.

Note

Flow style means that, with the use of a flow fixture object, the reference to the system under test does not need to be a public static variable, because it does not need to be accessed as a global variable from other fixture objects, as is the case with the core fixtures. Instead, any object references can be passed to a new fixture object when it is created in a method of the flow fixture object that is carrying out a DoFixture action.

Questions & Answers

What other things will an adapter method in a DoFixture be needed for?
The fixture method may map values in some way, such as between String values and ints.

It may need to make several calls into the system under test. The action may be expressive in the test but not correspond directly to the organization of the application code.

It may carry out an action through the user interface by clicking buttons and entering text in fields in dialog boxes, as we discuss in Chapter 32.

28.7 Setup

As we saw in Section 10.4 on p. 76, a SetUpFixture table may be used for setting up the data at the start of a test. This example is shown again in the second table of Figure 28.6.

The fixture class Discounts, a DoFixture, is shown in Listing 28.8. The method setUp() is called for the action *set up* in the first row of the second table. This returns a fixture object, of class SetUpDiscounts, which is used to interpret the rest of the table.

The fixture class SetUpDiscounts is a SetUpFixture, as shown in Listing 28.9. SetUpFixture reads the labels in the second row of the table and combines them into the name of a method. The "%" in the fourth label is converted into "percent", as defined by *extended camel casing* (see the Note on the next page). In this case, the method is

```
futureValueMaxBalanceMinPurchaseDiscountPercent()
```

This method takes four arguments, corresponding to the four columns of the table.

For each subsequent row of the table, SetUpFixture calls that method with the values from the row. As usual, a TypeAdapter is used to convert the cell contents into suitable values for the method.

In general:

- Before calling the method for the first time, the method startUp() is called. After all the rows have been processed, the method tearDown() is called. These methods can be overridden in a subclass of SetUpFixture to do pre- and postprocessing of the setup data.

- An exception thrown when calling the method is reported in the table.

- The setup method may be in the fixture itself or in the associated system under test, just as with DoFixture.

Questions & Answers

How do we know what extended camel casing translates to?
The simplest approach is to define the class for the relevant fixture and run the Fit test. The error message in the Fit report will tell you what program identifier is used.

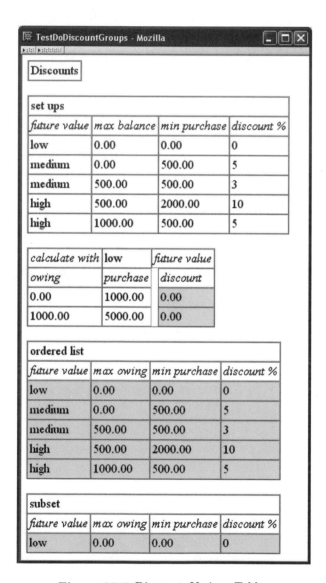

Figure 28.6 Discount: Various Tables

Listing 28.8 Discounts.java

```java
public class Discounts extends DoFixture {
   private DiscountApplication app = new DiscountApplication();

   public Fixture setUps() {
      return new SetUpDiscounts(app);
   }
   public Fixture orderedList() {
      return new ArrayFixture(app.getGroups());
   }
   public Fixture subset() {
      return new SubsetFixture(app.getGroups());
   }
   public Fixture calculateWithFutureValue(String futureValue) {
      return new CalculateDiscounts2(app,futureValue);
   }
}
```

Listing 28.9 SetUpDiscounts.java

```java
public class SetUpDiscounts extends SetUpFixture {
   private DiscountApplication app;

   public SetUpDiscounts(DiscountApplication app) {
      this.app = app;
   }
   public void futureValueMaxBalanceMinPurchaseDiscountPercent(
         String futureValue, double maxBalance, double minPurchase,
         double discountPercent) {
      app.addDiscountGroup(futureValue,maxBalance,
               minPurchase,discountPercent);
   }
}
```

Isn't it annoying to have to work out the name of the method involved and type it in when it can be so long?
There's no need. Simply define the fixture class and run Fit on the table. The report tells you the full name of the expected method.

Why does the method name depend on all the *given* columns as well?
If it didn't, someone could easily make a mistake with the *given* columns, such as in the order, that might go unnoticed.

Is there any point in using a SetUpFixture table if the corresponding DoFixture actions take no more space?
Maybe not, except that the form of the table makes it clear that it is setting up the data and/or state for the business rule that's being tested.

> **Note**
>
> As we saw in Chapter 21, *camel casing* removes the spaces from a label name and makes each word after the first start with an uppercase letter. *Extended camel casing* takes this further, to handle any characters in the label or keywords of any FitLibrary fixture tables. This means that the test writer can use whatever names make sense, without having to consider Java syntax.
>
> *Extended camel casing* defines how an arbitrary header name is converted into a valid Java identifier. Any character that is not permitted in a Java identifier, such as "%" or Unicode, is translated into a valid sequence of ASCII characters. *Camel casing* is applied to the result. Finally, if the resulting identifier is a Java keyword, it is modified to not be. (For other programming languages, Fit applies appropriate translation rules for each language.)

28.8   `CalculateFixture` Tables

The third table in Figure 28.6 makes use of a `CalculateFixture` table, `Calculate-Discounts2`, which is returned by the method `calculateWithFutureValue()` in Listing 28.8. The fixture class `CalculateDiscounts2` is shown in Listing 28.10. In a similar way to `SetUpFixture`, the labels in the second row of the table are combined to form a method name. Here, the method name `discountOwingPurchase()` is made up from the *expected* column label, followed by the *given* column labels.

For each of the following rows of the table, the method is called with two arguments from the two *given* columns. The result of the method call is checked against the *calculated* column for that row, and that cell is colored appropriately.

Listing 28.10 CalculateDiscounts2.java

```java
public class CalculateDiscounts2 extends CalculateFixture {
  private DiscountApplication app;
  private String futureValue;

  public CalculateDiscounts2(DiscountApplication app, String futureValue) {
    this.app = app;
    this.futureValue = futureValue;
  }
  public double discountOwingPurchase(double owing, double purchase) {
    return app.discount(futureValue,owing,purchase);
  }
}
```

In general:

- There may be several *calculated* columns. Each *calculated* column has a separate method made up of the *calculated* column label, followed by all the *given* column labels. For each row, the *calculated* columns are processed from left to right, calling the appropriate method.

- CalculateFixture may take a reference to an application object, just like with DoFixture. If the fixture doesn't declare a required method, the method in that object will be called instead.

- A CalculateFixture object may define a specific String for use in a *given* cell to mean to repeat the previous value in the column in the table. This is defined by calling the method setRepeatString() of the object, which takes the repeat String as an argument.

  By default, there is no repeat string. Compare this to ColumnFixture, in which an empty cell is used to repeat column values.

- A CalculateFixture object may also define a specific String for use in a result cell of the table where an exception is expected instead of a result value. This is defined by calling the method setExceptionString() of the object, which takes the repeat String as an argument.

  By default, there is no exception string. Compare this to ColumnFixture, in which a result cell value of *error* is used to signify that an exception is expected.

28.9 Ordered-List Tables

We now look at the use of ArrayFixture, as introduced in Section 10.6 on p. 78. The fourth table of Figure 28.6 starts with the action *ordered list*. This leads to a call of the method orderedList() in the flow fixture object of class Discounts, as shown in Listing 28.8.

This method returns an ArrayFixture that is created with the actual collection. The ArrayFixture checks this collection against the *expected* collection from the rest of the rows of the table. Figure 28.7 shows some of the interactions of tables and fixtures when Fit runs this table.

As well as taking account of the order of the elements of a collection, ArrayFixture and RowFixture have several differences.

- ArrayFixture accepts any Java Collection or an Iterator, as well as an array (Object[]). Any of these can be supplied through the constructor, so a subclass is not needed.

  To allow for collections whose elements are not object based, such as the collection shown by a JTable, ArrayFixture accepts a collection of Map. Each Map provides a mapping from a name to an object. Chapter 32 shows how this can be used in testing a GUI.

- With ArrayFixture, you don't specify the class of the elements of the collection.

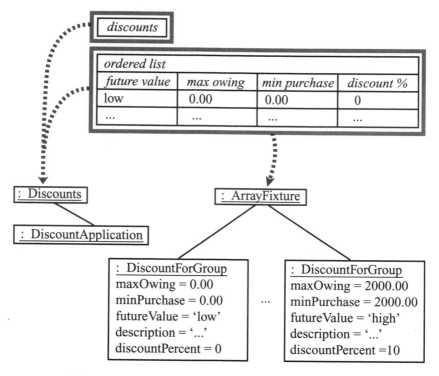

Figure 28.7 Fit Runs the Fourth Table of Figure 28.6

- **ArrayFixture** maps header labels to properties, as well as to `public` instance variables. For example, the label *name* would be mapped to the getter method `getName()`.

- **ArrayFixture** allows for mixed collections of objects. When a specific column doesn't apply to a particular object in the collection because it has no corresponding instance variable or property, the associated cell has to be empty.

    If a column applies to no elements of the collection, an error is given, as it's likely that a mistake has been made in the header label.

These differences also apply to `SetFixture` and `SubsetFixture`, which are closely related to `ArrayFixture`.

28.10   Testing Parts of a List

We now return to the example from Section 10.7 on p. 79, as shown again in Figure 28.6. The action in the fifth table of Figure 28.6 leads to a call of the method `subset()` in class `Discounts` as shown in Listing 28.8. This passes the actual collection to a fixture of class **SubsetFixture**, which checks the rows in the rest of the table against the actual elements.

SubsetFixture is the same as **SetFixture** but ignores the surplus rows: in the actual collection, those elements are not included in rows of the table.

28.11   Using Other Values in Flow Tables

As we saw in Section 25.2 on p. 214, a Fit fixture class overrides the method **parse()** to allow new types of values, such as **Money**, to be used in table cells. The FitLibrary fixtures, as in FitNesse, provide another approach, which avoids any duplication. These fixtures check whether the class of the value has a **static** method **parse()** that takes a **String** and returns an object of that class.

Sometimes, we want to handle values in a special way. For example, in Section 34.4 on p. 292, we want to write **Date** values without the seconds.

A **DoFixture** object, such as the flow fixture object, may call the **DoFixture** method **registerParseDelegate()** to register the current object as the one that handles the parsing of other values for any flow fixture objects.

28.12   Summary

We have covered the details of several FitLibrary fixtures in this chapter.

- A **DoFixture** flow fixture object maps actions with keywords into methods in the fixture or the underlying application object. Such methods may directly or indirectly return a fixture that is used to interpret the rest of the table.

- A **SetUpFixture** object is tailored to add data to set up a test.

- A **CalculateFixture** object is an alternative to **ColumnFixture**.

- Objects of the list fixtures **SetFixture**, **ArrayFixture**, and **SubsetFixture** all test collections in various ways. They do not need to be told the type of elements of the collection, can access properties and instance variables, and often don't need to be subclassed.

28.13   Exercises

1. Write fixtures for the tables developed for the exercises in Chapter 10.

Questions & Answers

What if the last row of a DoFixture table returns a fixture? Is it used in the next table?

A fixture resulting from the last row of a table is ignored. The next table in flow is interpreted by the flow fixture object anew.

Is there any way to have actions follow the rows of a RowFixture in a table?

No. RowFixture, the other list fixtures, SetUpFixture, and CalculateFixture all consume the rest of the rows of the table.

Wouldn't it be confusing if a method in the system under test were changed to return an object instead of void?

Yes, if that was called directly. The actions following in the table would then be incorrectly applied to that object. It's unlikely that there would be suitable methods, leading to an error.

Isn't this flow stuff too complex, compared to the core fixtures?

It seems more complex because it's introduced as a variation of the way the core fixtures work. But once you're familiar with the FitLibrary fixtures, you'll find it's simpler for both the Fit test writer and the programmer.

Note

One of the design goals of the FitLibrary fixtures was to enable inexperienced programmers to use Fit. Writing fixture code is confusing when students haven't yet learned about inheritance and writing subclasses.

The FitLibrary fixtures were designed to be used without the need to write any fixture code. This led to the automatic wrapping of returned values with fixtures, such as a List with an ArrayFixture and an Object with a DoFixture, which proved to be more generally convenient to use.

CHAPTER 29

Custom Table Fixtures

We now introduce the fixtures for the tables in Chapter 11. In that chapter, we argued that it can be valuable to develop custom Fit tables to be expressive for specific types of tests. In general, we'd expect that the effort involved in developing the fixture would be more than made up for in the reduced effort required in developing and maintaining the tests.

The first example table, for a business form, makes use of a `TableFixture`. The second example table, using graphics to test associations, makes use of a `DoFixture`. The third example table, using images to test a board game, makes use of an `ImageFixture`.

29.1 Business Forms

As we saw in Section 11.1 on p. 81, having a test that is similar in structure to a standard business form, such as an invoice, reduces the gap between the business world and the tests. Figure 29.1 shows again the example from Section 11.1.

Part of the fixture class for this test is shown in Listing 29.1. This class is a subclass of `TableFixture`,[1] which calls the method `doStaticTable()` with the number of table rows to check the various cells of the table. The text in a table cell is accessed by row and column, using the `TableFixture` method `getText()`, as shown in both `check()` methods in Listing 29.1. The second `check()` method has to explicitly convert the text into a `double`, as there is no automatic type conversion.

To provide feedback for the Fit report on whether a cell value is correct, the methods `right()` and `wrong()` are provided by class `TableFixture`. The methods take the position of the cell in the table; `wrong()` also takes the expected value, as a `String`.

---

[1] The class `fitnesse.fixtures.TableFixture` is supplied with FitNesse.

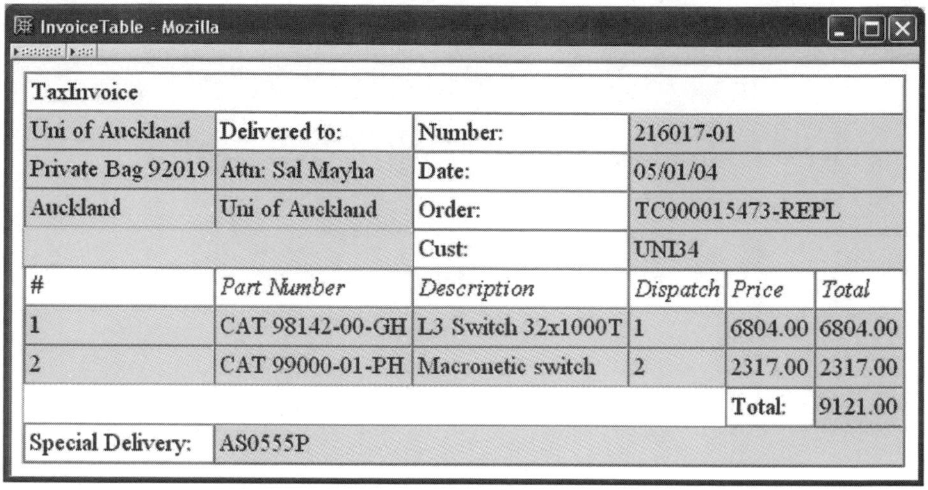

TaxInvoice					
Uni of Auckland	Delivered to:	Number:	216017-01		
Private Bag 92019	Attn: Sal Mayha	Date:	05/01/04		
Auckland	Uni of Auckland	Order:	TC000015473-REPL		
		Cust:	UNI34		
#	*Part Number*	*Description*	*Dispatch*	*Price*	*Total*
1	CAT 98142-00-GH	L3 Switch 32x1000T	1	6804.00	6804.00
2	CAT 99000-01-PH	Macronetic switch	2	2317.00	2317.00
				Total:	9121.00
Special Delivery:	AS0555P				

Figure 29.1 A Table Corresponding to an Invoice

29.2 Testing Associations

As we saw in Section 11.2 on p. 82, graphics can aid in the expressiveness of some tests. Figure 29.2 shows again the test from Section 11.2 for the occupancy of various users in various chat rooms (see also Plate 6).

The fixture class `UsersAndRooms` is shown in Listing 29.2. The method `users()` in Listing 29.2 returns a `DotGraphic` with a `String` containing a series of *Dot* commands corresponding to the expected graph. Because this method returns a `DotGraphic`, `DoFixture` expects that

- The expected value in the table cell is a GIF image file.
- A file containing the expected Dot[2] commands exists with the same name in the same folder but with the suffix .dot.

The image file referenced in the last cell of the second row of the Fit table is http://files/ChatGraph.gif, so the file http://files/ChatGraph.dot is also expected in that folder.

The method `users()` returns a `DotGraphic` with a `String` in *Dot* format, as follows:

```
digraph G {
lotr->luke;
lotr->anna;
}
```

This `string` defines three nodes—lotr, luke, and anna—with links from lotr to the other two nodes.

[2] See the following Note for details of *Dot*.

Listing 29.1 **TaxInvoice.java**

```java
public class TaxInvoice extends fitnesse.fixtures.TableFixture {
  private Invoice invoice = new Invoice();

  protected void doStaticTable(int rows) {
    check(3,3,invoice.getCustomer());
    checkAddress();
    checkDelivery();
    check(0,3,invoice.getAccountNumber());
    check(1,3,invoice.getDateAsString());
    check(2,3,invoice.getOrderNo());
    Order[] orderItems = invoice.getOrders();
    checkOrderItems(orderItems);
    checkSpecialDelivery(orderItems.length);
    checkTotal(orderItems.length);
  }
  private void checkOrderItems(Order[] orderItems) {
    int firstRow = 5;
    for (int row = 0; row < orderItems.length; row++) {
      Order item = orderItems[row];
      check(firstRow+row,0,""+item.getQuantity());
      check(firstRow+row,1,item.getPart());
      check(firstRow+row,2,""+item.getDescription());
      check(firstRow+row,3,""+item.getDispatched());
      check(firstRow+row,4,item.getPrice());
      check(firstRow+row,5,item.getTotal());
    }
  }
  private void check(int row, int column, String expected) {
    if (expected.equals(getText(row,column)))
      right(row,column);
    else
      wrong(row,column,expected);
  }
  private void check(int row, int column, double expected) {
    double actual = Double.valueOf(getText(row,column)).doubleValue();
    if (expected == actual)
      right(row,column);
    else
      wrong(row,column,""+expected);
  }
  // ...
}
```

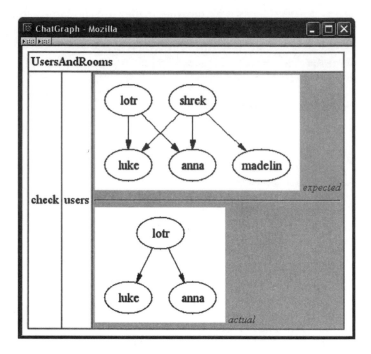

Figure 29.2 A Table Containing an Image

Listing 29.2 **UsersAndRooms.java**

```
public class UsersAndRooms extends DoFixture {
    private ChatServer chat = new ChatServer();

    public DotGraphic users() {
        String dot = "digraph G {\n";
        for (Iterator itRoom = chat.getRooms(); itRoom.hasNext(); ) {
            Room room = (Room)itRoom.next();
            for (Iterator itUser = room.users(); itUser.hasNext(); ) {
                User user = (User)itUser.next();
                dot += room.getName()+"->"+user.getName()+";\n";
            }
        }
        return new DotGraphic(dot+"}\n");
    }
}
```

The **String** in *Dot* format, as returned by the method **users()**, is compared against the contents of the **ChatGraph.dot** file. If they are the same, the test passes. Otherwise, the actual **String** returned by the **users()** method is written to a file in the same folder and *Dot* is run to generate a corresponding GIF file. The reported table then includes a reference to this new GIF file as the actual result.

Note

Dot is an application for laying out and producing graphs—made up of nodes and arcs—from a text file of commands that describe the graph. *Dot* is available free from [Dot], including a user manual.

Questions & Answers

Isn't it awkward to have to set up the expected GIF and *Dot* files?
It does require that you become familiar with the syntax of *Dot* files. But it's pretty simple.

Could this same technique be used with SVG files instead of GIFs?
Yes.

29.3 Two-Dimensional Images

Section 11.3 on p. 83 introduced the use of images in a two-dimensional structure. The fixture **StartSokoban** for this is shown in Listing 29.3. The method **board()** carries out the following sequence:

1. Collects a representation of the board, as an **int[][]**
2. Maps that to the file names of corresponding images, as a **String[][]**
3. Passes the resulting **String[][]** to a newly created **ImageFixture**
4. Returns that fixture

ImageFixture takes a **String[][]** as an expected argument and attempts to match the elements against the files names of the images in the cells in the rest of the Fit table. If they match, the test succeeds. Otherwise, the **ImageFixture** adds rows to the table in the report to show the actual array of images.

The **ImageFixture** class is covered in Section 38.3 on p. 314.

Listing 29.3 **StartSokoban.java**

```java
public class StartSokoban extends DoFixture {
    private static final String PREFIX = "/files/images/";
    private Sokoban sokoban = new Sokoban();

    public Fixture board() {
        int[][] pieces = sokoban.ge2DArrayOfValues();
        String[][] imageFileName = new String[pieces.length][];
        for (int row = 0; row < pieces.length; row++) {
            imageFileName[row] = new String[pieces[row].length];
            for (int col = 0; col < pieces[row].length; col++)
                imageFileName[row][col] = PREFIX+map(pieces[row][col]);
        }
        return new fit.ImageFixture(imageFileName);
    }
    private String map(int piece) {
        switch(piece) {
          case Sokoban.s: return "space.jpg";
          case Sokoban.e: return "shelf.jpg";
          case Sokoban.f: return "shelfwithbox.jpg";
          case Sokoban.b: return "box.jpg";
          case Sokoban.w: return "worker.jpg";
          case Sokoban.W: return "wall.jpg";
        }
        throw new RuntimeException("Unknown piece");
    }
}
```

29.4 Summary

We have covered two types of specialized fixtures for three examples of custom tables.

1. **TableFixture** allows random access to the cells of a Fit table, which is ideal when the table structure is not regular, such as when it represents an invoice.

2. FitLibrary fixtures allow for graphics to be used to test complex relationships.

3. **ImageFixture** allows for an array of images to be used for testing.

In general, it's not difficult to create specialized fixtures to support custom tables that aid in the expressiveness of specific Fit tests. We cover the development of such fixtures in Chapter 38.

PART IV

DEVELOPING FIXTURES FOR
RentAPartySoftware

CHAPTER 30

Fixtures and Adapting the Application

30.1   Introduction

In Chapter 12, we introduced RentAPartySoftware and the general issues that it was facing with *RentEz*, its software product. In Part II, we showed how Fit tables were introduced to deal with a variety of testing issues.

In this part, we present the programmers' perspective and show how fixtures were developed for the tables introduced in the chapters in Part II. We also show how those fixtures were connected to the system under test and the slow, focused evolution of the system to enable better testing where it was most needed. By the end of this part, we see the programmers carrying out new, agile development that is driven by Fit tests.

30.2   The Programmers' Perspective

Emily and Neo reported that all the RPS programmers had voiced several major concerns about the architecture and the development of *RentEz*.

> "We're concerned about the changes we will have to make to the system for testing. It's already difficult to change the system without breaking it, as it's so delicate.
>
> "This means that we're often slower to add new functionality than we (and everyone else) expect.
>
> "We know that the architecture needs rethinking. There's lots of duplicate code, and we need to change the structure of some of the classes. In some places, there's lots of conditional code that could be eliminated by introducing several subclasses. But it's very risky to change it, as it's easy to break working code in the process.

"We've got a backlog of work to be done, including many reported bugs, so management will not support long delays while we improve the system.

"But turning it into a Web application is going to force a lot of changes, so we need to tackle it somehow.

"Some of the code was written by people who have since left, and we're not familiar with it. We're bothered about changing such code, as we often introduce bugs in the process. Some of it is very stable, whereas other parts probably need to be replaced entirely.

"Our users keep changing their minds about what they require, which can waste a lot of time.

"And sometimes we add functionality that ends up not being used.

"It's a pain having to work overtime to avoid running too much over our deadlines for a release, especially as the code tends to be buggier than usual.

"Morale is lower than it's ever been. We used to be proud of the system, but not any more."

30.3   System Architecture

Emily gave a quick rundown of the architecture of the system, with brief sketches on the whiteboard. "The application is sort of structured as a three-layer system,[1] but not quite," she admitted. "Yes, we know there's business logic tied up with GUI code, but it's difficult to change it. We're behind in development and fixing bugs, so it's difficult to find time to tidy things up."

"But," added Neo, "we do need to separate the UI layer in order to introduce *RentEz* as a Web application. Or else duplicate the business logic code further. Neither approach is satisfactory."

"One reason for the problem," Emily suggested, "is that the GUI-building tools encourage development from the GUI, and that leads some of the programmers to include the business logic directly within the event-handling code. Another reason is that some of the programmers haven't got the point of having cleanly separated layers."

"Part of that," Neo added, "is that some of the business logic is closely related to the way the GUI works, such as which user interface operations can be carried out in a particular state of a client transaction."

"There's also a problem with the persistence layer," said Emily. "The database layer is not separated from the domain layer. We have SQL mixed up with the business logic. Luckily, that's not such an issue in the move to a Web application. But it causes problems when we have to make changes to the database schema or change the class structures."

"And when we need to improve database performance," added Neo.

---

[1] See the Note on 257.

Note

The **Three-Layer Architecture** [Fow02a] defines a layering to provide an important source of modularity. Ideally, it consists of three layers, as shown in Figure 30.1.

- The middle, *domain*, layer contains all the domain objects and the business logic and is independent of the particular user interface(s) that provide access to the user, as well as of the storage layer beneath it.

    This means that the top and bottom layers can be replaced or extended with minimal change to the middle layer. For example, with this approach, it is straightforward to add other types of user interfaces, as well as tests, in the top layer, as shown in Figure 30.2.

    The classes and pubic methods of this layer are often referred to as the *API* (application program interface) of the application.

- The top, *presentation*, layer provides the user interface. Objects in the user interface layer access objects in the domain layer, calling methods in the domain objects when the user carries out operations on the user interface. User interface objects also register—anonymously, as listeners— for changes with domain objects, so that the state of the user interface can be changed when the corresponding domain objects change. This layer provides a mapping between the objects in the *domain* and the user interface.

    The interaction between these two layers can be described in terms of the *Model-View-Controller* model or *MVC* [Fow02a] in which the Model is an object in the domain object layer and the View and Controller are in the user interface layer. Because of the MVC model, the middle layer is sometimes called the *model* layer.

- The bottom, *data source*, layer provides for persistence: storage of data, usually to files or a relational database system. This layer needs to load objects from the data store, update them when they change, and communicate to the middle layer any changes to the data store caused from elsewhere.

    This layer provides a mapping between the objects in the domain and the underlying data store. A range of tools is available to automate much of this mapping for relational databases.

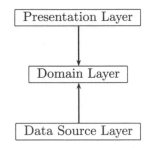

Figure 30.1 Three Layers

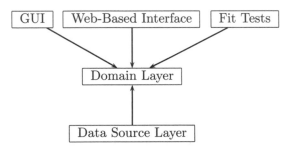

Figure 30.2 Several Presentation Layers

These issues are common in software development, as all the development effort goes into adding functionality and fixing bugs. Little or no time is put into structuring the software to manage change. It is not until the software gets larger and/or more complex that the need for flexibiity of the software is appreciated, by which time a lot of effort may be needed to rectify the problem. What's worse, time is rarely available to restructure for change, as so much time is spent on fighting the consequences of poor structure.

30.4   Test Infecting for Improvements

Luckily, it's not necessary to stop all further development and completely revise the software. The best way forward is to slowly make changes over time, in the areas that need to be changed anyway. Luckily, creating and running automated tests can support the restructuring process in two significant ways.

1. A suite of automated tests can be run to determine whether anything is broken during small steps of restructuring of the software. This process can give fast feedback, so that any problems can be dealt with while the recent changes are still in mind.

2. The software often needs to be restructured to support automated testing that gives sufficiently fast feedback, as we discuss later. Surprisingly, such

changes naturally lead to more modular and independent code, which is essential for changeability. The code also needs to be organized more around the calculation business rules, as we'll see in Chapter 31.

Erich Gamma calls "test infected" those programmers who use unit tests to drive software development [BG98]. This term has been generalized to the application code itself being "test infected" if it is structured to enable testing. This situation may come about because the code has been written test first, to pass tests that have been written first. Or it may be owing to changes carried out after the code has been written—"legacy" code [Fea04]—to enable automated testing.

The programmers at RPS were concerned about stopping their developments and code fixing in order to test infect their application in order to introduce unit tests. There's no need for that, and it's rarely realistic, anyway. The way to proceed is in an evolutionary manner, in small steps [Fow99], [Fea04]. Where to start?

Start test infecting where it's most needed: in the areas of change, owing to new functionality or to bugs in that code. Support those changes with Fit tests, to get feedback so that new errors are picked up quickly. As we'll see in Chapter 32, we can support test infecting and other changes by initially testing with Fit, indirectly, through the user interface.

This process may take months or years. Stable parts of the application code may never need to be touched. New developments can be carried out in a test-driven fashion, so that any new code is test infected from the start, as discussed in Chapter 33.

Questions & Answers

What happens if the three-layer architecture model is not used in an application? If there is no clear separation between the top two layers, the system under test will have to be tested through the user interface. As we discuss in Chapter 32, the Fit tests do not necessarily have to be written to explicitly use the user interface, however.

Does the code in the bottom layer ever need to be changed for testing? As we'll see in Chapter 33, a suite of Fit tests may run too slowly when they are applied to the whole system. Slow tests mean that feedback is delayed, which tends to encourage larger changes to be made before testing that the changes haven't broken the system.

So it pays to have the tests run quickly. There are two bottlenecks: testing through the user interface and database accesses. The first can be reduced by having more of the testing done directly through the domain layer. The second can be reduced by having more of the tests work without the data source layer connected at all.

But doesn't that mean that you're not testing the whole system and will miss bugs? Yes. However, there is an important trade off here, and there are ways to handle it, as we discuss in Chapter 33.

Our major problem is in understanding how our software can meet market need. How do Fit tests help us?

Fit tests can help in exploring and communicating what your system does, or can do. They can give you a way of discussing possibilities before implementing anything.

But the first step can be difficult, regardless of such tools. What significant issues do potential buyers face that are within the realm of your system? How can you solve their problems cost-effectively? How do you get their attention?

30.5   The Rest of This Part

The remaining chapters in this part provide a programmer's perspective on testing, Fit fixtures, and test infecting. We look at the development of fixtures for the RentAPartySoftware Fit tables that evolved in the chapters in Part II. We begin with simple fixtures and simple changes and move to larger-scale changes to the application.

The rest of the chapters of this part are as follows.

- Chapter 31 follows the development of Emily's first fixture, for a `ColumnFixture` table. She is able to make a simple alteration to the application to enable testing to occur easily.

- Chapter 32 follows the development of fixtures for workflow tests. We show how the workflow test fixtures are first implemented by driving the system under test through the GUI, as there is no clear API, or domain, layer.

- Chapter 33 covers the restructuring of an application to make it test infected. We overview an unfolding set of approaches to reducing dependencies between domain objects and other things, including the UI, persistence, and other domain objects.

- Chapter 34 shows how to control the date and time during testing through the use of a *mock* clock that is used in the application.

- Chapter 35 shows how to write fixtures for calculation tests that either work directly with the code for the business rules or that carry out the tests through workflow actions.

- Chapter 36 concludes this part.

CHAPTER 31

Emily's First Fixture

Programmers: The tables that use this fixture code are given in Chapter 13.

In starting to write fixtures for an existing application, it's good to build up experience step by step. It's likely to be easier to begin with fixtures for calculation tests.

To start integrating the first Fit tables for *late returns* into RPS, we worked with Emily. She had worked with Don previously, in Chapter 13, to develop the tables.

Emily started on a fixture for a calculating test table, as that was a good place to start. She was happy to change the application code to make the fixtures work without supporting tests, because that was what she was used to. It takes a while to realize that changing blind, without tests, is common but rather risky. It leaves incomplete work behind, which often needs to be tidied up later, when faults are found. Too often, such faults are found by the application's users.

31.1 The Table

In Chapter 13, Emily and Don developed `ColumnFixture` tables for testing late returns. One of the tables from that chapter is shown again in Figure 31.1.

rent.CalculateLateHours				
hours late	*grace*	*count grace*	*high demand*	*extra hours()*
0	1	yes	10	0
0.9	1	no	10	0
1	1	yes	5	6
1	1	no	12	0
9	1	no	10	18
19	2	no	100	117

Figure 31.1 Late Returns from Figure 13.8 on p. 99

31.2   Developing the Fixture

Later in the afternoon, we got together with Emily to discuss the fixture class. She mentioned in passing, "That other table dropped out easily; no trouble. Don is entering the tests now for those tables."

Emily had got the bare bones of the fixture class together, as shown in Listing 31.1.[1] However, she was unsure of the best way to hook it up to the application.

Listing 31.1   TestLate.java (version 1)

```
public class TestLate extends fit.ColumnFixture {
  public float hoursLate, grace, highDemand;
  public boolean countGrace;

  public int extraHours() {
    return 0;
  }
}
```

After suggesting to Emily that she change the return value of `extraHours()` to -1, she ran Fit on it. Of course, none of the tests passed.

Questions & Answers

Why did you change it to -1?
It's a good practice to make sure that the tests all fail initially. Then when you make a change to the code, such as hooking the fixture into the system under test, you see that your tests now pass because of that change.

Emily sketched the classes involved in handling *late returns*, as shown in Figure 31.2. The code for calculating the late return is in the class `Rental`, which depends on configuration information that's extracted from the database when the application starts.

What's the best way to hook it into the application? Emily mentioned the following possibilities as she thought of them, with some prompting and encouragement.

> "I could call my method inside `Rental` from the fixture. But it assumes associated `RentalItem` and `Client` objects, and that's kind of messy to set up. There needs to be a record in the database for all this stuff, and so on. I'm not sure how to set it up.
>
> "Or I could add a new method, `setUpTest()`, to `Rental`, which sets things up in the database before calling the normal method to do the calculation.

---

[1] See Chapter 21 for an introduction to writing `ColumnFixture` classes.

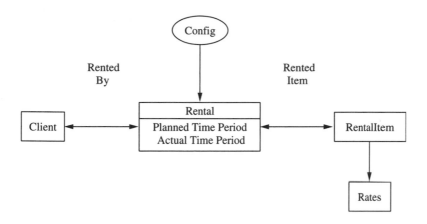

Figure 31.2 Emily's Sketch of the Application

"Better still, I could add a new method, `extraHours()`, to `Rental`, which takes all the information as parameters and returns the result. The fixture can call that directly. But it's odd to have it there if it doesn't use any of the information inside the `Rental` object!

"It would make more sense as a `static` method.

"Instead, I'll create a new class—say, `LateReturns`—that has a method, `extraHours()`, for doing those calculations. Then my method in the `Rental` object can gather up the information and call `extraHours()`. The calculations for the grace period can go in there, too. Then we can test that directly. We can create an object at startup for this, and it can hold the *late returns* configuration information."

Emily's fixture is now as shown in Listing 31.2. She's set up class `LateReturns` so that "it can later be fed all the *late returns* configuration info."

Listing 31.2 **TestLate.java (version 2)**

```
public class TestLate extends fit.ColumnFixture {
  public float hoursLate, grace, highDemand;
  public boolean countGrace;

  public int extraHours() {
    LateReturns lateReturns = new LateReturns(countGrace);
    return lateReturns.extraHours(hoursLate,grace,highDemand);
  }
}
```

She was eager to write the new class and change her code. But we suggested that she first write and test a separate **LateReturns** class.

Questions & Answers

Is it usual to call from fixture code into a part of the system under test?
Yes, especially in the case of testing calculations. Of course, it is important to test that the workflow also makes use of the underlying business logic code, as discussed in Chapter 35.

Then how do I automatically test that the new logic is actually used in workflow processing, as that's the only point where the user sees it?
There are two approaches. As we've mentioned before, whenever there are calculation tests, there needs to be some associated workflow tests that make sure that the calculations are correct during workflow. Another approach is to test business calculation rules by having the fixture itself carry out the workflow actions in order to carry out the test, as we discuss in Chapter 35.

Doesn't the first approach mean that we have to test all the possibilities again?
No, not necessarily. A few tests should confirm that the appropriate logic is being called. We take this issue up further in Chapter 35.

My instinct would be to change the application directly. Why do such a simple first step?
It was lower risk to test the new code in **LateReturns** before wiring the changes into the application. Simple steps give immediate feedback, so you know you're on the right track. This also encourages better modularity.

Here, Emily could develop and test **LateReturns** completely, without touching the application. When that was all working, she then altered the application to use the new class and tested it by running the whole application.

Emily spent the next few minutes developing class **LateReturns** to pass the test. She then altered the application code to use that new code.[2] She did some manual testing to show that the change had not broken anything obvious.

Don then appeared with a lot of tests, looking pleased with himself. He told us later that they'd run all the tests: "Whenever we saw red, we had fun arguing over whether the code or a test was wrong."

---

[2] This code is altered again when early returns are handled, as discussed in Chapter 35.

> **Note**
>
> The expected values for the calculation tests here are dependent entirely on the *given* values in the table. This meant that we could isolate the code in the system under test related to that business rule.
>
> In general, the aim is to create a `static` method that takes all the explicit and implied *given* values and returns a single result, without side effects, based only on those arguments. Prior to test infecting, such business logic code is likely to be tangled with workflow-style code, so it needs to be refactored out to be independent and able to be tested directly.
>
> The advantange of isolating the logic for a calculation-based business rule is that it is clearer and is likely to make it easier to handle a change to the business rule in the future.

31.3 Summary

It wasn't obvious to Emily how to connect the fixture to the application.

- Sometimes, a simple change to the system under test is all that's needed to expose or create the specific code that encodes a business rule. That was the case here. But this can be risky, as bugs may be introduced in the process.

- At other times, the system under test is poorly organized for directly testing business logic code. In that case, the fixtures for calculation tests may need to carry out a series of actions on the system under test, as we illustrate in Chapter 35.

Developing fixtures for calculation tests can be easier to start with than action tests. From a programmer's point of view, the following general characteristics can help in choosing an early area for introducing such Fit tests.

- A part needs attention because it really needs reorganizing soon, perhaps to separate the presentation layer or to introduce a new Web-based interface.

- The application is structured to permit the tests to be carried out on the domain layer, as introduced in Chapter 30, or only minor refactoring is required to provide this access.

- People who are familiar with the code are eager to participate and have time and the support of management to do so.

31.4   Exercises

1. Write a fixture for the *grace period* table(s) that you developed for the earlier exercises in Chapter 13.

2. Write one or more fixtures for the Fit tests for your own application's business rules, as you developed them for the later exercises in Chapter 13.

CHAPTER 32

Fixtures Testing Through the User Interface

Programmers: The tables that use this fixture code are given in Chapter 14.

In this chapter, we consider the issues of testing workflow with an existing application. Although the application code for handling calculation tests may be isolated in one or a few classes, this is not usually the case with workflow tests. When the GUI code and business logic are tangled, the Fit fixtures can test the system under test through the user interface.

32.1   Introduction

In Chapter 14, Don, Emily, and Sarah started to develop several Fit tables for testing workflow. Here, we see how Emily proceeded to write fixtures that connect those Fit tables to the system under test, even though those tables were developed further in Chapter 15.

Unfortunately, the *RentEz* software architecture is structured poorly; the GUI code and the business logic—the presentation and domain layers—are tangled.[1] So there is no clear domain layer with an API that can be tested directly. Emily considered several approaches, with prompting, to tackle this difficulty.

> "We could rewrite the Fit tests, using a scripting language that tests explicitly through the GUI. However, this doesn't allow us to make much progress and we end up with tests that are difficult to maintain (see the following Note).
>
> "We could write Fit fixtures that generate scripted tests instead of testing immediately. This approach is reasonable as our testers are

---

[1] The three layers are introduced in Section 30.3 on p. 256.

already familiar with a scripting tool—if they wish to continue using it. Any changes can then be made to the Fit tables rather than to the test scripts, improving maintenance. However, this approach doesn't use the reporting capability of Fit, as the generated test scripts are run separately to get feedback.

"We could rewrite the Fit tests so that they explicitly operate on the user interface. As with the first alternative, this would lead to maintenance difficulties and would complicate the tests with irrelevant, and potentially unstable, details.

"We could leave the tests in their current abstract form and change the application to expose the parts of the domain layer that are needed for those tests. We could do this in small steps, slowly getting the tests going and checking manually that the system hasn't been broken. But this means lots of manual testing to ensure that the effort in untangling the presentation and domain layers hasn't introduced errors.

"We could leave the tests in their current form and have the fixtures perform operations on the GUI. This means that the Fit tests remain concise and independent of the details of the GUI."

Note

Tests in many scripting languages can be recorded when the system is used and can be played back at another time. Unfortunately, the resulting test scripts are usually far too detailed and are difficult to alter and maintain. Some suffer from depending on the position of GUI components on the screen, so are vulnerable to simple layout changes.

The company had used various test scripting systems but was not inclined to continue with them. After much discussion, Emily decided to proceed with the last option. To get started on this approach, she decided to try it out on a simple system.

The *RentEz* GUI is written with Java Swing, so a way was needed to test through that interface. Fortunately, there are several open source tools for automating unit testing of Swing-based GUI systems. See the following Note for details of some of these
tools.

After exploring the various tool possibilities and seeking advice, Emily decided to use *jfcunit*. This tool is intended for unit testing, based on JUnit, so Emily used a `FitLibrary` class that made it easy to use from Fit fixtures.

Note

Following are several open source frameworks for unit testing Java Swing-based GUI systems:[a]

- *Abbot*, available at http://abbot.sourceforge.net

- *jfcunit*, available at http://sourceforge.net/projects/jfcunit

- *Jemmy*, available at http://jemmy.netbeans.org

- *Pounder*, available at http://pounder.sourceforge.net

- *Marathon*, available at http://marathonman.sourceforge.net

Several of these frameworks also have support for scripting tests in various forms, including using XML. Similar frameworks are available for other GUI systems.

Such systems have support for accessing the required component from the GUI and operating on it. Access to a component may be made in various ways, including its **name** property and its type.

---

[a] See the *Gui Tools* at www.junit.org for the latest list.

32.2 Spike

After some discussion about the best place to start, Emily decided to start with a simple mockup rather than with the full *RentEz* system. She developed the simple Fit test shown in Figure 32.1. This test includes a setup table to define two rental items, followed by a table to check the current set of rental items.

DoRentEze		
setup		
rental item	*count*	*$/hour*
coffee dispenser	10	8.20
hot water dispenser	12	8.00
rental items		
name	*count*	*$/hour*
coffee dispenser	10	8.20
hot water dispenser	12	8.00

Figure 32.1 Setup and Check

Emily then developed a much simplified user interface for part of *RentEz* to run this test. This UI is shown in Figure 32.2; when the user clicks the *Add* button, the dialog box shown in Figure 32.3 results.

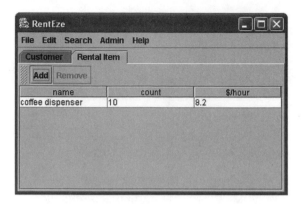

Figure 32.2 Spiked *RentEz* Application

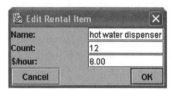

Figure 32.3 Dialog Box for Adding Rental Items

Note

In Extreme Programming, a *spike* is a short experiment with some technology or some possible solution to a problem. The idea is to learn from the experience and to then apply the improved understanding to the system under development.

32.3   The Fixtures

The fixture `DoRentEze` that Emily wrote for Figure 32.1 is shown in Listing 32.1. This fixture runs the GUI by constructing an `AdminFrame`, which is the Java Swing `JFrame` for the simple mockup. This GUI is passed to a `RentEzeUiAdapter`; this adapter [GHJV95] is responsible for carrying out the operations on the GUI.

`DoRentEze` defines two methods, corresponding to the actions in the first rows of the second and third tables in Figure 32.1. The `setUp()` method returns a `SetUpFixture` fixture object[2] to set up the rental item data. The `rentalItems()` method returns a `SetFixture` with the actual collection of rental items from the system under test.

---

[2] See Section 28.3 on p. 232 for an introduction to writing `SetUpFixture` classes.

Listing 32.1 **DoRentEze.java**

```
public class DoRentEze extends DoFixture {
   private RentEzeUiAdapter adapter =
        new RentEzeUiAdapter(new AdminFrame());

   public Fixture setUp() {
      return new RentalItemSetUp();
   }
   public Fixture rentalItems() throws Throwable {
      return new SetFixture(adapter.getRentalItems());
   }
   public class RentalItemSetUp extends SetUpFixture {
      public void rentalItemCountDollarSlashHour(String name,
            int count, double hourlyRate) throws Throwable {
         adapter.addRentalItem(name,count,hourlyRate);
      }
   }
}
```

32.4   The Adapter

Initially, Emily had encoded the GUI operations directly in the fixture, but she had realized that it would be better to have an adapter. The adapter code is shown in Listing 32.2. This code uses a GuiAdapter[3] to operate on the components, such as JButtons, of the running GUI.

The adapter provides two API methods, as called from the fixture. The first method, addRentalItem(), emulates the operations of the user through the GUI, as shown in Figure 32.2, to add the details of a new rental item.

- pressTab() clicks the second tab of the named JTabbedPane.

- pressButton() clicks the *Add* button now showing.

- getAdapterForFirstDialog() returns a GuiAdapter for the dialog that's expected to show, as shown in Figure 32.3.

- enterString() is used three times to enter text into named JTextFields in the dialog. The strings are as supplied from the Fit table.

- pressButton() clicks the *Add* button on the dialog to complete the data entry.

This GuiAdapter depends on the Swing components of interest being explicitly named. For example, the first JTextField is named "nameField", as shown in part of the code for the dialog box in Listing 32.3.

The second method of class RentEzeUiAdapter, getRentalItems(), is shown in Listing 32.2. This method passes the actual collection from the JTable, named

---

[3] This general-purpose class is available as a part of the FitLibrary.

Listing 32.2 **RentEzeUiAdapter.java**

```java
public class RentEzeUiAdapter {
    GuiAdapter frameAdapter;

    public RentEzeUiAdapter(JFrame frame) {
        frameAdapter = new GuiAdapter(frame);
    }
    public void addRentalItem(String name, int count,
            double hourlyRate) throws Throwable {
        frameAdapter.pressTab("tabbedPane",1); // Press tab for Rental
        frameAdapter.pressButton("addButton");
        GuiAdapter dialogAdapter = frameAdapter.getAdapterForFirstDialog();
        dialogAdapter.enterString("nameField",name);
        dialogAdapter.enterString("count",""+count);
        dialogAdapter.enterString("hourlyRateField",""+hourlyRate);
        dialogAdapter.pressButton("addButton");
    }
    public List getRentalItems() throws Throwable {
        frameAdapter.pressTab("tabbedPane",1); // Press tab for Rental
        return frameAdapter.collectionOfJTable("table");
    }
}
```

Listing 32.3 **EditRentalItemDialog.java**

```java
public class EditRentalItemDialog extends JDialog {
    private JTextField nameField = new JTextField(20);
    private JTextField countField = new JTextField();
    private JTextField hourlyRateField = new JTextField();

    public EditRentalItemDialog(JFrame frame, RentalItem item) {
        super(frame, "Edit Rental Item", false);
        // ...
        nameField.setName("nameField");
        hourlyRateField.setName("hourlyRateField");
        countField.setName("count");
    }
    // ...
}
```

"table", to a `SetFixture`. This method makes use of the general-purpose method `collectionOfJTable()` in class `GuiAdapter`, which takes the internal name of a `JTable` and returns a list of `Map` objects, one for each row in the table. A `Map` defines, for a row, the mapping between each `JTable` column name and the corresponding value from the table.

Figure 32.4 shows the interaction during setup of the first two tables of Figure 32.1 and the fixture, GUI, and application objects.

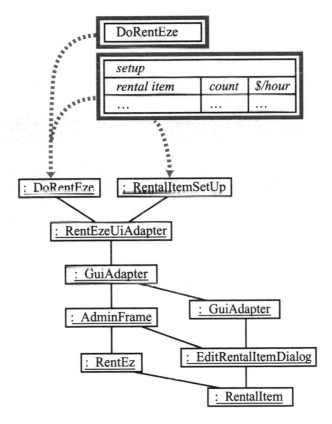

Figure 32.4 Testing Through the GUI

> **Note**
>
> The adapter acts as mapping layer that maps each API action into a sequence of operations on the GUI. Having a separate layer means that we can write the fixtures for the intended API, as it develops. Once this mapping layer is in place for a part of the API, the corresponding part of the system can be untangled. Once we have a means of switching the tests so that they can be run through the GUI or the API or both, we can be sure that mistakes aren't introduced and left.

> **Note**
>
> `SetFixture`, `ArrayFixture`, and `SubsetFixture` all interpret `Map` objects in an actual collection in a special way, as introduced in Section 28.9 on p. 243. Instead of checking for an instance variable or a property that corresponds to the Fit table header name, the fixture looks for a mapping from that name to a value. For consistency with the treatment of table headers, extended camel casing[a] is applied to a `JTable` column name before it is used as a key into the `Map`.
>
> ---
> [a] See Section 22.2 on p. 190 for an introduction to extended camel casing.

32.5   Showing Others

Once Emily had it all working, she was eager to show it to Don and Mitra. Mitra commented, "The beauty of this approach is that you can see the GUI working while the tests are running. This could be used to show a client how a part of the system works. I suppose it could also be used to generate user documentation as 'movies' or a sequence of screenshots."[4]

"Yes," replied Emily, "That would be easy to do. That's another good reason to use realistic data in the tests. And when the user interface changes, it would be trivial to regenerate the 'movies.'"

Don added, "I expect that you'd notice little odd things that weren't being picked up by the automated tests. It would also be handy to have automated tests that drive the application to a point where you want to do some exploratory testing."

"I'm now ready," Emily concluded, "to start applying this approach to *RentEz*."

---
[4] The Naked Objects system [PM02] uses this sort of approach to generate user documentation in HTML from programmed acceptance tests.

> **Note**
>
> Following are various frameworks for testing Web-based systems. Java-based open source frameworks include[a]
>
> - *HttpUnit*, available at www.httpunit.org
> - *HtmlUnit*, available at http://htmlunit.sourceforge.net
> - *JWebUnit*, available at http://jwebunit.sourceforge.net
> - *Canoo Web test*, available at http://webtest.canoo.com
>
> Of course, these frameworks can be used to test a Web site regardless of the language used to develop the Web application. Similar frameworks are available for other languages.
>
> *HtmlFixture* is a Fit fixture that in turn uses *HtmlUnit*. This fixture provides a fixed vocabulary of actions and checks for testing Web-based systems. It's available at http://fitness.org/FitNesse.HtmlFixture.
>
> ---
>
> [a] See the *Web Tools* at www.junit.org for the latest list.

32.6 Summary

In order to test some workflow of *RentEz*, it was necessary to test through the GUI. Rather than changing the Fit tests to do this explicitly, Emily decided to have the fixtures map from the tests into operations through the user interface.

To gain experience with this approach, Emily developed a simple mockup of *RentEz* for trying out this approach. She ended up introducing a mapping layer, an adapter, so that she could design the desired API for the domain layer in the process.

This approach has several advantages.

- The Fit tests remain independent of the GUI. A change in the GUI may simply require a change in one part of an adapter. By contrast, if the Fit tests are explicitly tested through the GUI, all the affected tests would need to be changed.

- The GUI can be seen in action, with the possibility of automatically recording the results for user documentation.

- Simple changes in the application, such as method name changes, are more likely to be picked up at compile time and/or handled automatically through the use of refactoring tools.

- A portion of the testing can be made through the GUI, tailored to get reasonable build times.

This approach has two disadvantages.

1. The tests are much slower when they go through the GUI. This leads to slower feedback after changes on whether any tests have been broken.

2. The tests are still dependent on the **name** properties of the Swing components. For example, if a component that is used in an adapter is removed, there is no compile-time check for this; it has to be checked by running the tests.

We take up these matters in the next chapter.

Questions & Answers

We'd like all our tests to go through the GUI, so that the GUI code is checked as well.

There are two assumptions here. One is that the tests will run quickly enough to give you quick feedback. If the build and test process is too slow, people will put off getting essential feedback because of the delays in getting it. One approach here is to run some tests through the GUI and some through the API; the choice can be made randomly when the tests are run, to give the right tradeoff between performance and coverage.

The second assumption is that there is significant code in the GUI that needs to be tested along with the functionality of the system. One approach is to reduce the GUI-specific code as much as possible [Fea02]. Another is to have separate tests that simply test that the user interface itself works correctly: that menu items are enabled appropriately, that the right information is displayed, and so on.

It would be great to create Fit tests for an existing system by simply using the system through the user interface.

Yes, that can be done by adding code into the system to record the tests at the right level of detail. For example, the code associated with a dialog box could generate an action for a Fit table when the *OK* button is clicked. This approach is used in *texttest* [Tex] and is also described in [MBA03].

What if information that needs to be checked is not available through the GUI?

In that case, it will be necessary to change the system under test to log such information when it's changed. Then the Fit test can check the log file for the information.

The notion of an adapter, as we introduced earlier, could be used here as well. Rather than encoding details of the log file format in the fixture, an adapter could provide the required API and do this. Then, when the relevant part of the domain layer has a suitable API, that could be used instead.

The general approach to using logs for testing is emphasized in the testing framework *texttest* [Tex].

CHAPTER 33

Restructuring the System for Testing

Chapter 30 introduced the motivation for changes to the application to accommodate testability. Chapter 32 showed one way to begin testing without such changes, by testing through the user interface. Such tests can then support the process of changing the application itself, helping to ensure that bugs are not introduced in the process.

In this chapter, we introduce the ways and means of test infecting an application. Surprisingly, the changes we need to make to enable direct testing also have huge benefits in other respects. Michael Feathers [Fea04] provides considerable help in working with legacy, or non-test-infected, code.

Sometimes, quite drastic changes are needed, and this can be off-putting because it looks like wasted work. The way forward is to make small changes that gradually test infect the code in areas that are changing anyway or are of low quality, so that the quality spreads in an organized, nonrisky manner.

To do this, a boot-strapping approach is needed. Once in place, a slow outer layer of tests can support the evolution of changes to the application to test infect it.

33.1 Test Infecting

Emily, pair programming with Neo, altered *RentEz* in small steps to pass the growing number of Fit tests, doing this for each test in turn, where needed. They had been getting familiar with agile development techniques and wanted to get more experience with pair programming (see the following Note).

They added a **name** property to those GUI components that needed to be accessed to enable the tests to run through the user interface (see Chapter 32). They took less time than they expected to make the changes for the first test—luckily, as it was a rather mechanical task. As Emily commented, "At least there's a low chance of introducing errors, because we're simply adding simple code to set names and not otherwise changing what's there."

> **Note**
>
> Pair programming [Wil02] is an effective technique to develop high-quality software that combines development and review in a single process. While one person is using the keyboard, the other is actively engaged in watching, thinking, and giving feedback. Together, the two are continuously considering and discussing various approaches to unit tests, code, and design.
>
> Although it appears that less work will be done with two people working together, experimental evidence indicates that this technique produces higher-quality systems, thus reducing longer-term costs owing to bugs and badly structured systems.

33.2   Slow Tests

Emily and Neo found that as the number of running tests grew, they ran too slowly to give fast-enough feedback after making changes. They waited while the tests ran, which was frustrating. As Neo said, "This is a pain; let's make more changes before we run the tests, so we make faster progress."

So they made more changes before checking that they hadn't broken anything. As Emily pointed out, however, "We're spending time debugging instead, which is even more frustrating. It's time to tackle the speed of the tests so we get faster feedback and make quick progress without frustration!"

After looking briefly into the cause of the speed problem, Emily and Neo figured that it was owing to the speed of the user interface and of the database. Neo was eager to start making changes. But Emily suggested, "Let's put some print statements in the fixture adapter code to see how frequently different parts of the GUI are used. It's better to know where the performance issues are, rather than guessing."

"Hmm, good idea," agreed Neo. "It's no different from understanding and improving any other performance problem"[Fow02b].

They subsequently found that the setup adapter code was executing most frequently. "It's obvious when you think about it," reflected Emily.

"It should be straightforward to add setup methods to the API," said Neo.

"Yes, let's do that next," replied Emily.

33.3   Setup

Before beginning to rewrite the fixtures, Emily and Neo reviewed the setup tables, as shown again in Figure 33.1.

"Let's start by writing a minimal `StartApplication` class," suggested Neo, "and add code in small steps."

rent.StartApplication					
setup					
rental item name	*count*	*$/hour*	*$/day*	*$/week*	*deposit*
coffee dispenser	10	1.50	8.20	60.00	0.00
hot water dispenser	12	1.50	8.00	50.00	0.00
cup	500	0.05	0.45	2.00	0.10

setup	
client name	*phone*
Joanna	373 7599

setup	
staff name	*phone*
Bill	555 9876

time is now	2004/05/06 09:01

Figure 33.1 Setup of Rentals for a Client

Listing 33.1 **StartApplication.java (version 1)**

```java
public class StartApplication extends DoFixture {
    private RentEz rentEz;
}
```

"Good idea," replied Emily, "why don't you start."

Neo created a fresh version of the class `StartApplication` for testing through the domain layer, as shown in Listing 33.1.

He then ran the test, which failed at the start of the second table of Figure 33.1, as expected. "Each of the setup tables starts with *setup*," said Neo, "so again we'll need a separate fixture, as with the GUI-based fixtures."

The change he made to `StartApplication` is shown in Listing 33.2. A single object of `GeneralSetUpFixture` is created once and is used for all setup tables.

Two of the methods of the fixture class `GeneralSetUpFixture` written by Neo are shown in Listing 33.3. These methods in turn call into the API of *RentEz*.

The next step was for Emily and Neo to extend the API with these methods and get them working. They talked to Sarah, who added a Fit test to check that the setup had worked correctly. This gave them fast feedback on whether their new code was working correctly. It took several hours for Neo and Emily, between them, to get the new code working.

The test passed. Figure 33.2 shows the interaction of the fixtures with `RentEz`.

With this change, the tests were running at a better pace but still not fast enough. It was time to start untangling the presentation and domain layers so that testing could occur directly through the API.

Listing 33.2 **StartApplication.java (version 2)**

```
public class StartApplication extends DoFixture {
    private RentEz rentEz;
    private GeneralSetUpFixture setUp;

    public StartApplication() throws Exception {
        rentEz = new RentEz();
        setUp = new GeneralSetUpFixture(rentEz);
    }
    public Fixture setup() {
        return setUp;
    }
}
```

Listing 33.3 **GeneralSetUpFixture.java**

```
public class GeneralSetUpFixture extends SetUpFixture {
    private RentEz rentEz;

    public GeneralSetUpFixture(RentEz phs) {
        this.rentEz = phs;
    }
    public void staffNamePhone(String name, String phone) throws Exception {
        rentEz.createStaffMember(admin(), name, phone);
    }
    public void clientNamePhone(String name, String phone) throws Exception {
        rentEz.createClient(admin(), name, phone);
    }
    // ...
    private StaffMember admin() throws MissingException {
        return rentEz.getStaffMember("Admin");
    }
}
```

33.4 Barriers to Testing

The major problem in speeding up test execution is tangled application code. Business logic in the presentation layer and database access code in the domain layer objects can make it difficult to test business rules in isolation. Even if the logic associated with a business rule is defined in a single class, it may still be impossible to test that logic without needing many other objects to be available.

This issue is primarily one of *modularity*. A lack of modularity has a big impact on the ease of changing a system; the more dependencies between different parts of a system, the more difficult it is to change it, let alone isolate and fix bugs in those parts. Many systems also have a problem with *redundancy* (see the Note).

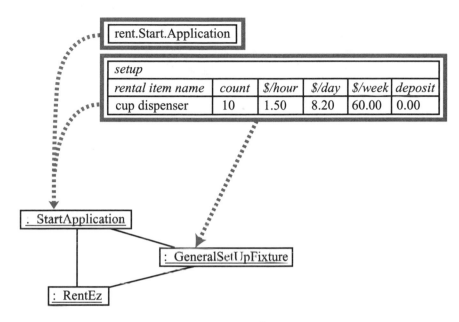

Figure 33.2 Setup

Note

Once a system grows complex and is difficult to change, pieces of code are much more likely to be duplicated rather than reused. To reuse existing code, it is often necessary to change it so that it is available in a useful form. That may simply mean extracting it into a new method, or it may require a change to the class structure of the application. Without tests, such *refactoring* changes are difficult to carry out without introducing new bugs [Fow99], [Ker04]. Even with a refactoring tool, some changes inevitably have to be done by hand, with a good chance of errors being made.

So as the complexity grows, the developers learn from bitter experience that it is better to not change the existing code. An alternative approach is to duplicate code, but that leads to *redundancy* and thus *inconsistency* [HT00]. It goes like this: We end up with two or more pieces of code that carry out some task—redundancy—but when it needs to be changed, only one piece is altered—inconsistency.

We now look at adapting the application incrementally, so as to avoid unnecessary risk.

33.5   Transactions

Chapter 15 introduced the notion of business transactions. Emily and Neo reviewed Figure 33.3, a Fit table from Section 15.4 on p. 119 that manages such transactions.

begin transaction for client	Joanna	staff	Bill			
rent	100		cup	for	2	weeks
pay with cash $	210.00					
complete transaction						

Figure 33.3 Handling Transactions

They then looked through the GUI code. "Hmmm," Emily commented, "there's such a lot of business logic in the GUI code. See how the current amount owing is encoded in that event-handling code."

"Yes," replied Neo, "the general handling of the whole transaction is tangled up in there. We'll need to pull that out in some way and put it in the domain layer."

After spending some time looking through the GUI code for transaction-specific business logic, Emily and Neo felt that they understood some of what was going on. Neo suggested, "Let's start refactoring out the business logic into a separate class, which can remain with the GUI until things get clearer."

"OK," replied Emily. "We need to pull out the notion of a transaction starting, the things that happen in the transaction, tracking the amount owing and paid, and the transaction completion. How about calling the new class `ClientTransaction`?"

In small steps, they extracted the transaction business logic into class `Client-Transaction`, running the GUI-based tests after each change to ensure that they hadn't broken anything. This was slow work that they had to do very carefully. They needed to understand how both the GUI and the transaction code worked, before pulling it apart. Several times, Neo started making a change that Emily questioned. It worked well having two minds working on this.

It was slow to begin with, but as `ClientTransaction` evolved, it got easier. They found redundant code in various parts of the GUI, which they eliminated with the new class. They were pleased with their new abstraction and felt that they understood better the notion of transactions. Having clear Fit tests helped considerably, as they could incorporate most of the "language" of the tests into the interface of `ClientTransaction`.

Their experience is very common; test infecting an application usually adds clarity and removes redundancy. The improved modularity makes it easier to find and fix bugs and to make changes in the future.

Having the fixtures call directly into the API also means that some changes, such as method name changes, will be automatically propagated into the fixture code by refactoring tools. Similarly, many inconsistencies will be picked up by the compiler.

This tighter coupling works well, compared to the loose coupling when tests are run through the GUI. For example, if a GUI component is removed or renamed, we won't discover a problem until the tests are run. This delays feedback.

33.6   Transaction Fixture

"Now we need a fixture that connects to the `ClientTransaction` in *RentEz* and carries out actions on it," Emily suggested.[1]

"Yes," replied Neo, "we can pass the `ClientTransaction` object to it when we create the `DoFixture`."

Emily added support for transactions through a separate `DoFixture` object. The method `beginTransactionForClientStaff()` in class `StartApplication`, as shown in Listing 33.4, corresponds to the first action in the Fit table in Figure 33.3.

Listing 33.4 **StartApplication.java (part 3)**

```
public class StartApplication extends DoFixture {
    private RentEz rentEz;

    public Fixture beginTransactionForClientStaff(String clientName,
            String staffMemberName) throws MissingException {
        ClientTransaction transaction = rentEz.beginClientTransaction(
            clientName,staffMemberName);
        return new TransActionFixture(rentEz,transaction);
    }
}
```

This method returns a new `TransActionFixture`, which defines methods corresponding to the actions used in a transaction table. For example, four of the methods of class `TransActionFixture` are shown in Listing 33.5.

Figure 33.4 shows the interaction of the tables, fixtures, and application objects for tests involving a business transaction. Note how the `TransActionFixture` object acts directly on the `ClientTransaction` object within the system under test.

Questions & Answers

Is it usual to have fixtures refer to other system under test objects, such as the `ClientTransaction`?

Yes, and it is desirable to do so, as it keeps the fixture simple and minimizes the dependency of the fixture code on other parts of the system. The fixture objects connect to the domain objects in much the same way that GUI objects do.

---

[1] See Section 28.5 on p. 234 for an introduction to this approach.

Listing 33.5 **TransActionFixture.java**

```java
public class TransActionFixture extends fit.DoFixture {
   private ClientTransaction transaction;
   private RentEz rentEz;

   public TransActionFixture(RentEz rentEz,
         ClientTransaction transaction) {
      this.rentEz = rentEz;
      this.transaction = transaction;
   }
   public Money rentForWeeks(int count, String hireItemName,
         int weeks) {
      return transaction.rent(count,getRentalItemType(hireItemName),
            new Duration(0,0,weeks));
   }
   public boolean payWithCashDollar(Money amount) {
      return transaction.payCash(amount);
   }
   public boolean refundCashDollar(Money cashAmount) {
      return transaction.refundCash(cashAmount);
   }
   public boolean completeTransaction() {
      return transaction.complete();
   }
   //...
}
```

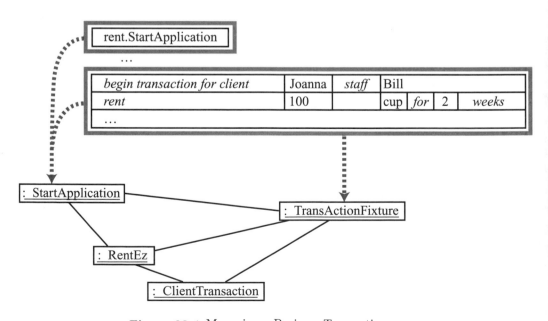

Figure 33.4 Managing a Business Transaction

With testing being run through the GUI, the setup time could, presumably, be reduced by writing setup data directly to the database.

Yes. If the domain and data source layers are still tangled, so that testing involves the database, the initial fixture can set up the data in the database directly. Then the setup fixtures have nothing to do. Or they could check that the setup data is as expected for the start of the test.

Wouldn't using the setup tables for checking mean that the setup tables would need to be changed to distinquish the various sorts of setup?

Yes. Instead of having just `set up` in the first row of each of the setup tables, we'd need something like `set up rental items`, `set up clients`, and so on.

As the separation of the domain objects and the UI is carried out, one roadblock to testing has been removed. The next hurdle is domain objects that have database management—or other forms of persistence—tangled within them.

33.7   Split Domain and Data Source Layers

Now that some of the tests were running directly against the API, they were somewhat faster. The database access times were now the bottleneck. We don't follow Emily and Neo as they tackle this problem, because it takes us well away from Fit, but we do give some general guidelines.

Carrying out tests when the domain objects include code for managing persistence is more difficult. The dependency between the objects and the database—or file system or whatever—may mean that a database connection is needed, even if the tests don't involve the database. Database or file access will slow down the tests, which becomes significant as the number of Fit tests grows into hundreds. The problem gets worse when a domain object refers to many other objects that are also persisted to the database.

The solution is similar to the one noted earlier.

- Focus on the parts that have the most impact on the speed of tests.

- Untangle the code by separating the persistence management layer.

- Make the changes slowly and incrementally where they will provide the best value in speedup and/or improvements to the modularity.

This untangling can have positive benefits beyond testing. For example, it may be possible to use a tool that automatically manages the mapping from the domain objects to the persistence store, getting rid of a lot of tedious code. Or it may be possible to autogenerate some of the persistence layer, using reflection on the domain objects. See Fowler [Fow02a] for further details of managing persistence in a layered fashion.

Once we have separated the data source layer, we can more easily manage the creation of objects from our fixtures during testing. For many tests, we can create temporary domain objects that are needed in the tests but don't need to be written to the database.

However, we still need some end-to-end tests, and that involves access to the database, as there is much scope for bugs in the SQL and code that manages that layer. Once the layers are separated, it is much easier to also use unit tests for the interaction between those bottom two layers. Relevant to this process is [FS03], which discusses the evolution of database design.

The next hurdle is that many of our domain objects have references to other objects. To create a domain object for testing, we need to create a lot of other objects as well. Much of the time, they are irrelevant to our tests.

Questions & Answers

What about the speed with the underlying database?
Yes, that can be a problem with the time it takes to run lots of Fit tests. At some point, we can't afford the database access time, just as we can't afford the GUI testing time.

What does that involve with the database?
It means separating the persistence management from the domain objects, such as **RentalItem**. In the same way, we'll need to separate the GUI layer from those objects so that different UIs are possible, including a Web browser interface, as well as tests.

That sounds like a lot of work!
Yes, it's never pretty to dissect a legacy system to test its innards. But the payback is considerable, and it gets easier as you make progress.

33.8   Reduce Interdependencies

Reducing the interdependence of domain objects makes it easier to test them. At the same time, we get other benefits, because the modularity will make it easier to make changes, reuse code, and find bugs.

However, it is more difficult to reduce these dependencies, because many of them are inherent in the associations that arise from the business rules. Others result from the architecture and are difficult to avoid.

Nevertheless, some surprisingly powerful techniques make use of suitable abstractions. For specific details of managing and reducing such dependencies, see [Mar02], [Fow97], and [Fow02a].

33.9   Summary

We have strongly advocated that Fit tests express the business rule tests as clearly as possible. This may seem difficult to do because it is so easy to get caught up in the way things are, or will be, implemented, instead of the essence of what's needed from a business perspective. It may also seem strange because it seems like rework, with the application having to change to aid testability.

We have seen how we can, step by step, eliminate dependencies that get in the way of testing. In the previous chapter, we started by rejecting the idea of testing through the UI explicitly in the Fit tables and showed how the fixtures could act as adapters to do that job.

We then looked at how to eliminate or reduce dependencies between the domain objects and the presentation and the data source layers and other domain objects. The adaptation of the application to enable testing needs to be done carefully, so as to minimize the risk of lowering quality. As tests are introduced from the outer level, the UI, they can support refactorings that enable still more test access.

There may be complex internal logic that is dependent only vaguely on the business logic and so will not be tested with the Fit tables. In that case, the process of adaptation needs to continue deeper into the application, with the support of programmer tests, such as in JUnit.

The changes we need to make to enable direct testing have huge benefits in other respects. Making a system testable for business-oriented tests and for programmer tests leads to strong modularity and a reduction in redundancy. It is not uncommon to add functionality to well-structured software by generalizing and *shrinking* the code.

Experience has shown that driving the development of the code with tests, at the business and programmer levels, can lead to high-quality systems that continue to be refreshed as they change. Doing a little refactoring all the time, as a part of the design process, can mean that development goes more quickly rather than more slowly. The reason is that much less effort is spent in bug fixing and rework, and it is much easier to enhance good-quality code.

Questions & Answers

What if the application is a real mess?
Rather than refactoring step by step what you have, it may be better to start with a fresh application that's developed test first and to slowly bring relevant pieces of code across step by step. This is especially good when required enhancements to the system break important assumptions about the current architecture. However, you may find it difficult to make a convincing case for this, as it appears as if it's going backwards, even though the result will be better and you will get there sooner.

What about domain objects that don't have a UI and that simply encode business rules?

The principle is still the same, in that modularity may need to be improved. However, there may be good reason to *add* UI for a newly isolated object that manages a business rule. A provided UI makes available to users a special business rule *calculator*. For example, they would be able to explore the consequences of various *given* values on the *calculated* values without having to commit data changes to find out.

CHAPTER 34

Mocks and Clocks

Programmers: The tables that use this fixture code are given in Chapter 15.

The tests in Chapter 15 were developed to advance the clock and set the time in order to test some parts of the system. Emily and Neo handled the changing date in the application by using the system clock indirectly. That meant that they could substitute a different clock that allows the date and time to be changed by the tests.

34.1   Introduction

Emily and Neo worked together to implement the fixtures for the tests in Chapter 15.

Those tests assume that the clock and time can be changed. "However," stressed Neo, "it would be a big mistake to try and fiddle with the real system clock."

"Yes, I agree," replied Emily, "so let's use a *mock object* for the date and time when running the tests. That will mean changing the application." (See the following Note on *mock objects*.)

> **Note**
>
> A *mock object* [MFC00] is designed to be substituted for the usual object in a system to simplify testing and to focus tests on a subset of the system. The use of *mock objects* is common in test-driven development and is a big topic in its own right [Bec02], [HT03], [Ast03], [RS04].

"At least," agreed Neo, "we can do the changes in small steps, and the tests will pick up any uses of the clock that we miss in *RentEz*."

Emily suggested, "Let's access the system clock indirectly in the application, through an object of a new class, `SystemClock`. In order to substitute a *mock* clock, we'll also need an interface: say, `Clock`."

290 Chapter 34 Mocks and Clocks

She took over the computer and coded the `SystemClock` class shown in Listing 34.1. "It simply returns information from the system clock: A new `Date` is set with the current date and time."

Listing 34.1 **SystemClock.java**
```
public class SystemClock implements Clock {
    public Date getTime() {
        return new Date();
    }
}
```

"The `Clock` interface is simple, with one method," added Emily. The interface code she entered is shown in Listing 34.2.

Listing 34.2 **Clock.java**
```
public interface Clock {
    public Date getTime();
}
```

"We need a single way for all the code to access the date and time," Emily offered.

"Yes," replied Neo, "let's have a method in *RentEz* for that."

Emily altered the application, *RentEz*, so that it creates a `SystemClock` as the clock to use, as shown in Listing 34.3.

Listing 34.3 **RentEz.java (version 1)**
```
public class RentEz {
    private Clock clock;

    public RentEz() {
        clock = new SystemClock();
    }
    public Date getTime() {
        return clock.getTime();
    }
    // ...
}
```

Neo noted, "So let's change the application code to call the `getTime()` method of *RentEz*, rather than accessing the system clock directly."

"Yes," replied Emily, "we can tackle one Fit test at a time and make only the changes that are needed to pass that test."

34.2   Changing the Date

"Let's review the way that the date is changed in the tests," suggested Emily. Figure 34.1 shows a table with the action *time is now* for changing the current date and time, as used in Chapter 15.

time is now	2004/05/06 09:01

Figure 34.1 Set the Date/Time

"So that means that we need a method `timeIsNow()` in the fixture, and we need a *mock* clock for testing," Neo suggested.

"Yes, and we'll need a way to change the current date/time in the mock," added Emily, "and we need to pass the mock clock to the application."

Listing 34.4 shows part of the fixture class `StartApplication`, which Emily altered to deal with the date. When an object of class `StartApplication` is created, it creates a `MockClock` object, which is passed in the constructor to the system under test, the `RentEz` object.

Listing 34.4 **StartApplication.java (part 1)**
```
public class StartApplication extends DoFixture {
    private final MockClock mockClock = new MockClock();
    private RentEz rentEz;

    public StartApplication() throws Exception {
        rentEz = new RentEz(mockClock);
    }
    public boolean timeIsNow(Date time) {
        mockClock.setTime(time);
        return true;
    }
    // ...
}
```

It works well to create the `MockClock` in the fixture and pass it into the application, because then the date/time can easily be changed by the fixture object. For the action `time is now` in Figure 34.1, the corresponding method `timeIsNow()` in Listing 34.4 calls the `setTime()` method of the `MockClock`.

The `timeIsNow()` method returns `true`, so the corresponding Fit action will be reported in green. This is what Don wanted, so he could see that the time had been changed.

Emily's class `MockClock` is shown in Listing 34.5. It simply maintains the last date/time that it was set to and supplies that `Date` in method `getTime()`.

The application needs to run in either test mode or in normal operation. To run in test mode, a `RentEz` object is created with a `MockClock` as an argument, as shown with the added constructor in class `RentEz` in Listing 34.6.

Listing 34.5 **MockClock.java**

```java
public class MockClock implements Clock {
  private Date currentTime;

  public void setTime(Date time) {
    currentTime = time;
  }
  public Date getTime() {
    return currentTime;
  }
}
```

Listing 34.6 **RentEz.java (version 2)**

```java
public class RentEz {
  private Clock clock;

  public RentEz(Clock clock) {
    this.clock = clock;
  }
  public RentEz() {
    clock = new SystemClock();
  }
  public Date getTime() {
    return clock.getTime();
  }
  // ...
}
```

34.3   Time-Related Object Interactions

Figure 34.2 shows the interaction of the fixtures with the system under test and the
MockClock. When the StartApplication object is created, it creates an object of
class RentEz, passing to it a MockClock. The system under test subsequently uses
that clock for the time, which is updated by *time is now* actions.

34.4   Date Formatting

When Emily and Neo ran the first test, they expected it to fail with the incorrect
date, as they had not yet altered the corresponding code in the application to use
the new Clock. But instead, the test failed because of the format of the date values
in the Fit table. The standard format for Date was incorrect because it included
seconds.

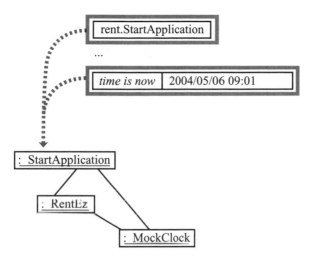

Figure 34.2 Using a Mock Clock

Emily extended the constructor in class `StartApplication` to call the `DoFixture` method `registerParseDelegate()`. This method specifies that `Date` values from the Fit tables are to be formatted without seconds, using a `DateFormat`, as shown in Listing 34.7.

Listing 34.7 **StartApplication.java (part 2)**

```java
public class StartApplication extends DoFixture {
    private final DateFormat dateFormat
        = new SimpleDateFormat("yyyy/MM/dd HH:mm");
    private RentEz rentEz;

    public StartApplication() throws Exception {
        // ...
        registerParseDelegate(Date.class,dateFormat);
    }
    // ...
}
```

34.5 Changing the Application in Small Steps

Once the first test was failing because of the incorrect actual date being that day's date, Emily and Neo started to change the application to access the `Clock` from class `RentEz`. Emily offered the driving seat to Neo.

Together, they traced from the test fixture into the code to see specifically where the application was accessing the system clock as it affected that test. Neo then changed that code to access the date through `RentEz`.

After one change, the test passed, surprising them both. They then chose the next Fit test involving dates and ran it to see it fail. After some time tracing through the code, they found another point that needed to be changed to use the new Clock. "There seems to be some redundancy here," remarked Neo.

"Let's mark it in the code and come back to it later," suggested Emily. "By using the tests to drive the change, we can be sure that all the changes have been tested."

Questions & Answers

What if you notice some code that needs to be changed, but there's no test to force the change?
At some point, it would be wise to think about the test that would be needed to use that code. That may take some careful thinking. However, it may not be possible to create such a test, if the code is completely redundant. It may have been left there after a change and no one was sure about removing it.

34.6   Summary

We have seen a useful pattern to follow when a system depends on another, independent system, such as the system clock. Emily and Neo introduced a normal and a mock form of the clock so that it was easy to switch between them. The test fixture creates the mock clock and passes it to the system under test, making it easy for the fixture to alter the date and time.

Questions & Answers

Can this *mocking* approach be used with other sorts of independent systems?
Yes. There is a tradeoff in doing this, however. The increase in speed of running the tests leads to a reduction in the quality of the testing. A good approach is to run the faster tests more frequently but still run the end-to-end tests involving the whole system regularly.

This approach to mocking is handy to use in programmer tests with JUnit as well. It allows subsystems to be tested by removing their dependence on other parts of the system. See [HT03], [RS04] for further details.

CHAPTER 35

Running Calculation Tests Indirectly

Programmers: The tables that use this fixture code are given in Chapter 16.

In Chapter 16, we showed that many similar action tests may being used to test several business rules, including rules that are better handled as calculation tests. We now show two ways that Emily and Neo implemented the fixtures for those calculation tests. One approach is to have a fixture that calls directly into the specific logic that handles that business rule. This approach is good when the business rule is encoded as a distinct piece of logic, ideally as a function that can be called directly.

The other, indirect, approach is similar to the approach Emily used in Chapter 32, when there was no API that she could test through. There she tested through operations on the GUI. In this approach here, the fixture calls a sequence of actions, creating sufficient objects to make it work.

35.1 Testing Directly

As we saw in Chapter 31, one approach to implementing fixtures for calculation tests is to call a specific method within the application that does only that calculation for a business rule. For example, consider the fair charge table from Chapter 16 shown again in Figure 35.1.

The `DoFixture` class `CalculateFairCharge` that Neo and Emily developed is shown in Listing 35.1.[1]

This method simply returns a `CalculateFixture` object of class `FairCharge`, as shown in Listing 35.2. Class `FairCharge` uses a `Duration`, which encodes the hours, days, and weeks of a rental. `Duration` values in this and the following Fit tables are handled automatically by the FitLibrary fixtures because a `static parse()` method exists in class `Duration`. This method translates a `String` into a `Duration`.

---

[1] This makes use of the application class `Rates`, which manages the charging rates of rentals.

rent.CalculateFairCharge						
rates $		5.00	*per hour*	45.00	*per day*	200.00	*per week*
duration		*fair*				
1 day		1 day				
8 hours		8 hours				
9 hours		1 day				
23 hours		1 day				
3 days 4 hours		3 days 4 hours				

rates $	1.00	*per hour*	45.00	*per day*	200.00	*per week*
duration		*fair*				
23 hours		23 hours				

rates $		5.00	*per hour*	45.00	*per day*	200.00	*per week*
duration		*fair*				
4 days		4 days				
5 days		1 week				
6 days 5 hours		1 week				

Figure 35.1 Testing a Part of the Application

Listing 35.1 **CalculateFairCharge.java**

```java
public class CalculateFairCharge extends DoFixture {
  public Fixture ratesDollarPerHourPerDayPerWeek(Money perHour,
        Money perDay, Money perWeek) {
    return new FairCharge(new Rates(perHour,perDay,perWeek));
  }
}
```

Listing 35.2 **FairCharge.java**

```java
public class FairCharge extends CalculateFixture {
  private Rates rates;

  public FairCharge(Rates rates) {
    this.rates = rates;
  }
  public Duration fairDuration(Duration duration) {
    return rates.fairDuration(duration);
  }
}
```

The **Rates** object encodes the business rule. This object is used in **FairCharge** to calculate the fair duration, based on the actual charge rates.

35.2   Testing Indirectly

Another approach is to carry out, through the API, actions that emulate the user's actions. This approach has the advantage of checking that the calculation business rules are handled in the workflow. This may be the only way if the corresponding logic is awkwardly embedded and if test support is needed to untangle it in order to later test it directly.

Part of the test from Chapter 16 is shown in Figure 35.2. (The fixture name in the initial table is altered, however, so that it can make use of the fixtures that were developed for other Fit tests in the past few chapters.)

rent.StartApplication						
refund $	5.00	*per hour*	45.00	*per day*	200.00	*per week*
paid time	*actual time*		*refund*			
3 hours	3 hours		0.00			
3 hours	2 hours		5.00			
5 hours	1 hours		20.00			

Figure 35.2 Testing Through the Application

The action in the first row of the second table results in a call of the method **refundDollarPerHourPerDayPerWeek()** of the **StartApplication** object, as shown in Listing 35.3. This creates temporary client and staff objects; **makeDummyClient()** in Listing 35.3, for example, is used by a variety of such tests. This method also creates a rental item object with the appropriate charge rates to use. It returns a **Refunder CalculateFixture** object, which is used for the rest of the table rows.

The **CalculateFixture** class **Refunder** is shown in Listing 35.4. For each row of the second table, from the third row on, the method **refundPaidTimeActualTime()** is called with two **Durations**.

The **refundPaidTimeActualTime()** method makes use of **TransActionFixture** methods to carry out the operations, rather than duplicating code. The method creates a start date and an end date, with the given duration between them. With the first transaction, created with the start date—equivalent to the action *time is now*—it rents an item until the end date, pays the cost, and completes the transaction.

Listing 35.3 **StartApplication.java**

```java
public class StartApplication extends DoFixture {
    private RentEz rentEz;

    public Fixture refundDollarPerHourPerDayPerWeek(Money perHour,
            Money perDay, Money perWeek) throws Exception {
        StaffMember staff = makeDummyStaff();
        Client client = makeDummyClient();
        RentalItemType item = makeDummyRentalItem(
                new Rates(perHour, perDay, perWeek));
        return new Refunder(rentEz,staff,client,item.getName());
    }
    private RentalItemType makeDummyRentalItem(Rates rates) {
        final String name = "dummy-rental";
        final int count = 1;
        final Money bond = new Money(0);
        rentEz.removeRentalItemType(name);
        rentEz.createRentalItemType(name,count,rates,bond);
        return rentEz.getRentalItemType(name);
    }
    private Client makeDummyClient() throws RpsException {
        final String name = "dummy-client";
        try {
            return getClient(name);
        } catch (MissingException e) {
            rentEz.createClient(rentEz.getAdminStaff(), name, "phone");
            return getClient(name);
        }
    }
    // ...
}
```

The second transaction is created with a date corresponding to the end of the actual duration. Then the rental item is returned, the refund is made, and the transaction is completed. The method returns the refund amount.

Questions & Answers

Why not simply run the whole application?
At this stage of revision, there are time overheads in running tests on the application, because of the need to set up the database data anew at the start of each test. We introduced this and related issues in Chapter 33.

Listing 35.4 Refunder.java

```java
public class Refunder extends CalculateFixture {
    private RentEz rentEz;
    private StaffMember staff;
    private Client client;
    private String rentalItemName;

    public Refunder(RentEz rentEz, StaffMember staff,
            Client client, String rentalItemName) {
        this.rentEz = rentEz;
        this.staff = staff;
        this.client = client;
        this.rentalItemName = rentalItemName;
    }
    public Money refundPaidTimeActualTime(Duration paidDuration,
            Duration actual) {
        final int count = 1;
        final Date startDate = new Date();
        final Date endDate = paidDuration.dateAfter(startDate);

        // Use a transaction to rent the item for the period
        TransActionFixture transAction = new TransActionFixture(rentEz,
                new ClientTransaction(rentEz,startDate,staff,client));
        Money cost = transAction.rentFor(count,rentalItemName,paidDuration);
        transAction.payWithCashDollar(cost);
        transAction.completeTransaction();

        // Use a transaction to return the item after the required delay
        TransActionFixture finalTransAction = new TransActionFixture(rentEz,
                new ClientTransaction(rentEz,endDate,staff,client));
        Money refund = finalTransAction.returnItems(count,rentalItemName);
        finalTransAction.refundCashDollar(refund);
        finalTransAction.completeTransaction();
        return refund;
    }
}
```

Isn't there a potential problem if the RentEz object is reused for each test row here? Yes. If the state of the **RentEz** object is not restored after each test, it will affect the next one. However, it takes time to restart the system under test each time, so it's good to avoid this.

Given that this is the responsibility of the fixture code in **Refunder**, rather than the Fit tests themselves, it seems like a reasonable compromise. If we decided to change the fixture so a new system under test was used for each test row, it wouldn't make any difference to the Fit tables.

35.3 Summary

Calculation tests can be carried out in two ways.

1. The fixtures for the Fit tables call directly into a method in the domain layer that encodes the business rule.

2. The fixtures carry out a series of actions, either on the domain layer or through the user interface, creating auxiliary objects as needed. To reuse existing code, the fixtures can make use of other fixtures for driving the actions, thus emulating Fit action tables.

The tests will run faster with the first approach, but they will test less of the system. The system under test may be structured so that we're unable to take this approach initially.

The tests will test more of the system with the second approach, but they will run slower, depending on whether they test through the user interface. Such tests are a useful first step with a legacy system. Once they're in place, the system can be test infected to allow the first approach.

CHAPTER 36

Closing for Programmers at RPS

36.1 The Value of Fit Tables

As we saw in Chapter 19, Fit tables help solve three major problems in software development. We now look at those problems from a programmer's perspective.

1. *Communication*: Providing a way for businesspeople who want a system to communicate their needs in a concrete way. The tests help us to see that we've completed work. They provide concrete examples of business rules.

2. *Balance*: Spending less time on gaining balance by reducing the number and severity of problems, catching them early, and making sure they don't return. As software systems age, they're inclined to get more and more difficult to change. Effort is needed, through refactorings, to keep systems in balance. To do this effectively, however, fast, automated tests are needed to help ensure that changes don't introduce bugs.

3. *Agility*: Keeping the software in good shape so that changes can be made quickly and effectively to support business change.

36.2 Getting Fit at RPS

The RPS programmers had originally voiced several major concerns with the architecture, Fit tests, and the development of *RentEz*. Let's review progress on their concerns, and see what Emily, Neo, and the other programmers report now.

- *We're concerned about the changes we will have to make to the system for testing. It's already difficult to change the system without breaking it, as it's so delicate.* "It was slow to get the Fit tests in place and then to get them working quickly. As we've test infected the system, it's delicate only in some parts. Everyone is more at ease about refactoring to improve it. It's weird to think that we were so fearful of making changes to it."

- *This means that we're often slower to add new functionality than we, and everyone else, expect.* "This is still so for changes that involve the disorganized parts. But changes in the refactored parts often go faster than expected. Having the automated tests for fast feedback means that any code we break during a change doesn't stay broken for long."

- *We know that the architecture needs rethinking. There's lots of duplicate code, and we need to change the structure of some of the classes. In some places, there's lots of conditional code that could be eliminated by introducing several subclasses. But it's very risky to change it, as it's easy to break working code in the process.* "We're starting to be proud of the code again. As we make changes, supported by tests, we remove redundancy. We sometimes find now that adding functionality leads to code shrinkage, as we're able to introduce useful abstractions."

- *We've got a backlog of work to be done, including many reported bugs, so management will not support long delays while we improve the system.* "The backlog remains as we make progress on the changes. I imagine that it won't be long before we're going faster and can reduce the backlog. The number of reported bugs is way down on the last release, which is brilliant."

- *But turning it into a Web application is going to force a lot of changes, so we need to tackle it somehow.* "That's going surprisingly well. We were not looking forward to doing that. Now it drops out of the process of separating the presentation and domain layers. This has raised some new ideas about the best way of presenting information in both the GUI and the Web interface."

- *Some of the code was written by people who have since left, and we're not familiar with it. We're bothered about changing such code, as we often introduce bugs in the process. Some of it is very stable, whereas other parts probably need to be replaced entirely.* "Where we've had to deal with such code, owing to bugs or new developments, pair programming has eased some of the pain. In some cases, we've discarded code and redeveloped it test first. Often, it's quicker to do that than to try and understand and fix what's there. We expect this to be a nonproblem in future, as we no longer have code ownership."

- *Our users keep changing their minds about what they require, which can waste a lot of time.* "We realize that some change is inevitable. The small iterations to give quick feedback to the customers seems to really help here. The feedback we get now is much more useful, too."

- *And sometimes we add functionality that ends up not being used.* "At least we don't spend so long on it before it gets scrapped."

- *It's a pain having to work overtime to avoid running too much over our deadlines for a release, especially as the code tends to be buggier than usual.* "The iterations have helped here, too. Others now understand about the effort it takes, and our estimates have gotten better. There is less pressure for releases. However, we find that pair programming is tiring; it's hard to slack off with someone there, keeping you to task."

- *Morale is lower than it's ever been. We used to be proud of the system, but not anymore.* "Morale is improving all the time. We all enjoy our work so much more. Two programmers talked of leaving but now seem quite settled. It would have been a shame to lose them, as they really contribute to the team."

PART V

CUSTOM DEVELOPMENT

CHAPTER 37

The Architecture of Fit

This chapter is relevant to you if you are interested in knowing about the inner details of Fit and how it works. You will need to know about this topic if you want to develop custom fixtures (see Chapter 38) or custom runners (see Chapter 39).

37.1 Running Fit

We'll get into the architecture of Fit by looking at what happens, step by step, when we use a FileRunner to run a table from an HTML file, as we saw in Chapter 26. The file contains only the TestOccupants table in HTML, as shown in Figure 37.1.

OccupantList		
user	*login time*	*entry time*
anna	15:45	15:48
luke	16.03	17:14

Figure 37.1 Fit Table for Testing Occupants

Figure 37.2 summarizes the following steps in running the table in Figure 37.1:

1. A FileRunner object (FileRunner#1) uses a Parse to read the HTML from the file and create a tree of Parse objects (Parse#1).

2. FileRunner#1 passes Parse#1 to the method doTables() of a new object of class Fixture that it creates, Fixture#1.

3. Fixture#1 gets the name of the fixture from the first row of the table: TestOccupants, a subclass of ColumnFixture. The fixture creates TestOccupants#1, an object of that class, and calls its method doTable() with Parse#2, the Parse subtree corresponding to that table.

4. TestOccupants#1, the fixture object, runs the tests by accessing the cells in the table via Parse#2. The fixture object marks the cells of passing tests by calling the method right(), inherited from Fixture, on Parse#3, one of the table cells.

5. The `right()` method, in turn, calls the method `addToTag()` of `Parse#3` to add the coloring.

Once it has run all the tables in a file, `FileRunner` writes out the updated `Parse` tree to a report file. This file shows all the markings carried out during the testing.

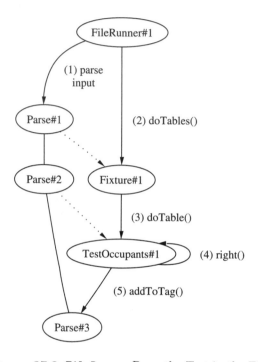

Figure 37.2 `FileRunner` Runs the Test in the File

37.2 Parse Tree

A sequence of tables in a file and the subcomponents of those tables are represented by objects of class `Parse`. The `Parse` structure for the table in Figure 37.1 is shown in Figure 37.3. We have shown four `Parse` fields here: (1) the type of `Parse`—table, tr, or td, corresponding to the HTML tags; (2) the text within a cell—only in tr objects; (3) the `parts`; and (4) the `more`.

The top `Parse` object represents the whole table; `parts` refers to a sequence of tr `Parse` objects that represent the rows of the table; `more` refers to the next table, if any. Each tr (row) object in turn refers to a sequence of td (column) objects; the sequence of components is formed by following the `more` values.

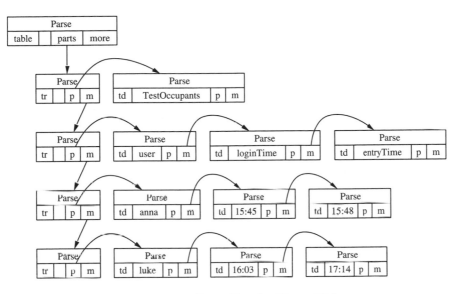

Figure 37.3 Parse Tree for Figure 37.1

37.3 doTable()

When it calls the doTable() method of a new fixture object, the Fixture object passes the tree of Parse objects for that table. By default, as defined in class Fixture, the doTable() method of a fixture object in turn calls methods to process individual rows (doRow()) and cells (doCell()), as shown in Figure 37.4.

A fixture class overrides some of this behavior. For example, ActionFixture overrides the doCells() method to carry out the action on each row in turn. The fixture object accesses the first cell in the row to find the action to be carried out, gathers up other data from the subsequent cells, and carries out the action.

ColumnFixture overrides the doRows() method to gather the labels in the first row and then calls doRow() on the rest of the rows. The ColumnFixture object also overrides the doCell() method to interpret the text value in the cell, depending on whether it is *given* or *calculated*.

RowFixture overrides the doRows() method completely, as it needs to collect up the rows as *expected* elements. For each *surplus* element, the RowFixture object adds a new row to the table by constructing extra tr and td Parse objects and inserting them in the tree, to be reported.

See Section 28.6 for details on when the first table in a sequence is a DoFixture table.

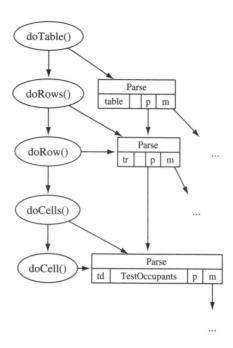

Figure 37.4 Method `doTable()`

37.4   Counts in Class `Fixture`

As we saw in Chapter 7, a `fit.Summary` table reports on the results of running all the previous tables in a file. This table also reports the details of the input and report files when a `FileRunner` is used. The counts of *right*, *wrong*, and so on, are gathered in `Fixture`.

Class `Fixture` has the following `public` instance variables.

- `Map summary` holds keyed information about the tests. This information is used by `Summary` to report on details of the tests. `Fixture` adds to it the run date and run elapsed time. When `FileRunner` is used, it includes the input file name, input update—last modified date of the input file—and the output file name.

- `Counts counts` holds the current counts of *right*, *wrong*, *ignored*, and *exceptions*. These counts are changed each time the corresponding methods in `Fixture` are called.

37.5   The `Fixture` Subclasses

The core fixture classes are subclasses of the class `Fixture`, as shown in Figure 37.5. The subclasses override relevant methods of `Fixture` to run the tests, as discussed in Section 37.3.

- **RowFixture** is a subclass of **ColumnFixture**, using some of the code in **ColumnFixture** to process column values.

- **TimedActionFixture** is a subclass of **ActionFixture**, acting the same as **ActionFixture** but also providing timing information in an extra column that is added to the reported table.

The subclasses also make use of utility methods in **Fixture**, such as the **right()** method, mentioned in Section 37.1.

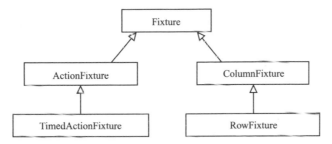

Figure 37.5 **Fixture** Classes

37.6 TypeAdapter

As we saw in Chapter 25, a **TypeAdapter** manages conversion between the text in table cells and Java values. More specifically, a **TypeAdapter** object provides the following methods:

- **get()**, to get data from a specified field of an object in the application
- **set()**, to set data into a specified field of an object
- **invoke()**, to call the specified method (with no arguments) in the object
- **toString()**, to provide a **String** form of the value, such as for use in the report
- **parse()**, to parse text from a table cell and convert it into a value of the appropriate data type
- **equals()**, to check that two values of that data type are equal

In addition, a **TypeAdapter** has several **public** instance variables. For our purposes, only the variable **target** is relevant to the following chapters of this part. To use a **TypeAdapter** with a particular object, such as to **get()** a value from it, we first need to assign that object to the **target** variable of the **TypeAdapter**. See the source code for **TypeAdapter** for further details.

Only some classes are managed by **TypeAdapter**, so a mechanism is provided to manage other classes, including those that are application specific. We saw in Chapter 25 that the conversion and comparison of classes, such as **Money**, are handled by overriding the **parse()** method in a fixture.

37.7   Summary

The architecture of Fit is based on the classes `Fixture`, `Parse`, and `TypeAdapter`.

- `Fixture` manages the overall running of the Fit tables and provides various utility methods. The standard fixtures extend `Fixture` to process a table in their own particular way.

- `Parse` is used to represent tables and is altered as the tests are run to provide feedback on them; it is written to a report file once the tests are run.

- `TypeAdapter` is used to manage interconversion between text values from table cells and underlying Java values and to make comparisons.

The architecture of Fit is sufficiently open and general to allow new types of fixtures to be easily created, to permit tests to be expressed as clearly as possible. In Chapter 38, we develop and use some new custom fixtures.

Runners handle the overall testing process, from input file to report. New types of runners can be easily developed and incorporated with Fit, as discussed in Chapter 39.

37.8   Exercises

1. Look at the code for `ActionFixture`, which is quite short. Follow through the code to see what happens when an *enter* action is carried out.

2. What happens if the corresponding method in the *actor* doesn't exist?

3. What happens if the *actor* is not yet *start*ed?

4. Note how `ActionFixture` calls the action methods, using reflection. Consider how you would subclass `ActionFixture` to provide other action methods, without changing `ActionFixture` itself.

5. Look at the code for `ColumnFixture` and note how the method `bind()` is called from `doRows()` with the header row. Note how a `TypeAdapter` is created for each column of the header row and is reused for each test row.

CHAPTER 38

Developing Custom Fixtures

As we pointed out in Chapter 11, using a custom format for a table can enable us to express tests more directly and clearly. We now look at the development of two simple general-purpose custom fixtures in order to encourage you to develop your own fixtures.

This chapter assumes that you are familiar with the Fit architecture, as introduced in Chapter 37.

38.1 Using `SetUpFixture`

A `SetUpFixture` table may be used for setting up the data at the start of a test, as we saw in Section 10.4 on p. 76. The setup table from that example is shown again in Figure 38.1. The fixture for that example was covered in Section 28.7 on p. 239, and is shown again in Listing 38.1.

set ups			
future value	*max balance*	*min purchase*	*discount %*
low	0.00	0.00	0
medium	0.00	500.00	5
medium	500.00	500.00	3
high	500.00	2000.00	10
high	1000.00	500.00	5

Figure 38.1 `SetUp` Table

The method `futureValueMaxBalanceMinPurchaseDiscountPercent()` in class `SetUpDiscounts` in Listing 38.1 is called for each data row in the table. The name of the method is derived from concatenating the labels in the header row of the table.

Listing 38.1 **SetUpDiscounts.java**

```
public class SetUpDiscounts extends SetUpFixture {
  private DiscountApplication app;

  public SetUpDiscounts(DiscountApplication app) {
    this.app = app;
  }
  public void futureValueMaxBalanceMinPurchaseDiscountPercent(
      String futureValue, double maxBalance, double minPurchase,
      double discountPercent) {
    app.addDiscountGroup(futureValue,maxBalance,
            minPurchase,discountPercent);
  }
}
```

38.2   SetUpFixture

Class `SetUpFixture` is an abstract subclass of `CalculateFixture`, as shown in Listing 38.2. To allow for actions before and after processing all the rows, the methods `startUp()` and `tearDown()` are provided. These methods can be overridden, for example, to make a database connection beforehand and shut it down once all the table rows have been added to the database.

As we see in Listing 38.2, `SetUpFixture` overrides `doTable()` of the superclass `CalculateFixture` to call the methods `startUp()` and `tearDown()` before and after processing the table. The `doTable()` code in `CalculateFixture` calls the method `bind()`, which is in turn overridden in `SetUpFixture`. If an exception occurs, details are provided in the report through a call to the `Fixture` method `exception()`.

The `bind()` method in Listing 38.2 is responsible for creating a `MethodTarget`, which can be used to call a method in an object with arguments from a row, as we will see shortly. The `bind()` method does this by concatenating each label in the header row, separated by spaces, and then turning this into a valid Java method name through a call on a `static` method in the class `ExtendedCamelCase`. Then it calls the method `findMethod()` in the superclass, which returns a `MethodTarget` if it is able to find a matching method in the fixture object or in the associated application object, if any.

Class `SetUpFixture` overrides `doRow()` to process each row. If there is no valid binding, the row is marked as being ignored, through a call to the `Fixture` method `ignore()`. If there is a binding, it calls the `invoke()` method on the `MethodTarget`, which converts each cell into the type of value that's required for the corresponding argument of the method concerned and calls the method reflectively.

38.3   ImageFixture

As we saw in Section 11.3 on p. 83, Fit table cells can contain images as well as text. In this section, we look briefly at the code for `ImageFixture`, a general-purpose

Listing 38.2 **SetUpFixture.java**

```java
public class SetUpFixture extends CalculateFixture {
   private MethodTarget target;

   public void doTable(Parse table) {
      try {
         setUp();
         super.doTable(table);
         tearDown();
      } catch (Exception e) {
         exception(table.at(0, 0, 0),e);
      }
   }
   protected void bind(Parse headerRow) {
      Parse cells = headerRow;
      argCount = cells.size();
      String argNames = "";
      while (cells != null) {
         argNames += " " + cells.text();
         cells = cells.more;
      }
      String methodName = ExtendedCamelCase.camel(argNames);
      try {
            target = findMethod(methodName,argCount);
            boundOK = true;
        } catch (Exception e) {
         exception(headerRow, e);
        }
   }
   public void doRow(Parse row) {
      if (!boundOK) {
         ignore(row.parts);
         return;
      }
      if (row.parts.size() != argCount) {
         exception(row.parts,"Row should be "+argCount+" cells wide");
         return;
      }
      try {
         target.invoke(row.parts);
      } catch (Exception e) {
         exception(row.parts,e);
      }
   }
   protected void setUp() throws Exception {
   }
   protected void tearDown() throws Exception {
   }
}
```

> **Note**
>
> FixtureFixture tables can be used in the test-driven development of
> custom Fit fixtures [Mug04]. FixtureFixture has been used to define the
> core and FitLibrary fixtures. The core fixtures are also defined with *fat*; see
> [Cun].

fixture to test such tables against a list that is supplied to it by the system under
test.

Class ImageFixture compares a 2D array of the names of image files, based on
the actual data, against the referenced images in the Fit table. The actual data is
supplied through the constructor.

Part of the class ImageFixture is shown in Listing 38.3.[1] Some of the error-
handling code is not shown in these methods.

The method doTable() first handles the case in which the collections are both
empty—table.parts.more refers to the second row of the table—in which case
it colors the header row green through a call to the Fixture method right().
Otherwise, doTable() calls rowsMatch() to match the *actual* and *expected*. If the
match fails, addActualRows() (not shown) appends all the actual data to the
bottom of the table. It is easier to understand the mismatches when the *actual*
images are shown underneath the *expected* ones, rather than interleaved with the
expected rows.

The rowsMatch() method in Listing 38.3 calls cellsMatch() to check each
actual row against what's *expected*. This method in turn calls cellMatches() to
check each individual cell, by accessing the HTML text in the cell to get the image
reference, such as img src="wall.gif" width=32 height=32. In cellMatches(),
we see the use of the Fixture method wrong() to color a table cell red.

38.4   Summary

It can be well worthwhile to create custom fixtures so that Fit tables can express
tests directly and clearly. We have looked at the development of two example
fixtures:

1. SetUpFixture, which is used to add the data from the rows of the table to
   set up the elements of a collection

2. ImageFixture, which checks the names of images in the table against a 2D
   array of expected names

---

[1] ImageFixture has since been generalized and included in the FitLibrary.

Listing 38.3 ImageFixture.java

```java
public class ImageFixture extends Fixture {
    private String[][] actual;

    public ImageFixture(String[][] actual2DArrayOfImageFileNames) {
        actual = actual2DArrayOfImageFileNames;
    }
    public void doTable(Parse table) {
        if (actual.length == 0 && table.parts.more == null)
            right(table.parts);
        else if (!rowsMatch(actual, table.parts))
            addActualRows(table.parts,actual);
    }
    private boolean rowsMatch(String[][] actual, Parse lastRow) {
        boolean matched = true;
        for (int i = 0; i < actual.length; i++) {
            lastRow = lastRow.more;
            if (!cellsMatch(actual[i],lastRow.parts))
                matched = false;
        }
        return markWrong(lastRow.more, matched);
    }
    private boolean cellsMatch(String[] actual, Parse allCells) {
        Parse cells = allCells;
        boolean matched = true;
        for (int i = 0; i < actual.length; i++) {
            if (!cellMatches(actual[i], cells))
                matched = false;
            cells = cells.more;
        }
        return markWrong(cells, matched);
    }
    private boolean cellMatches(String actual, Parse cell) {
        if (cell.body == null)
            return false;
        String image = getImageFileName(cell.body);
        boolean matches = finalFileName(actual).equals(finalFileName(image));
        if (matches)
            right(cell);
        else
            wrong(cell);
        return matches;
    }
    // ...
}
```

CHAPTER 39

Custom Runners

This chapter discusses how to develop custom runners. This topic is relevant if you already have lots of test data in other formats and don't wish to convert it into HTML tables. A custom runner can process that data and feed it into Fit, producing standard Fit reports.

We show two examples that read tests from plaintext and spreadsheet files and process them with Fit.

39.1 Runners

As we saw in Chapter 37, a runner carries out three functions in turn.

1. It inputs data in some form and converts it into a `Parse` tree. For example, a `FileRunner` inputs HTML from a file.

2. It creates a new `Fixture` object and calls its `doTables()` method, passing the `Parse` tree.

3. It writes the report. A `FileRunner` writes this to an HTML file. FitNesse returns this HTML as a wiki page.

To create a custom runner, we need to write code to carry out each of these steps. The FitLibrary class `CustomRunner` can be used to drastically simplify this task, allowing you to avoid knowing about most of the internal details of Fit.

39.2 Calculator Runner

In this example, the test data is already in a textual form, and it is convenient to leave it in that form. However, it would be handy to be able to run the tests, using Fit, and to present the results as an HTML report along with a summary.

For our example, we will write a runner that will read in the test data from a file and create internal Fit tables. After running the tests in the tables, a report is written out in HTML, as usual.

The file data format is a sequence of comma-separated numbers, with three per line. Here's a sample:

```
1, 2, 3
4, 5, 9
7, 8, 15
```

The report we want will have two tables, as shown in Figure 39.1. In the first table, the *calculated* column returns the *sum* of *a* and *b*, using Sum, a ColumnFixture. So we need to generate the first two rows of the table in our runner, followed by a row for each line in our file. The second table simply consists of a single row for the fixture name, fit.Summary; extra rows are added in the report.

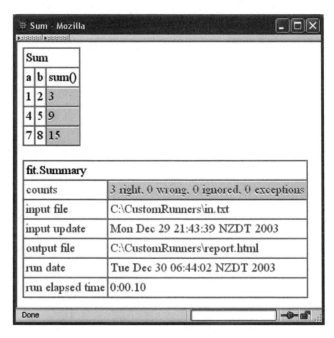

Figure 39.1 Fit Report for TestDiscount

39.3   Reading Tests from a Text File

Listing 39.1 shows the class SumRunner which processes the comma-separated test files, mapping the test into Fit. The main() method of the class expects two arguments: the input and report file names.

The constructor of SumRunner passes three things to the superclass: the title of the HTML file that's to be produced; the input File, so that the file details

Listing 39.1 **SumRunner.java**

```java
public class SumRunner extends CustomRunner {
   public static void main(String args[]) throws IOException {
      if (args.length != 2) {
         System.err.println(
         "Usage: java SumRunner inputFile.txt reportFile.html");
         System.exit(-1);
      }
      new SumRunner(new File(args[0]),args[1]);
   }
   public SumRunner(File inFile, String reportFileName)
                        throws IOException {
      super("Sum",inFile,reportFileName);
      BufferedReader in = new BufferedReader(
                  new FileReader(inFile));
      makeTable(in);
      runAndReportAndExit();
   }
   private void makeTable(BufferedReader in) throws IOException {
      addTable("Sum");
      addRow("a | b | sum()");
      while (true) {
         String line = in.readLine();
         if (line == null)
            break;
         addRow(line);
      }
      addTableWithLeaderText("fit.Summary","<BR>");
   }
}
```

can be added to the fixture; and the name of the report file. The constructor
then calls `makeTable()` to read the input file and create the internal form of
the Fit tables required. Then the tests are run and reported with a call to the
`runAndReportAndExit()` method of the superclass, `CustomRunner`. This method
runs Fit on the internal tables, writes the report, prints the count information to
`System.err`, and exits with a suitable error code.

The method `makeTable()` in Listing 39.1 calls the inherited `addTable()` to
create a new table with the first row value as argument. The method `addRow()`
creates a new row in the table. Finally, the second table is added, a `fit.Summary`,
with the text `"<BR>"` included before the table so that the tables are separated in
the report. Other functionality to ease writing custom runners is provided in class
`CustomRunner`; see the code for details.

Questions & Answers

Is the report always provided as HTML?
The Fit output need not be provided in HTML, although that is usually convenient. It would be possible to walk over the **Parse** tree, after the tests have been run, and produce some other output format; we don't consider that further here.

What if the test data file is huge?
In that case, building huge **Parse** trees may consume too much memory. It may be better, in the case of **ColumnFixture** tables, to produce several smaller tests and run them in sequence.

39.4   Reading Tests from a Spreadsheet

A similar approach can be taken when the tests are organized in a spreadsheet, such as the one shown in Figure 39.2. We want to produce the same report as the first example, as shown in Figure 39.1.

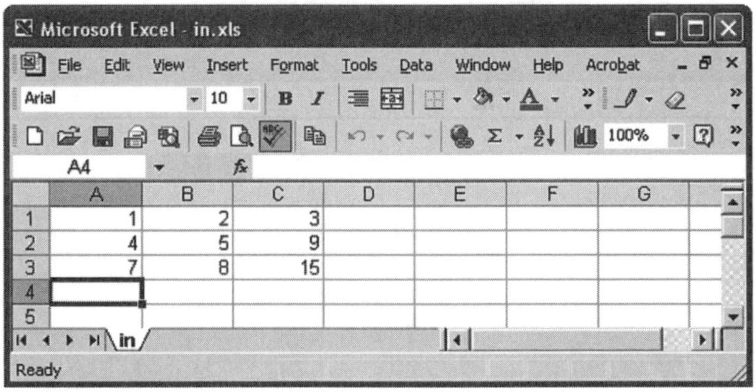

Figure **39.2** Spreadsheet Data

Poi is an open source package for reading from and writing to Excel spreadsheets. In the class **XlsSumRunner**, shown in Listing 39.2, we use *Poi* to read from the rows in the spreadsheet.

The **main()** method here creates an **XlsSumRunner** and then calls the method **runAndReportCounts()**, inherited by **XlsSumRunner** from **CustomRunner**. This means that the runner itself doesn't **exit()**, allowing for this runner to be used as a part of a test suite.

The constructor of **XlsSumRunner** shown in Listing 39.2 uses a *Poi* **HSSFWorkbook** to access the input Excel file. The constructor then calls the **makeTable()** method with a **HSSFSheet**, representing the first sheet of the spreadsheet, and then runs Fit on the resulting table, as in the previous section.

Listing 39.2 XlsSumRunner.java

```java
public class XlsSumRunner extends CustomRunner {
    public static void main(String args[]) throws IOException {
        if (args.length != 2) {
            System.err.println(
            "Usage: java XlsSumRunner inputFile.xls reportFile.html");
            System.exit(-1);
        }
        XlsSumRunner runner = new XlsSumRunner(new File(args[0]),args[1]);
        System.exit(runner.runAndReportCounts());
    }
    public XlsSumRunner(File inFile, String reportFileName)
                        throws IOException {
        super("Sum",inFile,reportFileName);
        HSSFWorkbook workbook = new HSSFWorkbook(new FileInputStream(inFile));
        makeTable(workbook.getSheetAt(0));
    }
    private void makeTable(HSSFSheet sheet) throws IOException {
        addTable("Sum");
        addRow("a | b | sum()");
        for (Iterator it = sheet.rowIterator(); it.hasNext();) {
            String[] cells = getCellValues((HSSFRow)it.next());
            if (cells.length == 0 || cells[0].equals(""))
               break;
            addRow(cells);
        }
        addTableWithLeaderText("fit.Summary","<BR>");
    }
    private String[] getCellValues(HSSFRow row) {
        // ..
    }
}
```

The `makeTable()` in turn processes each row in the HSSFSheet, calling the method `getCellValues()` to convert the value from each cell in the row into a suitably formatted string. This string is used to construct the next row in the Fit table.

Questions & Answers

Is it possible to select particular spreadsheet cells based on their color or borders or whatever?

Yes, *Poi* provides lots of information about the formatting of the cells in a spreadsheet. For example, the **SpreadSheetRunner** discussed in Chapter 26 makes use of this feature.

39.5   Summary

- A custom runner enables Fit to be used with test data in any format.
- We have looked at two simple custom runners, `SumRunner` and `XlsSumRunner`, to illustrate how to run tests from plaintext and spreadsheet files.
- The custom runners make use of the FitLibrary class `CustomRunner` to manage most of the details of creating internal Fit tables and running them.

CHAPTER 40

Model-Based Test Generation

In many cases, it's annoying to have to write huge numbers of tests for lots of combinations and situations. But it doesn't have to be like this. Often, it can be avoided by using model-based test generation.

The idea is to have a model, or a simulator, that encodes enough about a part of an application domain to generate useful tests. The important thing is for the model to be precise enough to determine the expected results. It would be too slow and laborious for a person to go through and decide what results to expect from generated tests.

Here, we show the basic idea with a test generator for a simple part of the RPS system. We'll use a particular approach to test generation that makes use of symmetries [Got03]

40.1 Symmetries: Operations That Cancel Each Other

Many business transactions have natural counterparts, as there is a kind of resource-balancing process going on. Goods are traded for cash, currencies are traded based on an exchange rate, time is exchanged for consulting fees, and bookings should all expire and bought goods replaced or returned.

With hiring in the RPS system, there is a balancing between the rental items going out and coming back or, occasionally, being exchanged for cash or written off because they weren't returned. So it's easy to write a program with a model for that process, involving multiple clients and rentals. Interleaving the rentals and returns is more likely to stretch the system and find errors, so we'll do that.

The design of model-based test generation entails several issues about how we generate the tests, run and report results, and develop the underlying model. One approach would be to generate Fit tables in files and run Fit on them as a group. But a more direct way is to generate the tables and run them with `CustomRunner`.

We don't want to have to manually run the tests and check the results afterward. It will be convenient to have the tests run automatically, maybe all the time. We want to be informed only when things go wrong, with sufficient information to be able to replicate any errors that are found.

Finally, we want to keep the model as simple as possible, for two reasons. One is to reduce the cost of creating it. The second is to reduce the chance of finding errors in the model rather than in our system.

40.2   Generate a Simple Sequence

As with development generally, it makes sense to go step by step. A sensible first step is to generate a simple test and see that it works. We can then extend our test generator as we get clearer about what it needs to do. We may find that a simple approach works fine and there is no point in making it more sophisticated. Or, after some use, we may find ways of improving it that weren't obvious initially. After all, it's just as hard for us to see the future clearly as it is for customers.

To generate a sequence, we will need to have a representation of the clients and rental items in our simulation. Then we can randomly pick a client and some rental items to be rented and later returned.

In this first step, we simply generate a single test that rents and then immediately returns each `RentalItem`. Listing 40.1 shows the first part of the code for class `Generate1`, a subclass of `CustomRunner`. Some initial setup data for clients and rental items is created in static arrays, and this is used in `makeSetUp()`.

The constructor for `Generate1` in Listing 40.1 creates the tables and runs the `CustomRunner` on them to produce a Fit report with title RPS. (See Chapter 39 for an introduction to the use of `CustomRunner`.)

The remainder of class `Generate1` is shown in Listing 40.2. The `makeTables()` method randomly chooses a `RentalItemModel` that has some items available for rental. The method generates one table to rent all those items and a second table to immediately return them.

The `makeCheck()` method in Listing 40.2 generates the final table, which checks that no RentalItems are outstanding. This could be improved by also checking that the rentals are back to their original numbers. (See the exercises at the end of the chapter.)

The method `makeSetUp()` in Listing 40.1 generates the Fit tables for initializing the setup data in the system under test. This uses the method `setUpRow()` in both `ClientModel` and `RentalItemModel` to return the relevant data to be inserted in the row of the setup table. Class `ClientModel` is shown in Listing 40.3, and class `RentalItemModel` is shown in Listing 40.4.

Listing 40.1 **Generate1.java (part 1)**

```java
public class Generate1 extends CustomRunner {
    private Random random = new Random();
    private static final RentalItemModel[] rentalItems = {
            new RentalItemModel("coffee urn", 10, 8.20),
            new RentalItemModel("hot water urn", 10, 8.00)
    };
    private static final ClientModel[] clients = {
            new ClientModel("Joanna", "3737599"),
            new ClientModel("Mistra", "4074707")
    };
    public Generate1() throws IOException {
        super("RPS");
        makeSetUp();
        makeTables();
        makeCheck();
        runAndReport();
    }
    private void makeSetUp() {
        addTable("rent.StartApplication");

        addTable("set up");
        addRow("rental item name | count | $/hour | $/day | $/week | deposit");
        for (int i = 0; i < rentalItems.length; i++)
            addRow(rentalItems[i].setUpRow());

        addTable("set up");
        addRow("staff name | phone");
        addRow("Bill | 555 9876");

        addTable("set up");
        addRow("client name | phone");
        for (int i = 0; i < clients.length; i++)
            addRow(clients[i].setUpRow());
        addTable("time is now | 2004/05/06 09:01");
    }
    // ...
}
```

Listing 40.2 **Generate1.java (part 2)**

```java
public class Generate1 extends CustomRunner {
    // ...
    private void makeTables() {
        RentalItemModel hireItem = getHireItem();
        addTable("begin transaction for client | Joanna | staff | Bill");
        addRow(hireItem.rentAll(1));
        addRow("pay with cash $ | 82.00");
        addRow("complete transaction");

        addTable("time is now | 2004/05/07 09:01");

        addTable("begin transaction for client | Joanna | staff | Bill");
        addRow(hireItem.returnAll(1));
        addRow("complete transaction");
    }
    private void makeCheck() {
        addTable("rentals for client | Joanna");
        addRow("rental item | count | start date | end date");

        addTable("fit.Summary");
    }
    private RentalItemModel getHireItem() {
        return rentalItems[random.nextInt(rentalItems.length)];
    }
}
```

Listing 40.3 **ClientModel.java**

```java
public class ClientModel {
  public String name, phone;

  public ClientModel(String name, String phone) {
    this.name = name;
    this.phone = phone;
  }
  public String setUpRow() {
    return name+" | "+phone;
  }
   public String getName() {
      return name;
   }
}
```

Listing 40.4 **RentalItemModel.java (version 1)**

```java
public class RentalItemModel {
    private String name;
    private int count;
    private double dailyRate;

    public RentalItemModel(String name, int count, double dailyRate) {
        this.name = name;
        this.count = count;
        this.dailyRate = dailyRate;
    }
    public String setUpRow() {
        return name+" | "+count+" | 0.00, "+dailyRate+"0 | 0.00 | 0.00";
    }
    public String rentAll(int days) {
        return "rent | "+count+" | | "+name+" | for | "+days+" days";
    }
    public String returnAll(int days) {
        return "return items | "+count+" | | "+name;
    }
}
```

40.3 Generate an Interleaved Sequence

We now extend the generator to randomly determine when RentalItemModels are returned. That way, rentals and returns are interleaved. By the end of a test sequence, all the RentalItemModels will be returned, with none outstanding. We also calculate the cost of a rental.

Whenever a RentalModel is made, we simply add a record of it to a list. Then we randomly choose between making a new rental with a client or making a return.

The makeTables() part of the class Generate2 refines the method originally given in Listing 40.2 and continues to use some of the methods that are shown in Listing 40.2. The new version of makeTables() in class Generate2, as shown in Listing 40.5, takes a parameter to specify how many random trials to use. For each trial, a random choice is made between the possible actions.

If a *rental* action is chosen, a random RentalItemModel is chosen in rental(). If any of that RentalItemModel are available for rent, a rental is made of a random subset, through the call to rentalSome() of class RentalItemModel, as shown in the revised class in Listing 40.6. A table is then generated to represent that rental, using the RentalModel, which is shown in Listing 40.7. This rental is added to the list of rentals, providing a source of possible returns.

If a *return* action is chosen, one of the RentalModels on the returns list is selected for return in returns() in class Generate2 in Listing 40.5. The appropriate table is then generated.

Listing 40.5 **Generate2.java**

```java
public class Generate2 extends CustomRunner {
    private List returns = new ArrayList();
    // ...
    private void makeTables(int trials) {
        for (int i = 0; i < trials; i++) {
            int choice = random.nextInt(100);
            if (choice < 60)
                rent();
            else
                returns();
        }
        while (returns.size() > 0)
            returns();
    }
    private void rent() {
        RentalItemModel rentalItem = getHireItem();
        if (rentalItem.none())
            return;
        ClientModel client = startTransaction();
        RentalModel rental = rentalItem.rentSome(client,1);
        returns.add(rental);
        addRow(rental.rentalRow());
        addRow("pay with cash $ | "+rental.getCost());
        addRow("complete transaction");
    }
    private ClientModel startTransaction() {
        ClientModel client = getClient();
        addTable("begin transaction for client | "+client.getName()+
        " | staff | Bill");
        return client;
    }
    private void returns() {
        if (returns.size() == 0)
            return;
        ClientModel client = startTransaction();
        RentalModel rental = getReturn();
        addRow(rental.returnRow());
        addRow("complete transaction");
    }
    private RentalModel getReturn() {
        int index = random.nextInt(returns.size());
        RentalModel rental = (RentalModel)returns.get(index);
        returns.remove(index);
        return rental;
    }
    private ClientModel getClient() {
        return clients[random.nextInt(clients.length)];
    }
}
```

Listing 40.6 **RentalItemModel.java (version 2)**

```java
public class RentalItemModel {
    // ...
    public RentalModel rentSome(ClientModel client, int days) {
        int rentedCount = count;
        if (count > 1)
            rentedCount = Generate2.random.nextInt(count-1)+1;
        count = count - rentedCount;
        return new RentalModel(client,this,rentedCount,days);
    }
    public boolean none() {
        return count == 0;
    }
    public String getName() {
        return name;
    }
}
```

Listing 40.7 **RentalModel.java**

```java
public class RentalModel {
    private ClientModel client;
    private RentalItemModel rentalItem;
    private int count;
    private int days;

    public RentalModel(ClientModel client, RentalItemModel hireItem,
            int count, int days) {
        this.client = client;
        this.rentalItem = hireItem;
        this.count = count;
        this.days = days;
    }
    public String rentalRow() {
        return "rent | "+count+" | | "+rentalItem.getName()+" | for | "+
            days+" days";
    }
    public String getCost() {
        return new Money(count*days*rentalItem.getDailyRate()).toString();
    }
    public String returnRow() {
        return "return items | "+count+" | | "+rentalItem.getName();
    }
}
```

40.4   Summary

Our example model to generate tests depends on a very simple model of the rental application. It is clear that this technique could be applied to a wide range of applications and could interleave more types of actions.

The generator makes changes that cancel out over the course of the whole test. For every rental that is made in the generated tests, we ensure that a corresponding return is made. Rentals and returns of different rental items by different clients are interleaved to make the tests more realistic and more likely to find errors.

See [Got03] for a formal introduction to testing based on symmetries. This paper also discusses techniques for reducing the generated test set without losing effectiveness. Cohen et al. [CGMC03] discuss various approaches to reducing test set size.

Other approaches to test generation may be more or less comprehensive. The more comprehensive the tests, the more comprehensive the model and the generator need to be. As with all testing, there are inevitable tradeoffs, so that limited testing resources can be used as effectively as possible.

Testing a system is based on the idea that having two or more different ideas of how a system will work may help pick up errors in either of them. It's important that the form of those approaches be different enough that we don't make the same wrong assumptions about the implementation.

However, one problem is very difficult to avoid: If there are misunderstandings about what is really required, the different approaches may simply encode the same mistakes. As Reinertsen [Rei97] points out, the major risk in design is in understanding *what* is needed, not *how* it will be provided.

40.5   Exercises

1. The tests would be strengthened if we also tested that the original rental items returned to their original state. Do this by generating another table at the end of the test to ensure this.

2. When a return is picked from the list of returns, all the rental items in that rental are returned. Change the test generator to make partial returns.

3. Rather than storing the setup data in the program, supply this data through Fit tables, with a special fixture to run the test generator.

PART VI

APPENDICES

Background Material

A.1 Testing

The art of testing is a big topic in its own right. Working with an experienced tester is a good way to pick up testing attitudes and skills and to learn about tools.

Many general books on software testing are complementary to this book [KBN+02, KBP02, Mar95]. Few, however, assume that tests are written up front as a way of expressing business requirements.

In *Testing Computer Software*, Kaner et al. [KBN+02] introduce testing in general. In *Lessons Learned in Software Testing*, Kaner, Bach, and Pettichord [KBP02] show how to apply testing successfully.

In *Integrated Test Design and Automation*, Buwalda, Janssen, and Pinkster [BJP02] cover the management and activities of testing from a tester's point of view, including automatic tests. Their design and use of "action words" have some similarity with the style of Fit, but they do not use a specific automation framework.

In *Testing Extreme Programming*, Crispin and House [CH03] discuss agile testing within the context of Extreme Programming and so share a common point of view with us about how to develop software incrementally.

Pragmatic Unit Testing by Hunt and Thomas [HT03] and *JUnit Recipes: Practical Methods for Programmer Testing* by Rainsberger and Stirling [RS04], are the closest in spirit to our book in that they also introduce a testing framework. However, JUnit is designed for programmers to use and plays a different role from Fit, which is intended for communication with businesspeople.

A.2 Agile Software Development

Agile software development builds on the ideas of evolutionary, or iterative, software development [LB03]. Among the many excellent books on agile development are [Bec04], [Coc01], [Mar02], [SB02], [PP03], [Hig04], [Coc04]. As introduced by Beck in *Extreme Programming Explained* [Bec04], Extreme Programming was especially instrumental in raising general awareness of agile thinking.

Stories play an important role in communication and planning in Extreme
Programming. For each story, automated acceptance tests are created to drive
development. In *User Stories Applied*, Cohn [Coh04] shows how to write XP stories.

Many developers may wish to move toward an agile approach but are stuck with
software that is far from agile. Feathers [Fea02] shows how to change such legacy
code to gain agility.

A.3   Ubiquitous Language

In *Domain Driven Design*, Eric Evans [Eva04] discusses the development of "ubiquitous languages" to aid communication about the requirements of systems. The
terminology impacts directly on the design of the software.

A ubiquitous language evolves as the understanding of the business needs of the
application evolve. This language is reflected directly in the classes, associations,
and methods of the software. UML diagrams can help in discussions about the
domain, making ongoing links between the business language and the form of the
implementation.

Businesspeople and software developers can thus speak a common, evolving
language, reducing the need to map between different realms and reducing misunderstandings. Evans suggests that some problems and issues that arise when coding
the application are best resolved by addressing the clarity of the current ubiquitous
language.

Fit tests are a natural way to help develop this ubiquitous language. Such tests
provide a comprehensive bridge between discussions of business need and software
design. Writing concrete examples as tests explores ways in which to use and evolve
the ubiquitous language for expressing business objects, constraints, and rules.

Book Resources Web Site

The following resources are available for this book at http://fit.c2.com/wiki.cgi?FitBook:

- The Java source code for all the examples covered in this book
- HTML files for all the Fit tests
- FitNesse pages for all the Fit tests

In addition, downloads and other information on Fit, FitNesse, and FitLibrary are available at

- http://fit.c2.com
- http://www.fitnesse.org
- http://sourceForge.net/projects/fitlibrary

Fit and Other Programming Languages

C.1 Table Portability

Parts I and II provide a general approach that is completely independent of the programming language used to develop Fit tables. In general, the same Fit tables may be used with different languages, although the fixture code will clearly be different. The C# code for fixtures is similar to the Java code shown in this book, so C# programmers will find the example code easy to follow and translate into C#.

C.2 Other Programming Languages

As well as Java, implementations of Fit are available for the following programming languages and systems:

- C# and the .Net platform
- C++
- Delphi
- Lisp
- Objective C
- Perl
- Python
- Ruby
- Smalltalk

See the Fit and FitNesse websites (http://fit.c2.com and www.fitnesse.org) for details of support for these other languages.

Bibliography

[Ast03]   David Astels. *Test Driven Development: A Practical Guide.* Prentice Hall, 2004.

[Bac]   James Bach. "What Is Exploratory Testing?" www.satisfice.com/articles/what_is_et.htm.

[Bec02]   Kent Beck. *Test-Driven Development: By Example.* Addison-Wesley, 2003.

[Bec04]   Kent Beck. *Extreme Programming Explained, Second Edition.* Addison-Wesley, 2005.

[BG98]   Kent Beck and Erich Gamma. "Test Infected: Programmers Love Writing Tests." *Java Report* 3(7): 37–50, July 1998.

[BJP02]   Hans Buwalda, Dennis Janssen, and Iris Pinkster. *Integrated Test Design and Automation.* Addison-Wesley, 2002.

[Boo94]   Grady Booch. *Object-Oriented Analysis and Design with Applications, Second Edition.* Addison-Wesley, 1994.

[CGMC03]   M. B. Cohen, P. B. Gibbons, W. B. Mugridge, and C. J. Colbourn. "Constructing Test Suites for Interaction Testing." In *ICSE 2003*, pp. 38–48, 2003.

[CH03]   Lisa Crispin and Tip House. *Testing Extreme Programming.* Addison-Wesley, 2003.

[Coc01]   Alistair Cockburn. *Agile Software Development.* Addison-Wesley, 2002.

[Coc04]   Alistair Cockburn. *Crystal Clear: A Human-Powered Methodology for Small Teams.* Addison-Wesley, 2005.

[Coh04]   Mike Cohn. *User Stories Applied: For Agile Software Development.* Addison-Wesley, 2004.

[Con]   "Context Driven Testing." www.context-driven-testing.com.

[Cun]   Ward Cunningham. "Fit: Framework for Integrated Test." http://fit.c2.com/.

[Dot]   "Graphviz—Graph Visualization Software." www.graphviz.org.

[Eva04]   Eric Evans. *Domain-Driven Design: Tackling Complexity in the Heart of Software*. Addison-Wesley, 2004.

[Fea02]   Michael Feathers. "The Humble Dialog Box." www.objectmentor.com /resources/articles/TheHumbleDialogBox.pdf, 2002.

[Fea04]   Michael Feathers. *Working Effectively with Legacy Code*. Prentice Hall, 2005.

[Fow97]   Martin Fowler. *Analysis Patterns: Reusable Object Models*. Addison-Wesley, 1997.

[Fow99]   Martin Fowler, Kent Beck, John Brant, William Opdyke, and Don Roberts. *Refactoring: Improving the Design of Existing Code*. Addison-Wesley, 1999.

[Fow02a]   Martin Fowler. *Patterns of Enterprise Application Architecture*. Addison-Wesley, 2003.

[Fow02b]   Martin Fowler. "Yet Another Optimization Article." *IEEE Software* May/June 2002.

[FS03]   Martin Fowler and Pramod Sadalage. "Evolutionary Database Design." www.martinfowler.com/articles/evodb.html, 2003.

[GHJV95]   Erich Gamma, Richard Helm, Ralph Johnson, and John Vlissides. *Design Patterns: Elements of Reusable Object-Oriented Software*. Addison-Wesley, 1995.

[Got03]   Arnaud Gotlieb. "Exploiting Symmetries to Test Programs." In *14th International Symposium on Software Reliability Engineering*, pp. 365–374. IEEE Comput. Soc., 2003.

[Hig04]   Jim Highsmith. *Agile Project Management: Creating Innovative Products*. Addison-Wesley, 2004.

[HT00]   Andrew Hunt and David Thomas. *The Pragmatic Programmer: From Journeyman to Master*. Addison-Wesley, 2000.

[HT03]   Andrew Hunt and David Thomas. "Pragmatic Unit Testing." www.pragmaticprogrammer.com, 2003.

[KBN+02]   Cem Kaner, James Bach, Hung Quoc Nguyen, Jack Falk, and Bob Johnson. *Testing Computer Software*, 2nd ed. Wiley, 1999.

[KBP02]   Cem Kaner, James Bach, and Bret Pettichord. *Lessons Learned in Software Testing: A Context-Driven Approach*. Wiley, 2002.

[Ker04]   Joshua Kerievsky. *Refactoring to Patterns*. Addison-Wesley, 2005.

[LB03]   Craig Larman and Victor R. Basili. "Iterative and Incremental Development: A Brief History. *IEEE Computer*, June 2003.

[LC01]   Bo Leuf and Ward Cunningham. *The Wiki Way: Collaboration and Sharing on the Internet*. Addison-Wesley, 2001.

[Mar]   Brian Marick. "Exploratory Testing." www.testingcraft.com/exploratory .html.

[Mar95]   Brian Marick. *The Craft of Software Testing.* Prentice Hall, 1995.

[Mar02]   Robert C. Martin. *Agile Software Development: Principles, Patterns and Practices.* Prentice Hall, 2003.

[MBA03]   Gerard Meszaros, Ralph Bohnet, and Jennitta Andreas. "Agile Regression Testing Using Record and Playback." In Frank Maurer and Don Wells, eds. *XP/Agile Universe 2003*, volume 2753 of *LNCS*, pp. 111–119. Springer, 2003.

[McC99]   Steve McConnell. *After the Gold Rush: Creating a True Profession of Software Engineering.* Microsoft Press, 1999.

[MFC00]   Tim MacKinnon, Steve Freeman, and Philip Craig. "Endo-Testing: Unit Testing with Mock Objects." In *XP2000*, Springer-Verlag, 2000.

[MSA03]   Gerard Meszaros, Shaun M. Smith, and Jennitta Andreas. "The Test Automation Manifesto." In Frank Maurer and Don Wells, eds. *XP/Agile Universe 2003*, volume 2753 of *LNCS*, pp. 73–81. Springer, 2003.

[Mug04]   Rick Mugridge. "Test Driving Custom Fit Fixtures." In *XP2004*, pp. 11–19. Springer-Verlag, 2004.

[PM02]   Richard Pawson and Robert Matthews. *Naked Objects.* Wiley, 2002.

[PP03]   Mary Poppendieck and Tom Poppendieck. *Lean Software Development: An Agile Toolkit for Software Development Managers.* Addison-Wesley, 2003.

[Rei97]   D. G. Reinertsen. *Managing the Design Factory.* The Free Press, 1997.

[RS04]   J. B. Rainsberger and Scott Stirling. *JUnit Recipes: Practical Methods for Programmer Testing.* Manning, 2004.

[SB02]   K. Schwaber and M. Beedle. *Scrum: Agile Software Development.* Prentice Hall, 2002.

[Tex]   "texttest." http://sourceforge.net/projects/texttest.

[Wil02]   Laurie Williams. *Pair Programming Illuminated.* Addison-Wesley, 2003.

Index

Abbot framework, 269
Action fixtures and ActionFixture tables,
    23, 187
  for buying items, 23–26, 187–189
  for cash rentals, 105
  for chat room state changes, 190–191
  for chat server actions, 26–28
  exercises, 29, 194
  vs. flow-style actions, 72–74
  operations of, 192–193
  summary, 28–29, 193–194
Action role for cash rentals, 105
Actions and action tests
  action fixtures for. *See* Action fixtures
    and ActionFixture tables
  designing, 161–165
  on domain objects, 75–76, 234–237
  expected errors with, 69
  flow-style, 71–74, 227–231
  smells
    convoluted setups, 165
    long tables, 162
    missing sad paths, 162
    missing tests, 163
    rambling workflow, 163–164
    similar setups, 164–165
    slow calculations, 162
    unclear workflow, 162–163
  transforming into calculation tests,
    127–128
    calculations in, 128–130
    durations in, 131–132
    exercises, 134–135
    reports in, 132–133
    summary, 133–134
Actors, 187–189
Actual values, 213–214
Adapters
  DoFixtures as, 231–232
  user interface for, 271–274
add method, 209, 211
addActualRows method, 316
addDiscountGroup method, 209
Adding to storytests, 147–148

addRentalItem method, 271–272
addRentalItemCountDollarsSlashHour method,
  271
addToTag method, 307
admin method, 280
Agile software development, 335–336
Agility, tables for, 3, 301
allowCredit method, 183
Analysts, Fit for, 3
Applications, connecting to tables. *See*
  Fixtures
Architecture, 307
  doTable method, 309–310
  exercises, 312
  Fixture class
    counts in, 310
    subclasses in, 310–311
  parse trees, 308–309
  running Fit, 307–308
  summary, 312
  system, 256–258
  TypeAdapter, 213, 311
ArrayFixture class, 243–244
Associations, 82–83, 248–251
Automated tests
  for restructuring, 258–259
  in table design, 170

Background material
  agile software development, 335–336
  for testing, 335
  ubiquitous languages, 336
Balance, tables for, 3, 301
Barriers in restructuring, 280–281
beginTransactionForClientStaff method, 283
Bibliography, 341–343
bind method, 314–315
blank keyword, 186
board method, 250
Books
  for background material, 335–336
  bibliography, 341–343
Borders for tables, 49
Brain twisters in business rules, 158–159

Bugs, tables for reducing, 171
Business analysts, Fit for, 3
Business forms, 81–82, 247–248
Business processes, business rules for, 10
Business rules
  for deposit charges, 115–118
  examples for, 16, 157
  for RentAParty software, 96
  smells
    brain twisters, 158–159
    long tables, 161
    meaningless numbers, 157–158
    poor names, 158
    split values, 160–161
    tangled tables, 159–160
    unnecessary detail, 159
  supporting text for, 157
  tables in
    custom, 161
    developing, 156–157
  test design for, 156–161
  types of, 10
Business transactions, date and time in,
    119–121
Businesspeople, Fit for, 3
buy method, 188
BuyActions class, 187–189
Buying items, 23–26, 187–189

CalculateCredit fixture, 16–18, 182–184
Calculated spreadsheet columns, 49
CalculateDiscount class, 13, 179–182
CalculateDiscounts class, 211
CalculateDiscounts2 class, 242
CalculateFairCharge class, 295–296
CalculateFirstPhoneNumber class, 184
CalculateFixture class, 78, 242–243, 314
calculateWithFutureValue method, 241
Calculation tests, 295
  designing, 165–167
  direct, 295–297
  indirect, 297–300
  smells in
    calculation problems, 166
    many columns, 165–166
    many rows, 167
    unrelated workflow, 167
  summary, 300
  transforming action tests into,
    127–128
    calculations in, 128–130
    durations in, 131–132
    exercises, 134–135

    reports in, 132–133
    summary, 133–134
Calculations
  in action tests, 162
  business rules for, 10
  ColumnFixture tables for. *See* Column
    fixtures and ColumnFixture tables
  in DoFixture, 238
  expected errors with, 67–68
  in storytests, 139–140
  tests for. *See* Calculation tests
Calculator runners, 319–320
Camel case, 183, 191, 242
Canoo Web test framework, 275
Carets (^) for subwikis, 61
Cash rentals
  background, 104–107
  clients in, 109–111
  exercises, 112–113
  introduction, 103–104
  split and restructure for, 107–109
  summary, 111–112
cellMatches method, 316–317
cellsMatch method, 316–317
Changes
  chat room, 39–43, 190–191
  dates, 291–292
  discount group, 43–46
  tests, 168–170
Charges, deposit, 115–118
Chat rooms
  changes, 39–43
  fixtures, 203–207
  state changes, 190–191
Chat server actions, 26–28
ChatServer2 class, 203–207
ChatServerActions class, 190–191
ChatStart class
  with adapters, 231–232
  for domain objects, 234–236
  for flow-style actions, 227–229
Check actions
  for action fixtures, 192
  for DoFixture, 237
  for flow-style actions, 73
check method
  in TableFixture, 247
  in TaxInvoice, 249
Check role for cash rentals, 105
checkOrderItems method, 249
ClientModel class, 328
clientNamePhone method, 280
Clients in cash rentals, 109–111

ClientTransaction class, 282–283
Clock interface, 290
Clocks, 289–290
  date changes, 291–292
  date formatting, 292–293
  summary, 294
  time-related object interactions, 292
Code for FitNesse, 223–224
collectionOfJTable method, 273
collectOccupants method
  in OccupantList, 196
  in OccupantList2, 208
  in OccupantListInRoom, 201
Color
  for expected errors, 69
  in reports, 14–16
Column fixtures and ColumnFixture tables,
    13, 179, 309
  CalculateDiscount, 179–182
  for cash rentals, 105
  for credit calculations, 16–18
  for credit extension, 182–184
  for discount calculations, 13–14
  exercises, 21–22, 186
  operations of, 185–186
  for phone number selections, 19, 184
  for reports, 14–16
  summary, 20–21, 186
Columns
  in calculation tests, 165–166
  labels for, 13
  in list tests, 167–168
  in spreadsheets, 49
Comments for business rules, 157
Communication
  tables for, 2, 10, 301
  tests for, 155–156
completeTransaction method, 284
connect method
  in ChatServer2, 206
  in ChatServerActions, 190
  in ChatStart, 234–236
Connecting tables to applications. *See*
    Fixtures
connectUser method, 227, 229
Converting text, 311
Convoluted setups, 165
Counts in Fixture, 310
CreateRentalTemplate story, 145–146
createsRoom method, 236
Creating tables, 49
  exercises, 55
  HTML for tests, 52–54

organizing tests, 50–52
spreadsheets for tests, 49–50
summary, 54
Credit calculations, 16–18, 182–184
creditLimit method, 183
Cunningham, Ward, 60
Custom fixtures, 247, 313
  association tests, 248–251
  business forms, 247–248
  ImageFixture for, 314–316
  SetUpFixture for, 313–314
  summary, 252, 316
  two-dimensional images, 251–252
Custom runners, 319
  calculator, 319–320
  reading tests
    from spreadsheets, 322–323
    from text files, 320–322
  summary, 324
Custom tables in business rules, 161
Customer Extreme Programming, 138

Data source layers
  in restructuring, 285–286
  in three-layer architecture, 257
Date and time tests, 115
  actions for, 118–119
  business transactions, 119–121
  deposit charges, 115–118
  exercises, 124–125
  introduction, 115
  reports for, 122–124
  sad paths for, 121–122
  summary, 124
Dates
  changing, 291–292
  formatting, 292–293
  setting, 118–119
Debugging FitNesse tests, 224–225
Decisions, business rules for, 10
Deposit charges, 115–118
Designing tests
  action, 161–165
  automation, 170
  for business rules, 156–161
  calculation, 165–167
  change in, 168–170
  list, 167–168
  principles of, 155–156
  summary, 170
Details
  in test design, 156
  unnecessary, 159

Developing
  fixtures, 262–265
  tables, 156–157
Development issues in RentAParty software,
  90
Direct calculation tests, 295–297
disconnect method, 206
disconnectUser method, 227, 229
discount method
  in CalculateDiscount, 180–181
  in CalculateDiscounts, 211
  in TestDiscount, 215
DiscountGroupOrderedList class, 197–200
DiscountGroupsEntry class, 211
discountOwingPurchase method, 242
Discounts
  CalculateDiscount for, 179–182
  CalculateDiscounts for, 211
  CalculateDiscounts2 for, 242
  ColumnFixture for, 13–14
  discount groups for
    additions to, 208–209, 211
    changes in, 43–46
    fixtures for, 208–211
    ordered lists, 197–200
Discounts class, 239–241
doCell method
  in ActionFixture, 309
  in ColumnFixture, 309
DoFixture tables
  as adapters, 231–232
  for cash rentals, 107
  domain object actions with, 75–76,
    234–237
  expected errors with, 74–75, 232–234
  flow-style actions with, 71–74, 227–231
  general operations, 237–239
  setup for, 76–77
Domain layers
  in restructuring, 285–286
  in three-layer architecture, 257
Domain objects, actions on, 75–76, 234–237
DoRentEze class, 270–271
doRow method, 314–315
doRows method
  in ColumnFixture, 309
  in RowFixture, 309
doStateTable method, 249
doStaticTable method, 247
doTable method
  in CalculateDiscount, 179
  in CalculateFixture, 314
  in ColumnFixture, 185

  in DiscountGroupOrderedList, 197
  in Fixture, 309–310
  in ImageFixture, 316–317
  in OccupantList, 195–197
  in SetUpFixture, 315
  in TestOccupants, 307
Duplication in tests, 169
Durations for charges, 131–132

Editing wikis, 60
Editors, HTML, 52–54
EditRentalItemDialog class, 272
Enter actions, 192
enterRoom method
  in ChatServer2, 206
  in ChatServerActions, 190
entersRoom method, 236
enterString method, 271
equals method
  in Money, 215–216
  in TypeAdapter, 311
Errors, expected. *See* Expected errors
Examples
  for business rules, 16, 157
  for communicating, 10
exception method, 314
Expected errors, 67
  with actions, 69
  with calculations, 67–68
  with DoFixture, 74–75, 232–234
  summary, 69
Expected values, 213–214
Exploratory testing, 151
Extended camel case, 183, 242, 314
ExtendedCamelCase class, 314
Extending credit, 182–184
extraHours method, 262–263
Extreme Programming
  customer, 138
  spike in, 270

FairCharge class, 295–297
fairDuration method, 296
FileRunner class, 307
findMethod method, 314
first method, 184
First tables for RentAParty software
  business rules for, 96
  exercises, 102
  grace periods in, 98–99
  high-demand items in, 99–100
  reports for, 100–101
  reviewing, 100–101

simplicity in, 97–98
starting, 95–96
summary, 101–102
Fit.jar file, 219
Fit overview
book resources for, 337
in business roles, 3–5
installation, 219
need for, 1–2
tables in. *See* Tables
FitLibrary class, 268
FitLibrary fixtures and tables, 71, 227
CalculateFixture, 78, 242–243
DoFixture
as adapters, 231–232
general operations, 237–239
domain object actions in, 75–76, 234–237
exercises, 80, 245–246
expected errors in, 74–75, 232–234
flow-style actions in, 71–74, 227–231
list parts tests, 79, 244–245
ordered list tables, 78, 243–244
other values in, 245
SetFixtures, 232
setup for, 76–77, 239–242
summary, 79, 245
values in, 217
FitNesse, 57
book resources for, 337
exercises, 64–65
installation, 223
code for, 223–224
debugging in, 224–225
exercises, 225–226
summary, 225
miscellaneous features, 64
for organizing tests with subwikis,
61–62
for ranges of values, 63–64
starting, 58–61
summary, 64
for test suites, 62–63
values in, 217
Fixture class
counts in, 310
subclasses in, 310–311
FixtureFixture tables, 316
Fixtures, 177
action. *See* Action fixtures and Action-
Fixture tables
column. *See* Column fixtures and Column-
Fixture tables
custom. *See* Custom fixtures

flow. *See* FitLibrary fixtures and tables
list. *See* Lists and list fixtures
sequences of tables, 203
chat rooms, 203–207
discount group, 208–211
exercises, 212
summary, 211
tables for, 11, 261
in traffic lights, 178
transaction, 283–285
user interfaces for. *See* User interface
writing, 177–178, 261
developing, 262–265
exercises, 266
summary, 265
tables for, 261
Folders
running on, 219–220
tests in, 51
Formatting
dates, 292–293
HTML files, 52
Forms, business, 81–82, 247–248
FrontPage
for FitNesse, 58
for HTML files, 53
futureValueMaxBalanceMinPurchaseDiscountPercent
method
in Discounts, 239, 241
in SetUpDiscounts, 313–314

GeneralSetUpFixture class, 279–280
Generate1 class, 326–328
Generate2 class, 329–331
get method, 311
getAdapterForFirstDialog method, 271
getApp method, 209
getCellValues method, 322
getClient method, 330
getCost method, 331
getHireItem method, 328
getName method
in ClientModel, 328
in RentalItemModel, 331
in User, 232
getRentalItems method, 271–273
getReturn method, 330
getTargetClass method
in DiscountGroupOrderedList, 197
in OccupantList, 195–197
in OccupantList2, 208
in OccupantListInRoom, 201
in ParamRowFixture, 230

getText method, 247
getTime method
  in Clock, 290
  in MockClock, 292
  in RentEz, 290, 292
  in SystemClock, 290
Goals of RentAParty software, 172–173
Grace periods for late fees, 98–99
Gray traffic light in reports, 14
Green traffic light in reports, 14
Groups, discount
  additions to, 208-209, 211
  changes in, 43–46
  fixtures for, 208–211
  ordered lists, 197–200
GuiAdapter class, 271, 273

hashCode method, 216
Headers
  for business rules, 157
  labels for, 13–14
High-demand items, 99–100
HSSFSheets, 322
HSSFWorkbooks, 322
HTML files
  running on, 220
  for tests, 52–54
HtmlFixture fixture, 275
HtmlUnit framework, 275
HttpUnit framework, 275

ignore method, 314
ImageFixture fixture, 314–317
Images, two-dimensional, 83–84, 251–252
Important order, testing lists with, 34–36
!include command, 64
Inconsistency, 281
Indirect calculation tests, 297–300
Infecting
  for improvements, 258–259
  for restructuring, 277–278
Initial plans for RentAParty software, 90–91
Installation
  Fit, 219
  FitNesse, 223
    code for, 223–224
    debugging in, 224–225
    exercises, 225–226
    summary, 225
Interdependencies in restructuring, 286–287
Interleaved sequences, 329–331
invoke method
  in MethodTarget, 314

  in TypeAdapter, 311
Issues in RentAParty software, 90, 171–172
Iterations
  in Customer Extreme Programming, 138
  in storytests, 148–150

Java command, 219–220
Java Swing, 268
Jemmy framework, 269
jfcunit tool, 268–269
JWebUnit framework, 275

Keywords for flow-style actions, 72

Labels, column, 13–14
Late fees, 95–96
  business rule for, 96
  grace periods for, 98–99
  simplifying, 97–98
LateReturns class, 263–264
Layers
  in restructuring, 285–286
  in three-layer architecture, 257
Lists and list fixtures, 195
  columns in, 167–168
  designing, 167–168
  exercises, 202
  ordered
    ArrayFixture for, 78
    for discount groups, 197–200
    for flow fixtures, 243–244
  with parameters, 201
  parts, 79, 244–245
  with RowFixture tables
    with ordering, 34–36
    without ordering, 31–34
  rows in, 168
  summary, 201–202
  unordered, 195–197
Long tables
  in action tests, 162
  in business rules, 161

makeCheck method, 326, 328
makeDummyClient method, 298
makeDummyRentalItem method, 297–298
makeSetUp method, 326–327
makeTable method
  in SumRunner, 321
  in XlsSumRunner, 322–323
makeTables method
  in Generate1, 328
  in Generate2, 329–330

Managers, Fit for, 3–4
Many columns in calculation tests, 165–166
Many rows in calculation tests, 167
map method, 250
map variable, 310
Marathon framework, 269
Markup in FitNesse, 64
Meaningful examples for business rules, 157
Meaningless numbers in business rules,
    157–158
Missing action tests, 163
Missing sad paths, 162
Mock objects, 289–290
   dates
      changing, 291–292
      formatting, 292–293
   for small step changes, 293–294
   summary, 294
   time-related object interactions, 292
MockClock class, 291–292
Model based test generation, 325
   exercises, 332
   interleaved sequences, 329–331
   simple sequences, 326–329
   summary, 332
   symmetries, 325–326
Model-View-Controller (MVC) model, 257
Modularity, 280
Money, values of, 214–217
Money class, 216–217
Mozilla for HTML files, 52–53
MSWord for HTML files, 52, 54
MVC (Model-View-Controller) model, 257

Names
   in business rules, 158
   for flow-style actions, 72
   in tables, 157
newRoom method
   in ChatServer2, 206
   in ChatServerActions, 190
none method, 331
Not actions in DoFixture, 237
Note actions in DoFixture, 237
Numbers, meaningless, 157–158

Occupancy class, 196
Occupancy2 class, 208
occupantCount method
   in ChatServer2, 206
   in ChatServerActions, 190–191
   in ChatStart, 228–229, 232, 235–236
OccupantList class, 195–197

OccupantList2 class, 206–208
OccupantListInRoom class, 201
Operations, symmetry, 325–326
Order of report rows, 15
Ordered lists
   ArrayFixture for, 78
   for discount groups, 197–200
   for flow fixtures, 243–244
OrderedDiscountList class, 199–200
orderedList method, 241
Organizing tests, 50–52

.PageFooter page, 62
.PageHeader page, 62
Pair programming, 278
Parameters, lists with, 201
ParamRowFixture class, 228, 230
parse method
   in Money, 216–217
   in TestDiscount, 215
   in TypeAdapter, 311
Parse trees, 308–309
payWithCashDollar method, 284
Phone number selections, 19, 184
Planning storytests, 143–147
Poi system, 220, 322
Poor names in business rules, 158
Portability of tables, 339
Pounder framework, 269
Presentation layers, 257
Press actions, 192
pressButton method, 271
pressTab method, 271
Previous rentals repeated storytests, 139
   planning for, 144
   story selection for, 146–147
   templates for, 145–146
price method, 188
Principles of test design, 155–156
Priorities in Customer Extreme Program-
   ming, 138
Programmers
   Fit for, 4–5
   perspective of, 255–256
Programming languages
   Fit implementations, 339
   table portability in, 339

query method
   in DiscountGroupOrderedList, 197
   in OccupantList, 195–197
   in OccupantList2, 208
   in OccupantListInRoom, 201

in ParamRowFixture, 230
Question marks (?) in FitNesse, 58

Rambling workflow, 163–164
Ranges of values, FitNesse for, 63–64
ratesDollarPerHourPerDayPerWeek method, 296
Reading
  tables, 11–12
  tests
    from spreadsheets, 322–323
    from text files, 320–322
Red traffic light in reports, 14
Redundancy, 169, 280–281
Refactoring tests, 281
refundCashDollar method, 284
refundDollarPerHourPerDayPerWeek method, 297–298
Refunder class, 299–300
refundPaidTimeActualTime method, 299
registerParseDelegate method
  in DoFixture, 245
  in StartApplication, 293
RegularTemplateAccepted story, 149–150
Reject actions, 237
Related workflow in calculation tests, 167
removeRoom method, 233
rent method, 330
RentalItemModel class, 329, 331
rentalItems method, 270–271
RentalItemSetUp class, 271
rentAll method, 329
RentalModel class, 331
rentalRow method, 331
RentAParty software, 89–90
  business rules for, 96
  cash rentals. *See* Cash rentals
  date and time tests. *See* Date and time tests
  development issues in, 90
  exercises, 93
  goals of, 172–173
  grace periods in, 98–99
  high-demand items in, 99
  initial plans for, 90–91
  issues in, 171–172
  people at, 91–92
  reports in, 100–101
  reviewing tables in, 100–101
  simplicity in, 97–98
  starting, 95–96
  storytests for. *See* Storytests
  summary, 92

transforming action tests into calculation tests, 127–128
  calculations in, 128–130
  durations in, 131–132
  exercises, 134–135
  reports in, 132–133
  summary, 133–134
RentEz class, 290, 292
RentEz GUI, 268
RentEzeUiAdapter class, 271–274
rentForWeeks method, 284
reportIndex.html file, 51
Reports
  for calculate tests, 132–133
  ColumnFixture tables for, 14–16
  for date and time tests, 122–124
  in FitNesse, 64
  for tables, 100–101
Resources, web sites, 337
Restructuring
  automated tests for, 258–259
  for cash rentals, 107–109
  interdependencies in, 286–287
  setup for, 278–280
  slow tests for, 278
  split domain data source layers in, 285–286
  summary, 287–288
  test barriers in, 280–281
  test infecting for, 277–278
  transaction fixtures, 283–285
  transactions for, 282–283
returnAll method, 329
returnRow method, 331
returns method, 329–330
right method
  in Fixture, 316
  in TableFixture, 247
  in TestOccupants, 307–308
room method
  in ChatServer2, 206
  in ChatServerActions, 190
  in ChatStart, 234–235
RowEntryFixture fixture, 76
RowFixture tables, 309, 311–312
  for cash rentals, 105
  exercises, 36–38
  summary, 36
  for testing lists
    with important order, 34–36
    with unimportant order, 31–34
Rows
  in calculation tests, 167

header, 13–14
    in list tests, 168
rowsMatch method, 316–317
RPS programmers, Fit for, 301–303
runAndReportAndExit method, 321
runAndReportCounts method, 322
Runners, custom, 319
    calculator, 319–320
    reading tests
        from spreadsheets, 322–323
        from text files, 320–322
    summary, 324
Running
    Fit, 307–308
    on folders, 219–220
    on HTML files, 220
    summary, 221
    tests, 220–221

Sad paths
    for date and time tests, 121–122
    missing, 162
Scripting languages, 268
Selections
    phone number, 19, 184
    storytests, 146–147
Sequences
    interleaved, 329–331
    simple, 326–329
Sequences of tables, 39
    for chat room changes, 39–43
    for discount group changes, 43–46
    exercises, 47
    fixtures for, 203
        chat rooms, 203–207
        discount group, 208–211
        exercises, 212
        summary, 211
    summary, 46
set method, 311
setExceptionString method, 243
SetFixture fixture, 232
setRepeatString method, 243
setTime method, 292
setUp method
    in Discounts, 239
    in DoRentEze, 270–271
    in SetUpFixture, 315
    in StartApplication, 280
SetUp page, 62–63
SetUp.xls file, 51
SetUpDiscounts class, 241, 313–314
SetUpFixture tables

    for cash rentals, 107
    for flow fixtures, 239
    working with, 313–316
setUpRow method
    in ClientModel, 328
    in RentalItemModel, 329
Setups
    for cash rentals, 105
    convoluted, 165
    for DoFixture, 76–77
    for FitLibrary fixtures, 239–242
    for restructuring, 278–280
    similar, 164–165
setUps method, 241
Show actions, 237
Similar setups, 164–165
Simple sequences, 326–329
Simplicity in tables, 97–98
Slow calculations, 162
Slow tests for restructuring, 278
Small step changes, mock objects for,
        293–294
Smells
    action tests
        convoluted setups, 165
        long tables, 162
        missing sad paths, 162
        missing tests, 163
        rambling workflow, 163–164
        similar setups, 164–165
        slow calculations, 162
        unclear workflow, 162–163
    business rules
        brain twisters, 158–159
        long tables, 161
        meaningless numbers, 157–158
        poor names, 158
        split values, 160–161
        tangled tables, 159–160
        unnecessary detail, 159
    calculation tests
        calculation problems, 166
        many columns, 165–166
        many rows, 167
        unrelated workflow, 167
    list tests
        many columns, 167–168
        many rows, 168
    test changes
        duplication, 169
        excessive, 169–170
Software architects, Fit for, 4–5
Software engineers, Fit for, 4–5

Sokoban program, 83–84
Spiked applications, 269–270
Split domains in restructuring, 285–286
Split tests in cash rentals, 107–109
Split values in business rules, 160–161
Spreadsheets
    vs. HTML, 54
    for tests, 49–50, 322–323
staffNamePhone method, 280
Standard values, 213–214
Start actions, 192
StartApplication class
    for dates, 291–293
    for flow tables, 245
    for indirect tests, 297–298
    for setup, 278–280
    for transaction fixtures, 283
StartSokoban class, 249–250
startTransaction method, 330
startUp method, 314
State changes in chat rooms, 190–191
Stories for communicating, 10
Storytests, 137
    adding to, 147–148
    exercises, 153
    exploratory testing in, 151
    introduction, 137–139
    planning, 143–147
    previous rentals repeated in, 139
    progress in, 148–150
    rental calculations in, 139–140
    selecting, 146–147
    summary, 151–153
    templates for, 140–143
Subclasses of Fixture, 310–311
Subfolders, tests in, 51
subset method, 241, 244–245
Subwikis, 61–62
SuiteSetUp page, 63
SuiteTearDown page, 63
SumRunner class, 320–321
Supporting text for business rules, 157
Symmetries, 325–326
System, restructuring. *See* Restructuring
System architecture, 256–258
SystemClock class, 289–290
Systems analysts, Fit for, 3
Systems under test, tables for, 11

Table of Contents table, 58
TableFixture class, 247
Tables, 9

ActionFixture. *See* Action fixtures and
    ActionFixture tables
for associations, 82–83
benefits of, 2–3
business forms, 81–82
for business rules, 156–157
ColumnFixture. *See* Column fixtures and
    ColumnFixture tables
for communicating, 2, 10, 301
connecting to applications. *See* Fixtures
creating. *See* Creating tables
custom, 161
exercises, 85
FitNesse for. *See* FitNesse
flow and FitLibrary. *See* FitLibrary
    fixtures and tables
for flow-style actions, 73
lists. *See* Lists and list fixtures
long, 161–162
portability of, 339
reading, 11–12
sequences of. *See* Sequences of tables
summary, 85
for systems under test, 11
tangled, 159–160
for testing, 11
two-dimensional images, 83–84
value of, 171, 301
TableWizard, 64
Tagged formatting, 52
Tangled tables, 159–160
TaxInvoice class, 249
TearDown.html file, 220
tearDown method, 314–315
TearDown page, 62–63
TearDown.xls file, 52, 220
Templates
    creating, 140–141
    inside templates, 142–143
    planning, 144–145
    for previous rentals repeated, 145–146
    working with, 141–142
TestDiscount class, 215
TestDiscountGroups.html file, 49–50
TestDiscountGroups.xls file, 49–50
Testers, Fit for, 4
TestLate class, 262–263
TestOccupants class, 307
Tests
    ActionFixture tables for. *See* Action
        fixtures and ActionFixture tables
    associations, 82–83, 248–251
    background material for, 335

barriers to, 280–281
calculation. *See* Calculation tests
cash rentals. *See* Cash rentals
date and time. *See* Date and time tests
designing. *See* Designing tests
HTML for, 52–54
lists. *See* Lists and list fixtures
missing, 163
organizing
   with subwikis, 61–62
   suites for, 50–52
refactoring, 280
restructuring for. *See* Restructuring
running, 220–221
with sequences of tables. *See* Sequences of tables
spreadsheets for, 49–50, 322–323
suites
   FitNesse for, 62–63
   organizing tests in, 50–52
tables for, 11
Text
   for business rules, 157
   TypeAdapter for, 311
Text files, reading tests from, 320–322
Three-layer architecture, 257
Time-related object interactions, 292
Time tests. *See* Date and time tests
TimedActionFixture class, 311
timeIsNow method, 291
toString method
   in Money, 216
   in Object, 215
   in TypeAdapter, 311
total method, 188
Traffic light metaphor
   fixtures in, 178
   in reports, 14–16
TransActionFixture class, 283–284
Transactions
   date and time in, 119–121
   restructuring, 282–285
Transforming action tests into calculation tests, 127–128
   calculations in, 128–130
   durations in, 131–132
   exercises, 134–135
   reports in, 132–133
   summary, 133–134
Trees, parse, 308–309
Two-dimensional images, 83–84, 251–252
TypeAdapter class
   capabilities of, 213–214

elements of, 311
labels for, 185

Ubiquitous languages, 336
Unclear workflow, 162–163
Unit tests, 259
Unnecessary detail in business rules, 159
Unordered lists, testing, 31–34, 195–197
User guides for FitNesse, 58
User interface, 267
   for adapters, 271–274
   examining, 274–275
   for fixtures, 270–271
   introduction, 267–268
   spiked applications, 269–270
   summary, 275–276
user method
   in ChatServer2, 206
   in ChatServerActions, 190
UserCopy class, 228–229
userCreatesRoom method, 227, 229
userEntersRoom method, 227, 229
UserFixture class, 236
users method, 248, 250–251
UsersAndRooms class, 248, 250
usersInRoom method, 227, 229, 232

Values
   exercises, 217–218
   in FitNesse and flow fixtures, 217
   of money, 214–217
   ranges of, 63–64
   split, 160–161
   standard, 213–214
   summary, 217
Virtual Wiki, 224

Web sites, 337
Wiki words
   adding, 58–59
   in tables, 61
Wikis, 60
Workflow
   rambling, 163–164
   related, 167
   unclear, 162–163
wrong method
   in Fixture, 316
   in TableFixture, 247

XlsSumRunner class, 322–323

Yellow traffic light in reports, 14